# Sharing the Past:
# Shaping the Future

This volume was made possible through the generosity of
**John Kelman Sutherland Reid CBE TD MA BD DD**
1910– 2002
padre, pastor, preacher, translator, teacher and theologian
to whom it is dedicated with admiration and appreciation.

## Acknowledgements

Our thanks to all who have agreed to have their material published in this format and especially The European Ethnological Research Centre and the Council of the Church Service Society for allowing us to republish material in their copyright.

Thanks are also due to photographer Gordon Young, Portrait House, Linlithgow, for the image used on the front cover.

Special thanks to the Convener of the Editorial Group, Dr Stewart Todd; Bill Hogg who undertook the secretarial work; together with Tom Davidson Kelly, Gerald Jones and Dr Henry Sefton.

## Editorial Note

The editors have aimed at a measure of consistency without altering the style of individual writers, for example variety of capitalisation and referencing in footnotes. Non-inclusive language was not adjusted in articles from an earlier generation. References for previously published material are given and those articles marked with an asterisk in the table of contents are published for the first time.

© copyright of all articles remains with the authors

Published by William T. Hogg

Printed by Meigle Colour Printers, Tweedbank
2009

ISBN 978-0-9562682-0-4

# Contents

Acknowledgements ........................................................................... v
Editorial Note .................................................................................. v
Preface ........................................................................................... viii
Contributors ................................................................................... ix

**THE CHURCH**

Our Christian Heritage ................................................................... 1
Henry R Sefton

On Being the Church in an Age of Religious Indifference ......... 24
A Stewart Todd

Why We Are a Parish Church ...................................................... 36
Marjory A MacLean

Church and State in Scotland, Today and Tomorrow ................ 48
James L Weatherhead

The Relentless Search for Christian Unity .................................. 60
Tom A Davidson Kelly

Creed and Confession ................................................................... 74
Henry J Wotherspoon

**WORSHIP - THE SETTING**

The Architectural Setting* ............................................................ 93
George Hay

Scottish Church Furnishings ...................................................... 105
Henry R Sefton

Church Furnishings ..................................................................... 114
A Stewart Todd

The Individual Cup ..................................................................... 122
Alastair K Robertson

## WORSHIP – THE CONTENT

Christian Worship - An Introduction* ....................................................... 137
Colin R Williamson

The Word in Worship* ............................................................................. 147
Colin R Williamson

The Divine Service and Morning Service: Their Common Structure* ... 162
A Stewart Todd

The Book of *Common Order* of the Church of Scotland ......................... 173
A Stewart Todd

The Christian Year* ................................................................................. 189
R Stuart Louden

Celebrating the Christian Year* .............................................................. 198
William T Hogg

Music for Worship* .................................................................................. 205
Douglas Galbraith

## MINISTRY

Our View of the Ministry Today ............................................................... 217
A Stewart Todd

Order, Ordination and the Ministry of Word and Sacrament ................... 227
John L McPake

The Ministry of the Eldership .................................................................. 246
Reports to the General Assembly of the Church of Scotland 1989

Leaflets from the Stewartry ..................................................................... 258
Colin R Williamson

# Preface

In days of recession and haste it seems there is a forgetfulness of the depth and breadth of the richly threaded story of the Church of Scotland. Many holding leadership positions in the Christian Church feel that they are managing decline. They feel unsupported, and adrift in an unfamiliar world. We are told that we live in a post-Christian, post-industrial, post-secular and post-modern world. Today's generation is learning in a stark way the truth that here we have no abiding city.

Nevertheless the prophet Jeremiah urges us, 'Stand at the crossroads, and look, and ask for the ancient paths, where the good way lies; and walk in it, and find rest for your souls.' The response of the Council of the Scottish Church Society is to offer to the Church, and especially to those seeking ordination, or newly ordained to the ministry of word and sacrament, an introduction to what has been the ethos and practice of our Church.

The late Professor JKS Reid gave generous legacies both to the Scottish Church Society and to the Church Service Society, of which he had been President from 1978-80. Professor Reid's presidential address to the latter society offered a scrutiny of the New Testament ideas and credal formulations based on them which lead us to a sacramental interpretation of the Communion of Saints.

The content of this volume expresses such ideas and concerns, drawing as it does on the work of scholarly ministers of the late Victorian and Edwardian eras, those of recent generations and our own: parish ministers, teachers at schools of divinity, and officials of the General Assembly. The single contribution by an elder combines the skills of a practising architect and architectural historian. A range of voices provides an awareness of the richness of theological reflection on the nature of the Church of our fathers and mothers.

At its best, during the time of Reformation and in more recent days the Kirk has been careful to avoid sectarian and narrow views. We believe that the Church of Scotland needs to retain its theological identity as part of Christ's worldwide body. The Scottish Church Society invites the Reformed and Presbyterian Church of Scotland to re-consider its catholic roots. In the words of a prayer in Prayers for Sunday Services (1980) '[We] pray that we may pass on to our children a heritage as rich as we ourselves received'.

Tom Davidson Kelly  
President, Scottish Church Society  
Ascensiontide 2009

# Contributors

**The Revd Tom A Davidson Kelly MA BD FSA Scot** is Minister Emeritus, Govan Old Parish Church, Glasgow. He was Secretary of the Scottish Church Society from 1980-82, and of the Church Service Society from 1994-97, becoming President from 2001-02. In 2006 he was elected President of the Scottish Church Society for a three-year term, and has a special interest in the historical development of Scottish ecclesiology.

**The Revd Douglas Galbraith MA BD BMus MPhil ARSCM** was until recently Co-ordinator of the Office for Worship, Doctrine, and Church Art and Architecture (Church of Scotland). Following retirement, he acted as Ecumenical Officer for the Church for a period of fifteen months. He has been Chair of the Scottish Committee of the Royal School of Church Music, and is a tutor in the Bangor University/RSCM International Centre for Sacred Music Studies, as well as in the certificate and diploma courses at the University of St Andrews. He also serves on the Steering Committee of the Scottish Churches Organist Training Scheme (SCOTS). Currently Precentor of the General Assembly, he edits the Scottish church music quarterly, *Different Voices*.

**George Hay MBE ARIBA ARIAS DLitt** was a Scottish architect, who spent much of his professional life with HM Office of Works in Edinburgh, and with the firm of Ian G Lindsay & Partners, in which he was a partner from 1952-60. Recognized as 'very much a Scottish Renaissance man', he gained early distinction for a thesis on the Scottish architectural woodwork of the 16th and 17th centuries, and later acquired a specialist knowledge of ancient monuments, churches and church furnishings. An elder in the Kirk of the Greyfriars, Edinburgh, he was a member of the General Assembly's Committee on Public Worship and Aids to Devotion. Among his publications *The Architecture of Scottish Post-Reformation Churches 1560-1843* (Oxford 1957) is arguably the most significant. Dr Hay died on 5 December 1986.

**The Revd William T Hogg MA BD** has been minister at Sanquhar St Bride's Parish Church since 2000, and is also Depute Clerk to the Presbytery of Dumfries and Kirkcudbright. Previously, he was minister at Glenorchy and Innishael with Strathfillan, and Clerk to the Presbytery of Lorn and Mull and to the Synod of Argyll. He has been Treasurer of the Scottish Church Society since 1988.

**The Revd W Gerald Jones MA BD ThM** has been minister at Kirkmichael with Straiton (St Cuthbert's) in the Presbytery of Ayr since 1985. He was a member of the General Assembly's Panel on Worship from 1987-91, and of the Council of the Church Service Society from 1986-98, and has been Secretary of the Scottish Church Society since 2004. He also serves as an Honorary Chaplain at York Minster.

**The Revd R Stuart Louden TD MA BD DD DLitt** was Minister at Greyfriars Kirk, Edinburgh, where he served from 1949-78, having previously been minister at Dailly Parish Church from 1945-49. Appointed a Chaplain to the Forces in 1939 (Middle East), he gave distinguished War service, and was taken prisoner of war at Tobruk in 1942. Dr Louden was Convener of the General Assembly's Colonial and Continental Committee from 1957-62, and of the Committee on Public Worship and Aids to Devotion from 1965-70. He served as Vice-Convener of the Church Hymnary Revision Committee from 1963-73, and as a Vice-President of the World Alliance of Reformed Churches from 1964-70. Dr Louden was President of the Church Service Society from 1964-66, and the Scottish Church Society from 1975-77. He was President of the Scottish Ecclesiological Society in its diamond jubilee year (1963). His significant publications are *The Church in the World* (Edinburgh 1957) and *The True Face of the Kirk* (London 1963). Dr Louden died on 26 March 1991.

**The Revd Marjory A MacLean LLB DipLP BD PhD** has been Depute Clerk of the General Assembly of the Church of Scotland since 1998, and is also Secretary of the Legal Questions Committee. From 2002-03 she was Acting Principal Clerk, and delivered the Chalmers Lectures in 2007-08 on 'The Crown Rights of the Redeemer: God, Sovereignty and the Church of Scotland'. Previously in the legal profession, Dr MacLean was minister at Stromness Parish Church, Orkney, from 1992-98, and is a member of the Court of the University of St Andrews from 2006-10.

**The Revd John L McPake BA BD PhD** has been minister at Mossneuk Parish Church, East Kilbride, since 2000. He was Convener of the General Assembly's Panel on Doctrine from 1999-2004, and Joint Convener of the Joint Commission on Doctrine with the Roman Catholic Church in Scotland from 2002-04.

**The Revd Alastair K Robertson MA BD PhD** was minister at Fort William Duncansburgh Parish Church from 1966 until his retiral in 1981. He was Secretary of the Scottish Church Society from 1955-67, and served as President of the Church Service Society from 1976-78. He was also Convener of the General Assembly's Committee on Public Worship and Aids to Devotion from 1970-74. His unpublished Edinburgh PhD thesis (1956), 'The Revival of Church Worship in the Church of Scotland from Dr Robert Lee (1804-67) to Dr H J Wotherspoon (1850-1930)', is widely acknowledged as a seminal study of the catholic revival in 19th century Scotland. Dr Robertson died on 17 April 1995.

**The Revd Henry R Sefton MA BD STM PhD** was previously Lecturer (1972-90) and Senior Lecturer in Church History (1991-92), and Co-ordinator in Christian Studies (1995-97) at Aberdeen University, and Master of Christ's College, Aberdeen from 1982-92. From 1962-66 he was minister at Newbattle Parish Church, and Assistant Secretary in the Church of Scotland Department of Education from 1966-72. He was also Chairman of the Association of University Teachers (Scotland) from 1982-84; Clerk to Aberdeen Presbytery from 1993-95; and Alexander Robertson Lecturer at Glasgow University in 1995. Dr Sefton was Secretary of the Scottish Church Society from 1967-72, President from 1988-91 and President of the Church Service Society from 1991-93.

**The Revd A Stewart Todd MA BD DD** is Minister Emeritus, St Machar's Cathedral, Old Aberdeen. He was a member of the Church Hymnary Revision Committee from 1963-73, and a member of the Church Hymnary Trust from 1965-2008. He was also Convener of the General Assembly's Committee on Public Worship and Aids to Devotion from 1974-78, and of the Panel on Doctrine from 1990-95. In 1991 he was appointed a Chaplain to the Queen in Scotland, and has been an Extra Chaplain since 1996. Dr Todd was President of the Church Service Society from 1980-82 and of the Scottish Church Society from 1985-88.

**The Very Revd James L Weatherhead CBE MA LLB DD** was Principal Clerk of the General Assembly of the Church of Scotland from 1985-93 and 1994-96, having been elected Moderator of the General Assembly in 1993. In 1991 he was appointed a Chaplain to the Queen in Scotland, and has been an Extra Chaplain since 2001. Dr Weatherhead previously had ministries in Rothesay and Montrose.

**The Revd Colin R Williamson LLB BD** is Minister Emeritus, The Stewartry of Strathearn, in the Presbytery of Perth. From 1980-84 he was Convener of the General Assembly's Panel on Worship, and was President of the Church Service Society from 1995-97, having served as its Secretary from 1980-94.

**The Revd Henry J Wotherspoon MA DD** was minister at St Oswald's, Edinburgh, from 1894-1923, and President of the Scottish Church Society from 1904-05 and from 1921-24. A distinguished liturgical scholar, with a particular interest in sacramental theology and ecclesiology, Dr Wotherspoon was influential in the Scoto-Catholic Movement, and in the founding of the Scottish Church Society in 1892. He was President of the Scottish Ecclesiological Society from 1914-15. In 1913 he was appointed Alexander Robertson Lecturer at Glasgow University, and delivered the Croall Lectures in 1926-27, published as *Religious Values in the Sacraments* (Edinburgh 1928). In another seminal study (with Dr J M Kirkpatrick), *A Manual of Church Doctrine According to the Church of Scotland* (London 1919), he sought to show continuity between the Church of Scotland and the Church Historic, not only in terms of doctrine, but with regard to the nature of the Church, and with particular regard to sacrament and ministry. Dr Wotherspoon died on 28 January 1930.

W Gerald Jones

# Our Christian Heritage
# The Story of the Scottish Churches[1]
## *Henry R Sefton*

**1. 1560 and All That**

The year 1560, the conventional date of the Scottish Reformation, has been widely thought to be a turning point in Scottish history – much as 1066 has been a date to conjure with in English history. But if we had been around in 1560 would we have noticed much difference between the beginning and the end of that year? Recent historians, notably Gordon Donaldson, have suggested that there is a remarkable amount of continuity in the Church before and after 1560. This means that the pre-Reformation Church in Scotland is a shared inheritance. All branches of the Christian Church owe something to it.

**The Gospel**

What then do we all owe to the pre-Reformation Church? Here are some suggestions:

We have inherited the Gospel, the faith once delivered to the saints. But which saints? Our patron saint, St Andrew, never reached Scotland in life, though the town of St Andrews bears his name and the Roman Catholic Cathedral of St Mary in Edinburgh enshrines a relic of him. St Ninian certainly came to Whithorn, probably about 397, but he was a bishop and bishops were not pioneer missionaries. So he was likely a second or even third generation Christian there. The answer seems to be that we do not know who first preached the Gospel in what is now Scotland.

---

[1] Originally published by ACTS 1994.

## The Celtic Church

Interest in the Celtic Church seems to be at an all-time high, judging from the spate of recent books about it. There are several recent books on Celtic spirituality (including, for instance, the prayers of David Adams). Prayers, hymns and devotions dating from the era of St Columba and St Aidan and their followers have a wide appeal. Those who are deeply concerned about the environment point to the Celtic saints' empathy with nature. Eager Presbyterians have even claimed that the Celtic Church was not unlike them in its organisation, while the Scottish Episcopal Church likes to think it is the inheritor of the Celtic Church.

The organisation of the Celtic Church was actually monastic. Celtic abbeys or monasteries were communities of men and women under the rule of an abbot and sometimes an abbess. They usually included a bishop who ordained priests but who was subject to the abbot. Celtic monasteries were outward looking and missionary. Celtic monks loved to go on a *peregrinatio*, a kind of pilgrimage not to a holy place but to desert places, from which they drove out evil in the name of the Lord God. The missionary impulse is a part of the Celtic way that all churches share.

## Scottish Identity

From the 7th century onwards the Church in what is now Scotland was under severe pressure to conform to the practice of the rest of the Western Church. Europeanization is no new thing! By the 12th century the diocesan episcopal system of Church government had replaced the old Celtic way and a beginning was made in establishing a parish system. But unlike other provinces of the Western Church Scotland had no archbishop until 1472. The Scottish Church, however, was determined not to own the jurisdiction of the archbishop either of York or Canterbury. The adoption of Andrew as patron saint had much to do with the fact that it was he who brought Peter to Jesus and Peter was the patron saint of York! Scotland was pleased when in 1188 Pope Clement III declared the Scottish Church to be the special daughter of the Roman see and therefore subject to no archbishop.

The Scottish bishops and abbots warmly supported the patriotic cause during the wars of independence. The Declaration of Independence of 1320, which takes the form of a letter to the Pope, was drafted by the Abbot of Arbroath, Bernard de Linton. Robert the Bruce's success owed much to their efforts.

In the 15th and 16th centuries there were signs that a distinctively Scottish style of worship might develop. The beautiful Arbuthnott service books, prepared for the Church of St Ternan at Arbuthnott in Kincardineshire (but now in the Paisley museum) give space to commemorating Scottish saints, including Ternan. One of the first books to be printed in Scotland was the Aberdeen Breviary compiled at the request of Bishop William Elphinstone for Aberdeen but probably intended for wider use. This daily service book includes many readings about the deeds of Scottish saints. Curiously enough both the Reformation and the Counter or Catholic reformation promoted closer following of European models.

**A Concern for Reform**
The name which is most often associated with reformation in Scotland is that of John Knox. Perhaps that is because he wrote a *History of the Reformation in Scotland* and did not feel any need to be modest about his own part! He is certainly less than fair to the concern for reform which was felt by John Hamilton, Archbishop of St Andrews from 1547 to 1571. The proceedings of the provincial councils called by Archbishop Hamilton show a deep concern for the state of the Church and point to ways in which things could be improved. Hamilton's programme of reform was not successful but then neither was the programme set out by Knox and his colleagues

in the Book of Discipline of 1561. Much of this also remained on paper and Knox included the text of the book in his *History* as a kind of testimony. But the principle of *Ecclesia semper reformanda*, a Church always needing to be reformed had been established.

**The Parish System**

Both Hamilton and Knox assumed the continuance of the parish system which had developed since the 12th century. The word parish derives from *par-oikia* the land round the house. In practice this meant the land controlled by the lord of the manor who built the church, appointed a priest and arranged for him to be supported by a tenth or teind of the annual crop. This system has lasted to the present day. Parish ministers have a responsibility for a territorial area, not just a congregation and in recognition of this teinds are still paid to the Church of Scotland. The amount was standardised in 1925 and takes no account of inflation so it is now little more than a historical relic. The Roman Catholic Church and the Scottish Episcopal Church also operate a parochial system. As far as the members of the Church are concerned only Roman Catholics today regularly observe parochial boundaries. In urban areas, and even in many rural areas, the parish system is more important to those outside the Church than to those within it.

**2. The Debate about Bishops**

The word 'bishop' is probably the most emotive term in Scottish ecclesiastical vocabulary. It is no accident that we had Bishops Wars in the 17th century and a furious pamphlet and newspaper war over bishops in the 1950s. Scots folk have been vehemently against bishops but have been equally loyal to them, even in troubled times and at risk of persecution.

Why bishops? Some of the reasons are theological and ecclesiastical but others are really political and constitutional. Bishops have been around in Scotland for a long time. We have already noted Bishop Ninian about 397. Even if he was not a pioneer missionary, it was felt even then that a bishop was necessary for the well-being of the Church. The abbots were the key-persons in the Celtic Church but monasteries nearly always included a bishop because only the bishop was thought to have the power to ordain priests. Down the centuries this has been regarded as a prime function of a bishop - the right and the duty of ordaining priests. The main challenge to this view comes from Churches which see this right as being vested in the presbytery or in the local church. This theological reason for bishops depends on one's interpretation of the guidance of Scripture and of the tradition of the Church but in Scotland it has tended to be overshadowed by the political and constitutional roles expected of bishops.

Traditionally bishops have been regarded as a focus for the unity of the Church - almost a personification of it. But after Kenneth MacAlpine, King of the Scots, became the King of the Picts in 844 he saw the Bishop of Alba based at Dunkeld as a focus for the unity of his enlarged kingdom. In the 10th century the bishop moved to the town formerly known as Kilrymont but renamed St Andrews after the bones of St Andrew had been enshrined there. The bishop was thus an important political figure as well as the leading ecclesiastic in the Kingdom.

The introduction of the diocesan system by Alexander I and David I was the counterpart of the feudal system which was developed during their reigns. Just as the secular great lords held lands from the king in return for services in war and peace, so did the bishops. The bishops were spiritual lords owing allegiance to the king for the lands they occupied. The double loyalty to the king and to the Church became increasingly a cause of tension and controversy. The question of military service was an obvious problem area. Great lords had to be ready to fight under the king's banner. Was it right for a spiritual lord to do so? Whether he did or not he was expected like any other lord to provide a band of fighting men when required by the king.

As government became more sophisticated so did the need increase for literate manpower. Unlike most of the great secular lords, bishops could read and write and so they were constantly in demand for the king's service. They held the great offices of state, like Lord Chancellor or Lord Treasurer, and also frequently served as ambassador to other kingdoms. The same was true of the lesser clergy, who effectively became the civil service. A bishop had to be very dedicated and as well organised, as was Bishop William Elphinstone of Aberdeen (1431-1514), to be both effective as a bishop and as a state official. Had all the medieval bishops been like Elphinstone the Reformation might have taken a very different course or might not have happened at all.

Because of the importance of the bishops in the administration of the kingdom the king became more and more interested in the appointment and although the election of a bishop should have been entirely an ecclesiastical process in practice the king was able to nominate his own candidate when a see fell vacant. In the later Middle Ages this right was often misused and highly born but illegitimate men and even boys were appointed to bishoprics. Even the see of St Andrews was not exempt and James Stewart and Alexander Stewart, royal but illegitimate, were successively archbishop of St Andrews.

Radical reformers like John Knox and Andrew Melville[2] considered that the bishoprics should be broken up and the revenues used to further the schemes for church extension, education and social care envisaged in the First and Second Books of Discipline. But King and

---

[2] Andrew Melville (1545 – 1622) was Principal of Glasgow University, and later St Mary's College at St Andrews. His advocacy established the system of presbyteries in Scotland.

Parliament, (or, more correctly, the 'Estates of Parliament') refused to do so and these considerable landholdings were an important pawn in the power struggles between Church and State in the 16th and 17th centuries. The Act of Revocation of 1586 gave King James VI control over all Church property and he used these resources very skilfully as he extended his control over both Church and State.

The prevailing group in the Church continued to press for the abolition of bishops and the establishment of a Presbyterian style of Church government. But although Presbyterianism was recognised by the Golden Acts of 1592 Episcopacy was not abolished and before long bishops were imposed on top of the Presbyterian structure by a series of royal and parliamentary measures.

Why was the king so anxious to retain bishops? It was partly because he felt that through them he could exercise more control over the Church. But more importantly it was because the bishops gave the king an effective means of controlling the Estates of Parliament. This was because of the peculiar way in which the Committee of Articles, the executive of the Parliament, was elected. Each of the three Estates (Nobles, Bishops, and Knights and Burgesses) had representatives but the Nobles chose the representatives of the Bishops and the Bishops chose the representatives of the Nobles. When these were chosen they in turn chose the representatives of the Knights and Burgesses. As long as the king could choose whom he wished as bishops he could control the Committee of Articles and therefore the Estates of Parliament. Bishops also continued to hold great offices of state to the great annoyance of the nobility. The king's ability to control Scotland depended on the continuance of the Estate of Bishops. Thus when the Claim of Right was presented to William and Mary bishops were included among the grievances to be rectified and in 1690 the office of bishops was officially abolished by the Act of Parliament establishing Presbyterian Church government in the Church of Scotland.

But bishops did not disappear from the Scottish scene for there were many who saw in them not tools for royal oppression in Church and State but rather Fathers in God to clergy and people and guarantors of the succession from the Apostles in faith and order. The doctrine of the apostolic succession through bishops[3] had been safe-guarded by the consecration of the new Scottish bishops by English bishops in 1612 and 1661. Great pains were now taken to continue the line by calling on English bishops who, like the Scots, refused to desert the Stuarts for Dutch William to consecrate bishops for Scotland. After the failure of the Risings of 1715 and 1745 the Episcopal Church took shape.

## 3. The Search for the 'Best Reformed Churches'

In 1643 a document was drawn up in the name of the Noblemen, Barons, Knights, Gentlemen, Burgesses, Ministers of the Gospel and Commons of all sorts in the kingdoms of Scotland, England and Ireland. This was the Solemn League and Covenant and it pledged those who signed it to the preservation of the reformed religion in the Church of Scotland and the reformation of religion in the kingdoms of England and Ireland in doctrine, worship, discipline and government according to the Word of God and the example of the best reformed Churches.

From the point of view of the English Parliamentarians the Solemn League and Covenant was a military alliance with the Scottish Parliamentarians in their common struggle against the absolutism of King Charles I. The Scots saw it very differently. They regarded the Solemn League primarily as a religious covenant and as the first stage in bringing the Church of God in the three kingdoms 'to the nearest conjunction and uniformity of religion, confession of faith, form of church government, directory for worship and catechising'. To this end they had accepted the invitation to send commissioners

---

[3] Apostolic succession' refers to the belief that authority has been passed down from the apostles from bishop to bishop in an unbroken line.

the Church of Scotland to an 'Assembly of Divines' which had been convened by the English Parliament to advise it in religious matters. The Scottish commissioners were few in number - only seven in an Assembly of over a hundred and thirty - but they were extremely able and exercised an influence out of all proportion to their number. Men like Samuel Rutherford, George Gillespie, Robert Baillie and Alexander Henderson, all ministers, and Archibald Johnston of Warriston, a lawyer and an elder, were a match for the keenest intellects in England.

The various documents agreed upon by the Assembly of Divines, *The Form of Presbyterial Church Government*, *The Directory for the Public Worship of God*, *The Confession of Faith* and the *Larger* and *Shorter Catechisms*, all bear a strong Scottish character.

Not surprisingly the Westminster documents found a ready acceptance in Scotland. They were approved by the General Assembly in 1645, 1647 and 1648. The *Directory* was approved by Parliament and the *Confession of Faith* (known as the 'Westminster Confession') was ratified and established by Acts of Parliament in 1649 and 1690 as the public and avowed Confession of the Church of Scotland. The Scots were convinced that these documents set out the doctrine, worship, discipline and government of the Church according to the Word of God and the example of the best reformed churches.

The General Assembly of 1650 were somewhat surprised to receive a letter from the invading General, Oliver Cromwell which contained this sentence: 'I beseech you, in the bowels of Christ, think it possible you may be mistaken'. The Scots refused to consider this possibility and so when the General Assembly attempted to convene at Dundee in 1651 Cromwell's troops dispersed the members. The Assembly was again prevented from meeting in 1653 and 1654 and did not meet again until 1690.

Synods, presbyteries and kirk sessions continued to meet throughout the Cromwellian occupation and after the bishops were restored in 1661 but Scotland was made aware during the 1650s that reformed churches need not be presbyterian in government. Indeed it is said that an astute English draughtsman suggested the phrase 'according to the Word of God and the example of the best reformed churches'. The Scots failed to see the ambiguity because they assumed that their model was according to the Word of God and was the best possible. They were outraged when the Commonwealth government insisted that toleration be given to all 'whose conscience was not satisfied with that form and bade them worship God in other Gospel ways.'

Few, if any, of Cromwell's soldiers were Presbyterians. They were either Independents[4] or Baptists. Cromwell wished to have gifted chaplains with his army who would preach ideas that he found congenial. Up to this point Independent views had found little acceptance in Scotland despite visits by Robert Browne in 1584 and John Penry 1588-90. The Scots had argued strongly in the Westminster Assembly against the view that each local congregation is autonomous and a full expression of the Church. It was to be the 18th century before Independent views took firm root in Scotland. Despite vigorous debates between the Commonwealth army chaplains and the parish ministers Independency did not survive the departure of the troops at the restoration of the monarchy.

The Scottish Reformers were strongly committed to infant baptism and it was not until the arrival of the English Commonwealth soldiers that Baptist teaching effectively reached Scotland. There were some native converts and there are records of baptisms at Bonnington Mill near Leith and at Cupar, Fife. The governor of Perth, General

---

[4] Independents later adopted the name 'Congregationalist'.

Overton was a Baptist and a letter dated 1653 refers to the brethren of Perth being in good health. But with the political changes of 1659 the Baptist churches vanished and many of the converts returned to the parish churches.

The Quakers (or more properly the Religious Society of Friends), make their first appearance in Scotland with Cromwell's army. They were especially active in North-East Scotland under the leadership of Robert Barclay (1648-90) and Alexander Jaffray, Provost of Aberdeen (1614-73).

In 1690 an Act passed by the Estates of Parliament decreed that Presbyterianism was to be 'the only government of Christ's Church within this kingdom'. This act was renewed in 1707 as part of the arrangements for union with England and it was also provided that each Sovereign on accession should swear to maintain the Presbyterian government of the Church. Despite this legislative support of the traditional Scottish view of what was meant by 'the example of the best reformed churches' other patterns emerged during the 18th century.

John Glas, minister at Tealing, published in 1725 a treatise entitled *The Testimony of the King of Martyrs* based on the text 'My Kingdom is not of this world' (John 18:36). In this Glas asserted the independence of Church and magistrate and gathered a group of seventy four people within the parish. When he was deposed from the ministry he set up an independent congregation in Dundee, known as the Glassites, supported by families from Tealing.

One of the lairds of Caithness, Sir William Sinclair of Dunbeath, served as a soldier in England and came into contact with Baptist views. On his return home he founded a Baptist church at Keiss in 1750.

In 1799 the Church of Scotland General Assembly passed an act forbidding ministers to allow into their pulpits anyone who had not been licensed to preach by a presbytery. The Assembly also decided to investigate the legal position of 'vagrant teachers and Sunday schools'. This was in reaction to the evangelistic efforts of the brothers Robert and James Haldane who have the unusual distinction of being involved in the development of two Christian denominations, the Congregationalists and the Baptists. It has been estimated that by 1805 some two hundred preachers trained and supported at Robert Haldane's expense were dispersed throughout Scotland. Their friend Greville Ewing was a brilliant organiser and he secured the foundation of the Congregational Union in 1812. But the Haldanes had become Baptists in 1808 and many of their converts followed them. The Baptist Union of Scotland was founded in 1843.

## 4. Minorities and Seceders

The relationship of Church and State has been a crucial factor in Scottish history. Again and again legislation has been passed which has marginalised some Christians or has caused them to secede from the established church.

The Estates of Parliament at their meeting in August 1560 passed legislation abolishing the authority of the Pope in Scotland and forbidding the celebration of mass. The Negative Confession of 1581 which was signed by all members of the King's administration was largely a denunciation of all things 'Popish'. During the 16th, 17th and 18th centuries there was legislation against 'unlawful hearers of mass'. The effect of this was to marginalise Roman Catholics and to make them non-citizens with no rights of any kind.

Despite all this a series of devoted Jesuit missionaries refused to give up on Scotland. The most famous of them, Father John Ogilvie, was imprisoned, tortured and put to death as a 'traitor' in 1615. But his fellow-Catholics considered that he had died as a martyr and in 1976 he was recognised as a saint and canonised by Pope Paul VI.

The Scottish mission was placed on a more regular basis by the appointment of Bishop Thomas Nicholson as the first vicar apostolic in 1694. He and his successors did much to reassure the Scots that the 'Papists' presented no threat to the security of the nation. In 1793 a Relief Act was passed under which Scottish Catholics were allowed freedom of worship and they were permitted to inherit and purchase land as freely as anyone else. The Catholic Emancipation Act of 1829 gave Catholics the right to vote and stand for Parliament.

The legislation of 1690 marginalised the bishops and others who considered that the oaths of allegiance they had given to King James VII were not transferable to William and Mary. Those who took this view soon came to be known as Jacobites from Jacobus the Latin form of James. The Toleration Act of 1712 was of no use to them for it gave freedom to worship according to the Book of Common Prayer and only to those who were willing to take the oath of allegiance to Queen Anne and to abjure the exiled Stuarts.

For most of the 18th century Episcopalians were persecuted by the British government. This was not because they were Episcopalians but because they were considered to be Jacobites. After the 1715 and 1745 risings the restrictions became greater and greater until it was declared illegal for a group of more than four persons to worship unless King George was prayed for by name and as king. The effect was to reduce Scottish Episcopalianism, in Sir Walter Scott's phrase, to 'a shadow of a shade'.

The key figure in the recovery of the Episcopal Church was Bishop John Skinner (1744-1816). It was he who arranged in 1784 for the consecration of Samuel Seabury in Aberdeen as the first bishop of the American Episcopal Church. After the death of Bonnie Prince Charlie in 1788 Bishop Skinner persuaded Episcopalians that they could now in good conscience pray for George III as king. This paved the way for the repeal of the Parliamentary acts against Episcopalians in 1792.

William of Orange was anxious that the Church of Scotland should be as comprehensive as possible and constantly urged moderation on the victorious Presbyterians. One group of Presbyterians, known as Cameronians after Richard Cameron, a Covenanting martyr, were not willing to be moderate. They regarded England and Ireland as still bound by the Solemn League and Covenant of 1643 and when neither showed any sign of establishing Presbyterianism, they refused to recognise the government of King William and Queen Mary and the government of their successors. The Reformed Presbyterian Church of Scotland maintains this protest today.

Another piece of Parliamentary legislation has been described as 'the parent of many grievous ills'. This was the Patronage Act passed by the Parliament of Great Britain in 1712. Patronage was no new thing and the Act restored a practice of long standing. Parish churches were in most cases built and endowed by the local landowner. In return for this the landowner claimed for himself and his successors the right of naming the priest, and later, minister who was to serve the parish. An Act of the Estates of Parliament of 1690 provided that they should be chosen by the heritors (landowners) as a whole and the elders of the parish rather than by a patron. This act was repealed by the 1712 act.

Despite many repeated protests the Patronage Act remained on the statute-book for a hundred and sixty-two years. The right of patronage could be sold or given away or could be forfeited to the Crown and frequently was. By the end of the 18th century fully a third of the parishes were in the gift of the Crown. For about a decade after 1712 patrons were usually careful to present ministers whom they knew were acceptable to the congregations concerned. But during the 1720s patrons and especially the officials exercising the Crown's patronage were less willing to conciliate local opinion and there were many disputed settlements.

Opinion in the Church of Scotland was divided on the subject of Patronage. No-one really liked it but most were prepared to put up with it. They spoke of 'our present happy constitution in Church and State' and regarded Patronage as a kind of fly in the ointment. Others, like Ebenezer Erskine, demanded to know what difference a piece of land should make between man and man in the Church of God and denounced the favour shown to the 'man with the gold ring and gay clothing'. Erskine refused to be silenced or even to accept a rebuke for his intemperate language and in 1733 he and his supporters solemnly seceded from 'the prevailing party in the Church of Scotland' and appealed to the first 'free, faithful and reforming General Assembly'. They formed themselves into a body called The Associate Presbytery.

In 1752 Thomas Gillespie was deposed from the ministry for refusing to take part in the induction of a minister presented to Inverkeithing but unacceptable to the inhabitants of the parish. In 1761 he and two other ministers similarly placed formed a Presbytery for the Relief of those oppressed by patronage.

Erskine, Gillespie and their followers considered that they were still part of the Church of Scotland. They had merely seceded from the misguided majority and looked forward to better times. The General Assembly took a very different view and the Act of 1799 closing the pulpits was aimed at the Seceders as well as the Haldanes.

## 5. Transformations

From the point of view of the twenty-first century the 19th century often seems to be a settled time of certainty. It is sometimes summed up in the phrase 'Victorian values'. But the 19th century was a period of profound change, more so than any preceding century. It is only because the 20th century saw even greater changes that the 19th seems so tranquil and undisturbed. The religious scene in Scotland was transformed during the 19th century and Professor A C Cheyne has described it as Victorian Scotland's religious revolution.

## The Presbyterians

At the beginning of the century Scotland was a predominantly Presbyterian country. The Church of Scotland was by far the largest religious communion. The Seceders had been fragmented into four groups and the Relief was now a Synod but the challenge of these Presbyterian dissenters to the Established Church was mainly in the central belt of the country and some of the larger towns. The Disruption of 1843, when the Kirk split into two ('Auld Kirk' and 'Free Kirk'), profoundly altered the balance of ecclesiastical influence in Scotland. For the first time the Church of Scotland was confronted by an alternative national Church supported by the prosperous rising bourgeoisie and embarking on a vigorous programme of church building. The Church of Scotland Free or Free Church of Scotland also provided schools, teacher training colleges, theological colleges and almost began to found a Free University.

To these two was added in 1847 a third major Church. The Union of two groups of Seceders - the 'New Light' Seceders and the Relief - to form the United Presbyterian Church of Scotland meant that there were three major presbyterian Churches in Scotland virtually identical in doctrine, discipline and worship but differing from each other in their attitude to the State. The Church of Scotland remained the Church established by law and, despite the tensions of the Ten Years Conflict between the Church courts and the Civil courts, was content to continue that relationship. The abolition by Parliament of Patronage in 1874 confirmed that view. The Free Church was committed to the principle of establishment but was opposed to the existing form of establishment which had enabled the Civil courts to 'interfere' in the internal discipline of the Church. The United Presbyterian Church was totally opposed to any control or support of the Church by the State and for the rest of the century spear-headed a vigorous campaign for the disestablishment of the Church of Scotland.

19th century Scotland also saw the rapid growth and consolidation of several of the existing Churches and the establishment of new ones.

**The Roman Catholics**
The growth of the Roman Catholic Church was aided not only by the repeal of penal legislation but also by the recruitment of Irish labour during the industrialisation of Scotland. When Father Andrew Scott was appointed to the Glasgow mission in 1808 his flock numbered less than five hundred. Within a few years it had risen to three thousand and he was able to build the imposing new church on the north bank of the Clyde which is now the cathedral of the archdiocese of Glasgow. In 1827 the numbers of Catholics had grown sufficiently to justify the division of Scotland into the Northern, Eastern and Western vicariates. In 1755 the Catholic population of Scotland had been estimated at 16,490 but in 1877 the figures were Western Vicariate 225,600, Eastern Vicariate 74,300

and Northern Vicariate 12,500. In 1878 Pope Leo XIII issued the Bull *Ex Supremo Apostolatus Apice* which recognised Scotland as a nation distinct from England and set up a Scottish hierarchy of two archbishops, one of St Andrews and Edinburgh who had under him the bishops of Argyll and Isles, Galloway, Dunkeld and Aberdeen and one of Glasgow who had no province but was independent. In 1947 Glasgow was made a province with an archbishop and bishops of Paisley and Motherwell.

**The Episcopal Church**
The 19th century also saw a notable revival in the Episcopal Church. The fourteen former dioceses were grouped into seven: Aberdeen and Orkney; Moray, Ross and Caithness; Argyll and the Isles; Brechin; St Andrews, Dunkeld and Dunblane; Glasgow and Galloway; Edinburgh. Each diocese was provided with a cathedral in the main centre of population. The number of churches increased from 73 to 150 during the twenty years from 1837 and clergy numbers increased over the same period from 78 to 163.

**The Methodists**
Methodism had reached Scotland in the 18th century and John Wesley visited the country twenty two times between 1751 and 1790. But the early Methodist preachers regarded a Scottish station as misery and banishment. The antagonism of the Church of Scotland and the refusal of some ministers to admit Methodists to the Lord's Supper led Wesley to ordain eleven ministers for Scotland and this led to an expansion in members 1790-1819. Methodism has been particularly successful in Shetland and reached a peak of 6000 in 1866. Despite its relatively small size in Scotland, Methodism has gained an entrance to the worship of all Churches through the hymns of Charles Wesley.

## The Congregationalists

The Congregational Union was formed in 1812 out of the uncertainty caused among Scottish Congregationalists by the withdrawal in 1808 of the Haldane brothers. It was defined in 1848 as a confraternity of Churches and not as an ecclesiastical court. On this basis its membership rose to 96 Churches by 1896. In that year it was united with the Evangelical Union which had been founded in 1843 by several Seceder ministers who had been deposed for their departure from Calvinist orthodoxy.

## The Baptists

Scottish Baptists were slow to unite because of strong views about the independency of the local Church and when the Baptist Union was formed in 1843 it contained only a minority of Churches and lasted only to 1856. The Baptist Union was refounded in 1869 with a membership of 51 Churches.

## Newcomers

During the 19th century there were several newcomers to the Scottish ecclesiastical scene. The first Catholic Apostolic congregation consisted of about 600 communicants who adhered to Edward Irving after he was deposed from the Scots Church in London in 1832. Because of its strong belief in the nearness of the Second Coming of Christ no provision was made to fill vacancies in the Apostolate on whom continuance of the ministry depended and few members now remain.

The Salvation Army came to Scotland in 1879 when a corps was established at Anderston in Glasgow. A young American, Henry Edmonds was appointed by General William Booth to expand the Scottish work and by 1888 there were 78 corps. Many Scots were helped by the Army to emigrate to new opportunities.

There is a reference to a 'little fragment of a flock' in Edinburgh in 1838 but the Brethren did not begin to expand in Scotland until after the split between Open and Exclusive wings in 1848. There were 80 Exclusive assemblies in 1880 and in 1887 there were 187 Open assemblies.

A new Presbyterian Church was formed in 1893 when the Free Presbyterians left the Free Church because of the latitude being allowed in relation to the Westminster Confession of Faith by the Declaratory Act of the Free Church Assembly.

## Organisations
Many of the organisations with which the contemporary Churches are familiar were founded during this century. These included the Scottish Sunday School Union (1899), the Boys' Brigade (1883) and the Girls' Guildry (1900).

## 6. God or Gods?
Do all these people worship the same God? This is the kind of question which has been asked by those who have been puzzled by the astonishing variety of Christian denominations. The variety of Presbyterian denominations in Scotland has perplexed many Scots as well as Christians in other countries.

The Presbyterians have responded by working for reunion with varying degrees of success. In 1900 the entire United Presbyterian Church and most of the Free Church of Scotland came together to form the United Free Church of Scotland. The minority who remained outside that union are represented today by the Free Church of Scotland. In 1929 occurred the union of the Church of Scotland with most of the United Free Church but a minority of the United Free Church felt unable to enter the union and maintains its separate witness today. On a smaller scale in 1956 some dozen congregations of the Original Secession Church joined the Church of Scotland but one congregation joined the Free Church. This reduced the number of Presbyterian Churches to five: The Church of Scotland, The Free Church of Scotland, The United Free Church of Scotland, The Reformed Presbyterian Church of Scotland (the Cameronians) and The Free Presbyterian Church of Scotland (dating from 1893). However in 1989 a sixth was formed when the Associated Presbyterian Churches broke with the Free Presbyterian Church over the controversy caused by one of the elders, Lord Mackay of Clashfern, attending requiem Masses for legal colleagues. In 2000 a seventh was formed by the secession of a group from the Free Church to form the Free Church of Scotland Continuing.

Presbyterian divisions are almost incomprehensible to those outside the Reformed tradition. The old question of the relationship of Church and State is still present. The United Free Church is voluntaryist and considers that the Church should neither be supported nor controlled by the State. The Reformed Presbyterians do not recognise an un-Covenanted State. The others believe in recognition of the Church by the State but differ in their views of how this should be. Doctrinal differences centre on the place given to the Westminster Confession of Faith and how much liberty of opinion is appropriate.

Despite their own divisions Scottish Presbyterians have been active in wider ecumenism. A Scottish Churches Council was formed in 1924 including representatives of the Church of Scotland, the United Free Church, the Episcopal Church, the Congregational Union, the Baptist Union and the Original Secession Church. Its function was to suggest when common action was necessary on questions of national importance and met quarterly until 1948. It was replaced by the Scottish Churches Ecumenical Committee which in turn was succeeded by the revival of the Scottish Churches Council in 1964.

There were several unsuccessful attempts at organic reunion during the 1950s and 1960s. Negotiations between the Church of Scotland, the Church of England, the Episcopal Church in Scotland and the Presbyterian Church of England produced a scheme of union on a bishops-in-presbytery basis which provoked much controversy in Scotland. Equally unsuccessful have been attempts to achieve union between the Church of Scotland and the Congregational Union, the Church of Scotland and the Methodist Synods in Scotland and Shetland and between the United Free Church and the Congregational Union. The Churches of Christ (heirs of the Haldane brothers and the Scottish-Irish American Alexander Campbell) united in 1981 with the United Reformed Church in England and Wales to form the United Reformed Church in the United Kingdom. The United Reformed Church was enlarged in Scotland by its union with the Scottish Congregational Church in 2000.

A highly significant step was taken in 1990 by the inauguration of ACTS (Action of Churches Together in Scotland) in which nine Churches participated: the Church of Scotland, the Roman Catholic Church in Scotland, the Scottish Episcopal Church, the Scottish Congregational Church, the Methodist Church in Scotland, the Religious Society of Friends in Scotland, the Salvation Army, the United Free Church of Scotland and the United Reformed Church.

Do all these people worship the same God? As the 20th century passed the question could be asked in a very different context from the situation prevailing about 1900. Scotland was then perceived to be a Christian country, the only notable non-Christian religious group being the Jewish community. Extensive immigration since then has led to a diversification of the religious scene so that Scotland can now be described as a pluralist society, a land of many faiths.

Much of this development has occurred since the Second World War but there have been Sikhs in Scotland since 1918, Hindus since the 1920s and the first Islamic mosque was opened in Glasgow in 1944. As a result of the Chinese occupation of Tibet in 1959 Chogyam Trungpa (1939-87) came to Scotland and founded the Samye Ling Buddhist monastery on Eskdalemuir. The Sikhs, the Hindus and the Muslims are largely ethnic communities of 'New Scots' but the Buddhists have actively encouraged inter-faith encounter. Scottish interest in the Baha'i faith goes back to the visit of Abdul Baha to Edinburgh in 1913 and since the establishment of the first Scottish Spiritual Assembly in 1948 many native Scots have been attracted to this inclusive faith.

It is nothing new to have racial labels attached to religious groups. The Episcopal Church has resented being described as the English Church and properly points to its deep Scottish roots. The Roman Catholic Church was once regarded as Irish, or sometimes Italian, but neither description is accurate or does justice to the second largest Church in Scotland, which has contributed so much to the community's well being. Similarly the Orthodox Churches in Scotland are not just Russian or Greek or Coptic but also attract to their services and their membership many who understand none of these languages.

For many people outside Scotland the typical Scot has been a dour, humourless Presbyterian. One Scot who actually claimed to be a Presbyterian atheist reinforced the stereotype. At the end of the 20th century many, perhaps most, Scots are not Presbyterians but their Scottishness is by no means thereby diminished.

# On Being the Church in an Age of Religious Indifference[1]

*A Stewart Todd*

**Presidential Address to the Scottish Church Society, 1988**

The Constitution of this Society speaks of the defence and advancement within the Church of Scotland of the doctrine of the One Holy Catholic and Apostolic Church as witnessed to in Holy Scripture and as set forth in the ancient Creeds. It speaks of the promotion of a true catholicity of life and practice in worship and in our relationship with the world. And then it spells out some of the implications of these grand objectives. And here are two of them. First, we are to affirm that the Church is 'a divine society, called into being, commissioned and sustained, not by men, but by the power of God'. Second, we are to foster the 'sense of the living continuity of the Church from Apostolic times under the guidance of the Holy Spirit'.

But we live in an age of religious indifference! Are these grand objectives, grandiloquently expressed, still valid or does the religious indifference of the age have the effect of marginalising them? It seemed to me this was a proper subject for a Presidential Address to be delivered in the octave of Pentecost; and if I fulfil the task involved only imperfectly, let me nevertheless assure you that it is offered as my earnest endeavour to repay the debt I owe to this Society and to acknowledge the honour you did me in electing me President three years ago.

Our experience of our own society (with a small 's') and our impression of the state of affairs in most of Western European society would lead us to believe that there is today indifference to religion on a massive scale. The devil whispers in our ear two more adjectives –

---

[1] First published 1989 by the Scottish Church Society as an occasional paper.

'unprecedented' and 'unparalleled'. The first point I would like to make is that if we are to be truly the Church we shall of course renounce the devil and all his works and eschew the sin of pessimism. The Church which acknowledges a living continuity from Apostolic times under the guidance of the Holy Spirit will know a bit of history and will remember that it has been guided by the Spirit through many strange and inhospitable times. Listen to this quotation from a four volume work on indifference written in 1827 by the Abbé Hugues Félicité Robert de Lammenais. The work was called *Essai sur l'indifférence en matière de religion*. He writes, 'The century that is really sick is not the one that is passionately involved in error, but the one that neglects and scorns truth. There is still power and consequently hope wherever violent outbursts occur, but what can be expected when there is no more movement, the pulse has ceased to beat and the heart is cold - only an imminent and inevitable breakup'. And then he goes on, 'It would be feeble to try to hide from ourselves the fact that European society is rapidly approaching that end-point. The rumbling noises in its breast and the shocks that rack it are not the most frightening symptoms that are visible to the observer. The worst symptom is undoubtedly the lethargy, indifference and deep drowsiness into which it is clearly sinking, and who will rescue it?' That was about religious indifference in 1827. In the New Testament Paul refers to God as God who, almost by definition, raised Jesus Christ from the dead: he also refers to God who, almost by definition, **'raises** the dead'. If the Abbé's account of religious indifference in 1827 is accurate then clearly the subsequent history of the 19th century proves Paul's definition accurate also. God is God who raises the dead or as our constitution puts it 'the Church is a divine society, called into being, commissioned and sustained not by men, but by the power of God.'

Being free from panic and pessimism we are to observe, then, that the religious indifference that characterises our times is not unprecedented. It would appear likewise to be not unparalleled. In September 1985 there was published by the Royal Society a report entitled *The Public Understanding of Science*. The Royal Society is usually described as the foremost learned scientific group in Britain. In that report, which was the result of a two-year study, they looked at ways in which the public understanding of science might be improved, and they listed proposals for action which were aimed at industry, education and the mass-media. The interesting thing was that among the things they saw themselves combating was not only hostility to science but indifference to science and technology among shop-floor workers, among managers, among investors, an indifference they believed was seriously weakening the nation's industry.

The Church inspired by the logic of the Gospel and reassured by observable historical facts cries 'sursum corda' to its people in times of religious indifference and eschews pessimism as a terrible sin. The Church, the true Church, will also resist the attractions of nationalism in times of religious indifference. The attractions are considerable.

In 15th century Scotland, Scottish liturgical use was basically Sarum. But Sarum was an elaborate use and the Sarum calendar of the 15th century was already so full of saints' festivals as to leave precious little opportunity to conduct the orderly and regular reading of the psalter and scriptures, which was the real content and purpose of the divine office. To the liturgical books of this complex rite you find the Scottish Church of the late 15th century and early 16th century, in nationalistic mood, adding yet more local saints' festivals, making the whole thing completely unmanageable. Scotland was not alone in Western Europe in perpetrating these liturgical follies but historians reckon it was probably the worst offender. Even the great Bishop Elphinstone, in whose cathedral I am privileged to work and worship - even the great Bishop Elphinstone was susceptible to the attractions of nationalism and, while part of his considerable liturgical contribution was to bring some order into the celebration of Scottish saints, it does nevertheless seem that it was to provide an emotional basis for the fashionable nationalism that the work was embraced as much as to reform the liturgy and serve the Church, since no attempt was made to demythologise the legends. The work therefore laid itself open to the criticisms of martyrologies and breviaries that for decades had been mounting in the Churches of the West, that they were overloaded with absurdities.

Nationalism still has its attractions and many seem to think that they will find here the spark that is needed in an age of indifference. And so there is grand talk of the national Church where it might sometimes be more appropriate to talk of a tiny pilgrim minority. Or else the *Book of Common Order (1979)* is criticised because, by giving pride of place to the Orders for Holy Communion and silently acknowledging thereby that the Eucharist is the norm of Christian Sunday worship, it does not reflect the ethos of the Church of Scotland! Or again we are all familiar with those pages of Scottish history which are accorded the respect of Holy Writ and which, if they were properly demythologised, would be seen to have more to do with the politics of nationalism than with religion; and yet these pages of history, undemythologised, still serve to inhibit ecumenical endeavour, and to portray the office of bishop, for example, as something to be resisted at all costs with vigour if not with venom.

The collocation of words in the title of our Society is significant and presumably not accidental. We call ourselves the Scottish Church Society. Our Scottishness, of which of course we can be proud, is nevertheless an adjunct to Church: the adjective forms an adjunct to the noun substantive. The adjective 'Scottish' is dependent upon the noun 'Church' as an attribute. Gratitude to God for one's heritage and one's native land and for the hand of God in one's history is one thing: but nationalism, concern for Scottishness that takes precedence over proper Church obedience to her Lord, nationalism that is embraced because it might stir the emotions of an indifferent people, may be some sort of palliative, but it is no cure. The lessons of history are worth noting. The good bishop's *Breviary*, which I have mentioned, never did achieve the promise of its launch and of its royal patronage. It was less than a commercial success and the publisher, soon after 1510, seems to have decided that there was not much future in liturgical books even with a nationalist emphasis. He turned his commercial energies to brewing instead.

The Church will resist the attractions of crude nationalism — the Church which sings: 'My soul there is a country afar beyond the stars', the Church which also sings of the glory of Jerusalem above, whose splendour 'challenges the souls that greatly dare and bids us seize the whole of life and build its glory there'.

In an age of indifference to religion the Church, the true Church, will avoid the sin of pessimism, will resist the attractions of nationalism and will also look askance at too much pragmatism. Pragmatism is the identifying of causes and results and lessons to be learned and the activity, often officious, of putting these lessons into practice. The massive indifference to religion in our times makes many people very nervous and sometimes desperate and they long to be doing something about it: pragmatism is appealing often and they do not always stop to consider the limitations of the pragmatist's view of things. What has been called liturgical renewal in recent decades was a case in point. Let me make it quite clear. I believe, I am sure we all believe, that liturgical revision was necessary and overdue. In our reformed Church, *semper reformanda*, we see it as something which from time to time has to be undertaken. Our whole desire is to be true to Christ and to new understanding and experience of him through the Spirit: our desire is also to be true to our people. The forms we use in worship must be appropriate to Christ and to the mystery of worship in which he is present and in which heaven intersects earth, the human and the divine interpenetrate. The forms we use in worship must be appropriate also to the people of the Church and their ability to use them. All of this requires effort, liturgical work and renewed effort from time to time. But clearly there were many in recent decades who embraced liturgical revision with unwonted fervour and sometimes with iconoclastic zeal because they believed that unreformed liturgy and archaic language were the cause of empty pews and that up-to-date liturgy with up-to-date language and musical idioms were going to fill the pews again. And patently they haven't! And the pragmatism has in some cases caused severe damage to the Church. An ill-considered use of forms because they were 20th century rather than because they were serviceable as vehicles of the truth has had the effect of trivialising worship to a degree that makes many of us profoundly sad.

I read recently contributions to the study of religious indifference by several sociologists. Now sociologists are not noted for their humility! But there were these distinguished sociologists acknowledging that while they could identify many possible causes of religious indifference, they could not validate the theses that relate any one of the causes to the phenomenon itself. From liturgical revision to inner city renewal, from relearning the grammar of dogmatics to feeding the hungry, from ecumenics to education of the young there is work to be done, an enormous volume of work; but the Church will do it in patient obedience to Christ, in quietness and confidence following the guidance of the Holy Spirit and not in upstart, ill-considered, headline-hitting pragmatism. The Church does not know all the answers: the Church does not even know all the questions.

I turn now to make adjustments to perspective which perhaps ought to be made. If for the moment I may substitute for religious indifference the words 'the secularised ethos of society', and I think that is permissible, it will enable me to refer to what seem to me wise words written eighteen years ago by Karl Rahner in a book called *Grace in Freedom*. In that book one chapter is entitled 'The **Christian** Character of the Secularised Ethos', and in that chapter Rahner calls for caution in our judgments about the secularity of contemporary life. Noting that the plough and the sickle were secular objects, as secular as the tractor and the combine harvester that have replaced them, he points out that there will be even more man-made reality in this world of ours, reality which is neither 'numinous' nature nor is profane in the bad sense. This man-made reality may obstruct the religious view because it is so large and so fascinating but it will be there by right and we must accept it. Rahner wrote, 'To say it quite simply: the loaf of bread has become much bigger, thank God, but man can still realize that he does not live by bread alone, for he has always been tempted, not only now, to think the opposite'. Rahner points out, very sensibly, that we make secularisation only more dangerous if we dramatise it and, he asks the question, 'is it really so certain that formerly, when religion and the Church played a greater part in public life, men really had more true faith hope and charity?' Think back to our 1827 quotation. Is it not also true that the seemingly secularised ethos of our time which speaks of the freedom and dignity of man, of responsibility and the love of one's neighbour - is it not true that this is the legitimate son of Christianity, even though it is often a prodigal squandering his property far from his father's house. Rahner concludes his brief discussion by saying that if we want to avoid the world's being submerged by a pagan secularism without God and without hope then we ought not to go on compiling statistics and making forecasts and concentrate instead on bearing our Christian witness by word and deed. Everything else we can and must leave to God.

Let me now make another adjustment to perspective in the whole matter of religious indifference. It is suggested by the earlier throw-away line about the Church not knowing all the answers nor all the questions. It is about the relationship between religious indifference and agnosticism. Now of course there is a clear distinction between these two. Religious indifference in the strict sense does not reflect upon itself: if it did it would emerge from its state of lack of interest and, by reflecting, religious indifference would turn into scepticism or agnosticism. Agnosticism is aware of itself. The agnostic has thought and doesn't know. But it has to be asked whether in the real world the distinction between indifference and agnosticism can always be made. Is everyone outside the Church indifferent all the time, victims of bored nihilism, or are they some of the time or to some extent agnostic? Helping to bring religious indifference to awareness of itself may seem a very small contribution for the Church to make but it is worth making if this awareness can take the form of agnosticism. Agnosticism is not Philistine: it may be a stance of extreme sensibility. You can't really apply the Laodicean reference in Revelation 3:16 to the agnostics: they are not lukewarm. To mention Rahner again: he claims that conscious agnosticism is the contemporary expression of what theology has taught as the incomprehensibility of God. In other words I am suggesting the Church will not despair about current religious indifference because people are not uniformly bored and nihilistic: in reality people probably oscillate between indifference and agnosticism and agnosticism not only admits of an option in favour of Christian faith but also agnosticism and Church can travel together if Church is humble enough to acknowledge that it doesn't have all the answers. Both share '*agnosia*' which is as respectable outside the Church as it is within the Church. But it is important therefore in these circumstances that our apologetic is humble and not harsh. Likewise our public prayer and praise will more appropriately be reverend, and decorous: I can't imagine who it is that really wants these ecclesiastical chat-shows that are fashionable. It certainly isn't the person outside the Church who sometimes wonders about religion. The superficially indifferent in our society who in their better moments are agnostic will perhaps warm more readily to our '*agnosia*' than they do to smug claims to superior 'gnosis' and a hot line to God. The Church's message concerns the love of Christ, the breadth and length and height and depth of it and the knowing of it, though as Paul adds significantly, it is beyond knowledge. The Church's worship like its apologetic will surely reflect this 'not knowing'. Our joyful hymns will be sobered with awe and our sad hymns will be not just protest songs but sad songs solaced with the immortal hopes and unstinted optimism of the Gospel. 'Unspeakable' is another characteristic New Testament adjective to qualify Christian joy or glory — joy unspeakable — something we can't know or put into words. So the Church will love the agnostic because his is a state of mind which to some extent we share and the Church will love the indifferent because Christ died for them too of course: we shall also, however, bear in mind that their indifferences may sometimes be a cloak for embarrassed but honest agnosticism. We shall remember Elijah whimpering under his juniper tree, 'I have been very jealous for the Lord God of Hosts: because the children of Israel have forsaken thy covenant, thrown down thine altars, and slain thy prophets with the sword: and I even I only am left and they seek my life to take it away'. And the Lord said unto Elijah, 'Yet I have left me seven thousand in Israel, all the knees that have not bowed unto Baal, and every mouth which hath not kissed him.' The classic sermons on that passage speak of the 'hidden Church.'

These adjustments to perspective I think are necessary and helpful. They do not excuse us however from the serious task of doing theology in an age of religious indifference. The constitution of our Society speaks of defending and advancing doctrine. The Church has to think what it is saying about God if what it is saying seems to produce in so many a complete lack of curiosity and ennui. I believe we have to think about our knowledge of God and learn the grammar of it which is trinitarian. I think it is also important to say this task is not to be thought of as belonging only to the full-time academic theologian. We are all theologians, especially those of us who have responsibility for the conduct of worship. You may not thank me for taking refuge in Latin, even less for the ambiguity of the Latin tag I shall trot out: *Lex orandi, Lex credendi* is a suggestive ring of words nevertheless. There is an interplay between worship and doctrine in practice, between what we say in our prayer *lex orandi*, and what we believe *lex credendi*. Geoffrey Wainwright published his systematic theology in 1980 and entitled it *Doxology*. The Lutheran theologian Edmund Schlink, noting that members of separated churches can pray together and worship together more readily than they can make common doctrinal statements, calls for a re-translation of dogmatic statements into the doxological context out of which they developed, in order to facilitate understanding of their original intention. Many of us here are doing liturgy and therefore doing theology every Sunday. The task is not marginalised just because so many are indifferent to it. The task is as central as ever it was. God's name is to be hallowed on earth as it is hallowed in heaven. The prodigal will return one day and when he does he shall want to find his father's house in good order: he shall not be particularly pleased to learn that his father, neglecting the homestead, has gone off to tell the prodigal's erstwhile employer how to run his pig farm.

I am speaking now and in conclusion of doxology/theology as a distinctive task of the Church requiring our best efforts continuously, for God's sake and for his children's sake, whether the times be propitious or unpropitious. I am speaking of a primary task and I am speaking on behalf of a society dedicated to safeguarding that primacy. Let me tell you about a bit of research that was written up recently by a Roman Catholic scholar and published in Volume XVI of *Studia Liturgica*. The subject is the Offertory in the Mass or what is now called the Preparation of the Altar and Gifts, in particular that part of it which was the prayer known as *super oblata*, now called the 'Prayer over the gifts'. Now of course different emphases have been made in those prayers over the centuries, now on the sacrifice to follow, now on the gifts as part of the created order. In our own tradition the corresponding prayers said in association with the receiving of money offerings and preceded by a procession are still in many churches an occasion for some pomp and Pelagianism.

The study shows however that the emphasis in many of the early *super oblata* prayers in western liturgies and in eastern liturgies was not on the gifts nor on the givers nor on what was going to be done with the gifts and their relation to the sacrifice of Christ. No: the emphasis in many of these prayers was on the utter unworthiness of the celebrant to speak the eucharistic prayer he was about to pray, in other words his inadequacy for the task of doxology/theology. And so having made brief reference certainly to the gifts which were on the altar and on tables around (and which would have been collected untidily and without procession), the celebrant, in some liturgies, turns to the people and says: 'Pray for me' and the people answer in this fashion: 'May the Lord be in your heart and in your mouth and may he receive an acceptable sacrifice from your mouth and from your hands for our salvation and for the salvation of all men'. In the Sarum Rite, used throughout Scotland in the medieval period, the response began, '*Spiritus Sancti gratia illuminet cor tuum et labia tua*': May the grace of the Holy Spirit impart light to your heart and to your lips. The researcher believes that the original reference to sacrifice in many prayers is a reference to the sacrifice of praise rather than as later understood to the sacrifice of Christ in the mass. He also makes the linguistic point that prayer *super oblata* need not mean 'over' the offering but prayer said in a position next to the offering or after the offering.

Eucharistic prayer, and by that I mean the kind of thanksgiving that we make in our services as the climax of worship whether or not we have elements of bread and wine on the table, – eucharistic prayer has always been and will always be solemn and spacious blessing of God, God equally versatile in creation and in salvation. It is a great challenge and we do indeed need the Holy Spirit to grace our hearts and our lips: it is also a great privilege and, if God will, our people can be helped to remember and gradually to identify with Christ and with his sacrifice and with his victory and with his presence and with his purpose for the world and in heart and mind to surrender self devoutly.

That prayer I believe is the great work of the Church be society ever so indifferent, the great work which is the inspiration of all other works out in the world. I would say let the Church be the Church, let us do our works; especially those works that are most properly and characteristically our own. And let us do our works in quiet confidence remembering the lines of Wordsworth

> Think you mid all this mighty sum
> Of things for ever speaking,
> That nothing of itself will come
> But we must still be seeking;

remembering also Paul who speaks of our works but also of the fruit of the Spirit (fruit grows by itself); and finally remembering the words of our Constitution: 'The Church is a divine society, called into being, commissioned and sustained, not by man but by the power of God'.

# Why We Are a Parish Church[1]

## *Marjory A MacLean*

I intend to answer this question twice, with different results. 'Why' can have a causative reference (why were you late in arriving from Forfar? - there was a rhinoceros loose on the Tay Bridge); 'why' can have a purposive reference (why on earth did you come over the Tay Bridge? - I wanted to see the rhinoceros). When I ask the question "why we are a parish Church" in a causative way the answers will emerge from the history of the Church of Scotland between 1560 and 1921; when I ask it in a purposive way some contemporary contentions will arise.

## I The Causative Background of the Parish System

Many institutions can appear nonsensical and incoherent if we do not look at them with a sense of history. The English language, for example, is full of inconsistencies which profoundly irritate non-native learners but which are perfectly explicable with a little etymological history. In the same way the character of the Church of Scotland is more easily grasped with the help of the institutions and developments that shaped it in earlier ages. The curious thing, though, is that most of the causative influences I shall talk about are entirely historical; they no longer exist. It is like looking at a building and knowing that the builders erected scaffolding first of all, constructed the building inside the scaffolding and then removed every piece of scaffolding once the building was able to support its own weight. I shall suggest a handful of pieces of the Church's scaffolding, almost all of them cleared away long since, leaving the edifice we are struggling to maintain, and determined to love, in our own day. Where there do seem to be scaffolding poles still lying about I shall point them out.

---

[1] This paper was read to the Scottish Church Society 15 November 1999 and published in the *Report*, 1999-2000.

## i) *Establishment*

At various historical points the principle of Establishment has been asserted. The vast social and religious revolution[2] mobilised by Knox for the Scots common weal was expressed as a political principle in 1592. In 1690[3] it was reasserted as the triumph over James VII's divine-right absolutism and optimistic pro-Catholicism. In 1707 it was underlined in the Act of Security, to redd the marches, so to speak, between the polities of England and Scotland.

The common assertion of each fresh declaration was Establishment as a monopoly privilege.

Establishment, in the mouths of its theological enemies of the 19th century, was always presented as a burden on the Church, but it was originally seen as the responsibility of the Christian state to maintain its Church. Christendom understood the sphere of influence of a single Church to be coterminous with that of the secular power; indeed the medieval origin of this co-ordinate jurisdiction of Church and State was in a single jurisdiction. The burden of establishment lay on the State in all its reaches and throughout its jurisdiction; the civil power was not exempt from the maintenance of the Presbyterian religion in places where Catholicism or Episcopalianism happened to be stronger. If the privilege of the Church extended throughout the land, it was partly because that privilege was held against the State and throughout its area of sovereign rule. For example, the Burgess Oath introduced in 1745,[4] remembered for causing one of the splits of the First Secession, was an anti-Jacobite measure which attempted

---

[2] Michael Lynch, 'From Privy Kirk to Burgh Church: An Alternative View of the Process of Protestantisation' in Norman MacDougall, ed, *Church, Politics and Society: Scotland 1408-1929*, Edinburgh: John Donald, 1983.

[3] Act 1690 c.5.

[4] Finlay A J Macdonald, 'Law and Doctrine in the Church of Scotland with Particular Reference to Confessions of Faith', St. Andrews unpublished PhD thesis 1983, ch. XI.

to weed all but the adherents of 'true religion' out of the government and business life of the cities, and somehow remained on the statute book until 1819, rending asunder the very confession it was designed to protect. Or one can look to the present debate about the Act of Settlement[5] and Act of Security, and wonder a little whether the Accession Oath that is reaffirmed in part annually by the monarch to the General Assembly is any kind of protection of the Church of Scotland. Is it really a piece of the scaffolding still visible on the site, or is it what Bagehot referred to as merely one of the ceremonial elements of the State?

For several centuries after the Reformation, then, the principle of Establishment tied the Church of Scotland to the whole people of Scotland, good-willed and disinterested alike, even when the purpose and passion of the principle had crumbled away to next to nothing before the negotiation of the 1921 settlement. That binding tie is one reason why we are a parish Church.

## ii) *Endowment*

The patrimony of the Church was one of the most enduring pieces of luggage of the Established Church and a bequest from history that the modern Church cannot isolate and return. From the wealth of the whole nation came a providence that confirmed the ties between Church and community.

Even as late as the early nineteenth century the Church was prevented from determining its own stipends.[6] I remember the late Leonard Small mischievously claiming to have been dismayed to discover that the stipend of St Cuthbert's Church, Edinburgh, was calculated

---

[5] At the time of writing, peers and MSPs are seeking to open parliamentary debate about its future.

[6] John Cunningham, *The Church History of Scotland from the Commencement of the Christian Era to the Present Time*, 2nd edition, James Thin, 1882, II. XXVII.

as a quotient of the value of the annual wheat crop grown in Charlotte Square. I also remember being just wise enough an assistant minister not to take everything he said altogether seriously.

But the main inheritance was the teinds, largely taken over from the pre-Reformation Church, and capitalised in terms of the 1925 legislation to the dismay of James Barr's United Free rebels, who constituted the continuing minority in 1929. According to Barr[7], the intention of Knox was that such funds would be used largely for education and poor relief, functions of the Church after the Reformation, but scarcely so in 1925. His logic was that their capitalisation should not create a windfall for the Church:

> The public resources of the State are to be turned over permanently to the private possession of the Church. This is not disendowment; it is capitalised, complete, final, and irretrievable endowment. <u>It is not a stroke for national justice: it is a raid on national funds.</u>[8]

However far one may agree with Barr's opinion of the proper destination of the capitalised teinds, it remains true that their source was from a tax imposed without religious discrimination in an era of religious monopoly for a social purpose benefiting the whole country.

By the time of the modern settlement religion was regarded as a largely privatised activity, something it had not entirely been since the time of Constantine the Great and the end of Christian persecution. The model of a State financially maintaining a solitary Church which in turn provided or co-ordinated most public services no longer represented Scottish public life, but the shape of the Church had been established in the age when it had. As by legal Establishment, so by financial

---

[7] James Barr, *The Scottish Church Question*, James Clarke, 1920 chs V and VI.
[8] Ibid. p.37.

Endowment, the Church of Scotland was tied to a sense of the service of the whole population long after an ethos of spiritual voluntaryism had untied the people's commitment to the national Church.

### iii) *Patronage*

At its least objectionable patronage was an 'exercise in civic virtue'[9] in the late 17th century, when elders and heritors nominated a minister for the approval of the congregation. At its worst, during the Ten Years' Conflict, it left one third of the Church feeling disenfranchised and tyrannised. The Reformed version of patronage was another exchange of responsibility and right. Patrons or heritors, whose status passed as a real heritable property right, bore the burden of the maintenance of church and minister. This appears to be a somewhat feudal extension of Calvin's notion of the spiritual responsibility of the civil magistrate. Since feudal rights and burdens are matters of private not public law, the significance of the system is the impinging of the burdens of Establishment upon the realm of private property law.

The 1874 Act abolished patronage by an historic measure with an instant effect. The Court of Session must have been not a little surprised, therefore, by the bizarre Ballantyne case[10] sixty years later. The 1874 Act was cited by a congregation which was being prevented by its Presbytery from calling a new minister. The reasons for Presbytery's refusal are immaterial, but the congregation relied on the Act because it declared the right of a congregation to call its own minister, which they interpreted as a right against all parties, including, for their purposes, the Presbytery. It is almost disappointing that the Court of Session did not issue the case because of want of jurisdiction. It would have been instructive to see what the civil law

---

[9] Richard Sher and Alexander Murdoch, 'Patronage and Party in the Church of Scotland 1750-1800' in MacDougall, op. cit. ch. 11.
[10] Ballantyne v. Presbytery of Wigtown, 1936 SC 625.

would have made of an interpretation of the Act which effectively cast a court of the Church in the role of patron, as this would have constituted an attempt by an agency of the Church (the congregation) to assert a civil right (the Act) against an external interference which turned out to be its immediately superior ecclesiastical court.

For the present purpose, it suffices to conclude that the system of patronage, tying the spiritual rights of a congregation to the private rights of the feudal system, was another piece of that scaffolding that created the national Church as a body thirled to the whole people and culture of every part of Scotland.

### iv) *Jurisdiction*

It is a commonplace amongst church lawyers that when the State made a 'grant' of spiritual jurisdiction to the Church, it was a grant in the sense of 'acknowledgement', not in the sense of 'conferral'.[11] It was the acknowledgement of an existing, historical set of rights, not the creation of new ones: the spiritual jurisdiction had no single point of origin, then, and in the post-Reformation era the relationship between it and the civil order changed and developed.

According to Donaldson,[12] for example, the separation of civil and ecclesiastical courts was a gradual process, and in the post-Reformation period there was confusion about jurisdiction in consistorial cases. The Church enjoyed a judicial role which gave her an authority far beyond her formal membership.

Similarly, in the executive field, the Church had responsibility *quoad omnia* for education, poor relief etc. and of course that still echoes in the constitution of some older congregations.

---

[11] Macdonald, op. cit. ch V.
[12] Gordon Donaldson, *Scottish Church History*, Scottish Academic Press, 1985 ch 5 section 10.

This illustrates a significant principle, that the territorial ministry of the national, Established Church extended not only throughout the whole country, but throughout each individual parish, beyond the *spiritualia*, beyond the congregation's membership, and beyond what the medieval Conciliarists would have recognised as the wielding of the spiritual sword.

Any parish minister who has had access to ancient Session records can tell blood-chilling tales of the extent of the jurisdiction enjoyed by elders long ago, exercised with remarkable diligence and received often with awe-inspiring meekness. From Stromness in the years around 1700 the most attractive and memorable problems faced by the Session were the occasion when the elders (whose unvarying pronouncement in cases of unmarried pregnancy was an instruction to marry within 40 days and spend the intervening Sundays on the cutty stool) were presented with one young man and his two pregnant girlfriends, and another meeting which requested the heritor's servantman to repair the cutty stool while he was trimming up the pulpit, since the former was showing signs of wear from heavy usage.

By its universal reach throughout the life of the parish area, the national Church established a sense of responsibility over every life, and this is today expressed by many Sessions, ministers and congregations as a sense of pastoral concern and outreach in a way quite different from the social activity of other Churches, even within the Scottish Reformed tradition.

### v) *Disestablishment*
Curiously perhaps, the 20th century attempts at disestablishment may be as significant as the old elements of Establishment in explaining why we became irreducibly, irresistibly a parish Church. Here are certainly some pieces of the scaffolding still lying about.

If Barr's invective quoted earlier was right, for instance, we are forever tainted with civic money buried deep in our capital assets, so the principle of Voluntaryism did not start with a clean sheet in 1929. Another example that survived the 1920s is the Crown and the Church: the monarch renews her oath annually to the only church body (the General Assembly of the Church of Scotland) to which she sends her personal representative, and the only Church which provides her chaplains in Scotland. Whatever the relation of crown and people presently is, it has the Church of Scotland somehow attached and somehow privileged.

The 1921 settlement cannot be underestimated as the best possible compromise in the circumstances where there were so many principles dear to so many people and so little that conscience could yield. But it created what was only nearly a neat entity, achieved what was only nearly dis-Establishment, made room only nearly for the voluntaryist principle, and, as the examples above illustrate, barely impinged on the fundamental characteristic of a Church responsible as much to the people of the parish as to the members of the congregation, as much to the culture of power as to the needs of the individual, as much to the common weal of Scotland as to the well-being of the single believer.

Those, in the causative sense of the question, are some of the reasons why we are a parish Church.

## II  The Purposive Intentions of the Parish System

But in the present what matters more to us is the purposive sense of the question 'why we are a parish Church'.

### i) *The Church as the Soul of Society?*

To pick up the pre-Reformation theme of the common weal of Scotland, many theologians understand the function of the Church to be in part the provision of a spiritual element in the life of the body of the State, to be as it were the soul of a corporate being.[13] The idea of the State as a personality is remarkably modern, though. When the civil and ecclesiastical jurisdictions separated in the late Middle Ages, the concept of corporate entity, quite natural in ecclesiology, was not applied to the emerging concept of the State except by some writers of the Counter-Reformation who were clinging to the *via antiqua*. Even as late as Hobbes the legal fiction of state personality had not been completed - in *Leviathan*[14] he confined himself to the representative theory of government and statehood. The State as an entity with a spiritual potential is conventionally credited to Hegel, long after the Scottish Reformation had set the pattern of church-state engagement. So to interpret the Articles Declaratory of the Church of Scotland as expressing an ancient relationship of Church and State as if they were two legal *personae* would be, it seems to me, incoherent.

I much prefer the definition of the State as 'social geometry' which suggests that the Church ministers not to a discrete state entity,[15] but rather witnesses and prophesies within the infinitely complicated network of society or the common weal. The anomaly alluded to earlier of the patronage system producing private feudal liabilities and rights, would appear to exemplify the unlimited possibilities of social exchange the Church had always enjoyed. The idea of Church and State as two socially identifiable beings defining their mutual relations may be the Declaratory Articles' way of conceptualising the exercise of disestablishment, but modern state theory suggests something more integrated, more complex, more difficult.

---

[13] See Karl Barth, *Against the Stream: Shorter Post-War Writings 1946-1952*, London: SCM, 1954 Part I 'The Christian Community and the Civil Community' for this kind of argument.

[14] Thomas Hobbes, *Leviathan: or the Matter, Forme and Power of a Commonwealth Ecclesiastical and Civil*, edited with introduction by Michael Oakshott, Oxford: Basil Blackwell, 1946.

[15] Bertrand De Jouvenel, *Sovereignty: An Inquiry into the Political Good*, translated by J F Huntington, Cambridge: CUP, 1951.

## ii) *The Parish as the Location of Social Ministry?*

A related problem is therefore how to reach the people of the common weal with the ministry of the Church, and the parish system has always seemed to be a neat way to ensure blanket coverage of the territorial extent of Scotland. Until the present century the experience of public and corporate life was largely through the local parish; now the social geometry has a different shape and scale and a new complexity. While the parish in which we meet today[16], and the parish in which I served as minister until last year[17] come as close as is still possible to being old fashioned parishes where the primary services of education, culture, religion and social care are delivered universally as they were in past ages, society is losing that pattern in so many places that the parish system is rarely the most efficient channel for the delivery of our ministry and mission. Yet our faith in the parish system and Declaratory Article III's territorial ministry is a shibboleth of speeches to the General Assembly, an irreducible minimum of our orthodoxy.

Part of the problem was what Harvey Cox famously described as a non-pejorative version of secularism[18], the immense change in the network of public and private relationships, primary and secondary contacts in a large-scale society and a kind of urbanised context[19] of which the Reformers had no notion. There is no point, he says, in Christians deploring the modern metropolis, which fails to fit their old patterns. In other words our parishes no longer contain our society, and in them our reach is severely limited.

---

[16] Ceres parish in the Presbytery of St. Andrews.
[17] Stromness parish in the Presbytery of Orkney.
[18] Harvey Cox, *The Secular City: Secularization and Urbanization in Theological Perspective*, SCM, 1965.
[19] Ibid. ch. 2.

### iii) *The Parish as the Sphere of Ministerial Sovereignty?*

Some people within the Church are less concerned about the parish system as our channel for reaching the people of our country and more concerned about the kind of protective cell a parish provides for each ordained minister. The experience of the Board of Practice and Procedure in advising ministers and Presbytery Clerks is that there is a diversity of age, a diversity of opinion and of practice, and a theological breadth in the Church. The experience of those ministered to by the Church has, therefore, an alarming inconsistency about it. Minister X will baptize any baby presented, minister Y adheres passionately to the letter of the Assembly's Act. Minister A ministers to the parish, minister B nurtures a gathered congregation of the convinced. Time and time again the natural justice arguments that are resorted to by the puzzled and discriminated-against in local communities put in question the kind of sovereignty the Church tries to leave in the hands of ministers and Kirk Sessions in their territorial sphere.

The Board is examining this in the case of Presbyteries as part of the task of reappraising Presbytery sizes. The question has arisen - does our recent affirmation of commitment to the principles of the European Convention on Human Rights[20] require us to prioritise consistency of practice in comparable cases above the sovereign right of each Presbytery to exercise its unique discretion? Will the Church end up either with legislation for everything to ensure consistency between regions, which would amount to an intolerable retention of power by the Assembly, or else with a Confederation of Presbyteries for the standardising of practice? Kirk Sessions, in their jurisdiction, have the same pressures to face.

---

[20] General Assembly 1999, Report of the Board of Practice and Procedure, Deliverance s.10.

The point is not to change the ambition of the Church, a timeless ambition, one it has not needed to change in 450 years: to miss no-one in sounding the note of the gospel in the ears of the people, to exclude no-one from the pastoral care of the Church, to speak of the prophecy of the Kingdom to the institutions of the world and not only to its individuals.

But in conceding with courage that the institutions of our society include very few of our old parishes these days, we can take comfort from John Oman, this century's seminal Scottish ecclesiologist, writing between the wars:

> Instead of mourning over the present loss of privilege, should [the Church] not rather recognise the dispensation of a wise Providence, appointed to teach her the wealth of her own resources, to give her a higher idea of the patience of God, and to show her a truer view of the Kingdom of His children, whom, by the sole method of truth and obedience, He has set free?[21]

For the task is still as Professor Gill has described it:

> Part of the business of the churches is to spill over into secular society and to alter its moral quality.[22]

Parish ministers in contemplating the purpose of their ministry must wonder, not why we are a parish Church, but whether we are a parish Church, whether we should be, whether we can be. They must wonder if their allegiance to that model is genuine conviction or sheer familiarity. They must wonder what will replace it in the ministry of my generation and how a new and faithful pattern can be recognisably consistent with our Reformation principles.

---

[21] John Oman, *Vision and Authority*, Hodder and Stoughton, 1928 p.317.
[22] Robin Gill, 'Church and Society - Possibilities and Constraints' in A Elliot, and D Forrester, eds, *The Scottish Churches and the Political Process Today*. Edinburgh: CTPI, 1986 p.59.

# Church and State in Scotland, Today and Tomorrow[1]

*James L Weatherhead*

**Read to the Scottish Church Society, 22 May 1998**

It is beyond reasonable doubt that the history of the Church of Scotland from 1560 to 1929 can be understood in terms of tensions between Church and State. For example, we understand the early contentions between presbyterian and episcopal polity in terms of monarchs endeavouring to control the Church by the appointment of bishops, and the Church endeavouring to assert its independence by the establishment of Church courts, through which the Church would be self-governing. To this early period belongs Andrew Melville's famous statement about two kings and two kingdoms in Scotland.

The resolution of these early tensions came about in 1690, with the establishment of the Presbyterian system. That system was further secured in 1707, by the Act which was an integral part of the Treaty of Union: the Act for securing the Protestant religion and Presbyterian Church Government in Scotland. Statements in that Act, and in the Treaty itself, to the effect that certain provisions were to prevail in all time coming, were an attempt to ensure that the new Parliament, which would have a majority of English members, could not use that majority to remove the distinctive rights of the Scottish minority.

Some Scottish constitutional lawyers argue that this Treaty was fundamental law, and the clauses in it which referred to all time coming were entrenched clauses which the new Parliament could not alter. In other words, the new United Kingdom Parliament was a new body, and the Treaty of Union was the written constitution of the United Kingdom.

---

[1] First published by the Scottish Church Society in the *Report*, 1997-1998.

However, it soon became clear that in practice the new Parliament would be regarded as the English Parliament, with Scottish members added to it. So the new Parliament claimed that it had absolute sovereignty, as the previous English Parliament had.

One consequence of this was the view that no Parliament could bind its successors, because it was the Parliament in being which was sovereign. Consequently, even entrenched clauses could be altered. So it was that, only a few years after the Treaty of Union, patronage was reintroduced by Parliament to the Church of Scotland, and the sad story of conflict between Church and State began again, leading eventually to the Disruption.

The Free Church, as its name declared, was determined to be free from State interference, but that freedom was shown to be insubstantial when, following the formation of the United Free Church in 1900, those of the Free Church who stayed out of the Union claimed that they were still legally the Free Church, and therefore owners of all the property. The case in the civil courts went to the House of Lords, who decided in favour of the Free Church, by a majority.

The basis of the judgement was that the Church was essentially a trust, and that trustees are not free to alter the terms of the trust deed under which they operated. I was interested to discover that one of the minority judges in this case said, in a later case, 'The great use of a trustee is to commit judicious breaches of trust.'

It is interesting that the judgement in the Free Church case has never been reversed. What happened was that there was a recognition that, in law, when trustees are unable to carry out their responsibilities, these responsibilities have to be transferred to people who can carry them out. So, in accordance with the law, Parliament set up a commission which went laboriously through all the properties involved, and allocated some to the Free Church, and some to the United Free Church (UF). Thus an equitable distribution of property was arranged; but the decision of the House of Lords still stands as a precedent.

When the Union of the UF Church with the Church of Scotland was being contemplated, attention had to be given to finding a constitution which would be acceptable to those who had maintained the old establishment principle, and also to those who emphasised the spiritual freedom of the Church; and a means had to be found of preventing a recurrence of the House of Lords case, by changing the legal position in such a way that the precedent would not apply.

So a large committee of members from both Churches laboured to produce the Declaratory Articles. Discussions were long and protracted, and the outcome was remarkable.

First, there had to be some definitive statement of the identity of the Church, and clearly that had to be doctrinal. So the First Article was composed, very deliberately, to include only the basic essentials.

Attempts to include too many specific doctrines, as for example the Virgin Birth, were successfully resisted. There was to be nothing laid down which would mean that, if the Church adopted a substantial theological change, that could lead to a challenge in the civil courts on the grounds that the Church had, by that change, lost its identity as the Church of Scotland, and consequently its rights to property.

So Article I is declared to be essential to the identity and corporate life of the Church. That means that, if the Church repudiated any doctrine in Article I, it would cease to be, legally, the Church of Scotland.

It is clear that if the Church repudiated the Doctrine of the Trinity, the minority who wanted to adhere to that doctrine could claim that they were the real Church of Scotland, and so claim legal title to all the property.

The same would be true if the Church decided no longer to adhere to the Scottish Reformation. It is unlikely that the Church would do so explicitly, but it has been argued that, if the Church departed entirely from Presbyterianism and adopted episcopacy, it would have departed from the Scottish Reformation.

However, the Church has the right to interpret the First Article.

As long as the Church is careful to act on the basis of its own interpretation of the First Article, it should therefore be safe; but the point which might be taken to a civil court would be whether a declared interpretation by the Church was really interpretation or actually substantial change. You could hardly get away with a statement that the Trinitarian doctrine in Article I was consistent with a Unitarian doctrine, and with calling that interpretation.

What would or would not be a legitimate interpretation of adherence to the Scottish Reformation is a much more complex question, but I am of the opinion that *ecclesia reformata, semper reformanda* is a relevant factor.

Adherence to the Scottish Reformation is not therefore an absolute obstacle to ecumenical progress.

It is significant in this context that Article VII asserts the right of the Church to unite with other Churches, without loss of identity, provided that in any such other Church it finds that the Word is purely preached, the sacraments administered according to Christ's ordinance, and discipline rightly exercised; but it does not say that we have to find that they are Presbyterian. You will of course recognise the marks of the true Kirk from the Scots Confession of 1560 in these criteria in Article VII. The phrase 'without loss of identity' is there to prevent any legal action similar to that of 1900.

The matter of the Church's right to legislate and adjudicate in matters of doctrine, worship, government and discipline, without interference by civil authority is unequivocally stated in the Articles.

In short, the Declaratory Articles in their final form dealt effectively with all the major concerns of both Churches, and paved the way for the Union of 1929.

In terms of Church and State, the most interesting and significant point, however, is the manner in which Parliament dealt with them, in the Church of Scotland Act, 1921.

This Act does not purport to grant independence to the Church. It recognises the Church's claim to be independent. That is clear in the terms of the Act, and it is further emphasised by the fact that the Act provides that it will not come into force until the Articles have been approved by the Church. What this means is that the State has recognised that the sovereignty of Parliament does not include jurisdiction over the Church of Scotland in spiritual matters.

It is a specific recognition of a limitation on the sovereignty of Parliament, and as such it is a distinctive and unique piece of legislation.

One immediate consequence of this today is that, whatever the UK Parliament may have devolved to the new Scottish Parliament, it cannot have devolved a power or authority which it has explicitly recognised that it does not have. By the same token, the State cannot have passed on, by treaty, to any European or international court, a power or authority which it does not have. If therefore the Scottish Parliament were to pass legislation purportedly exercising jurisdiction over the Church, that legislation would be *ultra vires,* and we might reasonably expect civil courts to declare this to be the case; but we cannot be sure that civil courts would live up to this reasonable expectation.

In relation to European courts, the position ought to be the same, but there is need for caution here, in that we cannot be sure how European courts would react. On the one hand, it appears to be the case that European authorities are sensitive to religious and ecclesiastical differences, and would not be inclined to interfere in spiritual matters. On the other hand, it is perhaps not impossible to imagine that a European court could declare the 1921 Act *ultra vires,* on the grounds that a State has no right to divest itself of responsibility for the human rights of its citizens.

The question of human rights has been raised in the UK, and the Board of Practice and Procedure produced a report on this, which was discussed on the opening day of this General Assembly. The situation described there is basically that an Act about human rights might provide, or appear to provide, a way to the civil courts for people who felt that their human rights had been denied by the Church.

This is partly a problem of definition, as to whether the provisions of the Bill apply to Church courts.

It is also a matter of law, since, if the new legislation is construed as applying to the Church, the question then arises as to whether such legislation is nevertheless excluded by the 1921 Act, or whether new legislation prevails over the 1921 Act.

In the normal case, later legislation would be held to prevail over earlier legislation. In other words, there would be an implied repeal, even if there was not a specific repeal. That, however, raises a question as to whether the 1929 Act is ordinary legislation or fundamental law.

It could certainly be argued that the 1921 Act, since it was passed on condition that the Church agreed to it, could not be repealed without the agreement of the Church. There is also a question of how far the State, having recognised a limitation on its sovereignty, could now unilaterally withdraw that recognition, since one implication of the 1921 Act would be that the State has no power to do this.

Two consequences of this for the future can clearly be identified.

First, we must be constantly vigilant. There may be no likelihood of a direct attempt to amend or repeal the 1921 Act; but an indirect threat may exist in other legislation.

For example, the Law Reform (Miscellaneous Provisions) (Scotland) Act, 1990, as first drafted, contained provisions which could have allowed a Government Minister to remove a parish minister from office; and it took a considerable amount of negotiation to ensure that the independence of the Church in this matter was safeguarded.

The human rights legislation is another case in point. The fact that the government has declined to make the Church's position absolutely clear in the Bill is worrying. On the one hand they say that the exclusive jurisdiction of the Church in matters spiritual is not threatened; but on the other hand they decline to insert a reference to the 1921 Act into the Bill, which would put the matter beyond doubt.

So we do face what may be unlikely, and yet possible in the opinion of some lawyers, namely that the terms of the Human Rights Bill, if enacted, would allow a civil court to claim some degree of jurisdiction over a Church court in a case involving human rights.

On Saturday, therefore, the General Assembly passed a deliverance as follows:

The General Assembly: -

(a) Approve the actions of the Board with regard to the Bill to incorporate the European convention on Human Rights into United Kingdom law, and fully endorse the representations made to Her Majesty's Government by the Board in the name of the Church.

(b) Deeply regret that Her Majesty's Government has, despite the representations of the Board, failed to agree to an amendment of the Human Rights Bill which would state explicitly that the position of the Church of Scotland in terms of the Church of Scotland Act, 1921, is not affected by the Bill.

(c) Affirm that the 1921 Act is *inter alia* a clear recognition by the State that it has no authority over the Church in matters spiritual, and that, as long as the 1921 Act remains in force, the honour and integrity of the State require it to act in a manner consistent with that recognition.

(d) Declare that the Church would continue to be bound by its own Constitution, set out in the Declaratory Articles, as recognised by the 1921 Act, even if the State were to amend that Act.

(e) Believe that Her Majesty's Government has no desire to create a situation of conflict between Church and State.

(f) Accordingly, urge Her Majesty's Government either to give an assurance that the Human Rights Bill is entirely consistent with the provisions of the 1921 Act or to amend the Bill to ensure that it will be so consistent.

(g) Instruct the Principal Clerk to send this Section of the Deliverance to Her Majesty's Government.

(h) Authorise the Board of Practice and Procedure to take any action it may consider necessary to pursue this matter in accordance with its Report and this section of the Deliverance.

All the above points are important, but it is particularly important, whenever any question of legislative change in the 1921 Act is discussed, to remember that all Parliament could purport to do would be to amend or repeal its recognition of the Declaratory Articles. It could not repeal the Articles themselves, because it did not enact them. And the Church could not change Article I, without loss of identity; nor could it change any of the other Articles except by the special procedure laid down in Article VIII.

Accordingly, unlikely though we hope and believe it to be, there is still a possibility that, in a particular case, a civil court could intervene in a Church case in such a way that someone might have to decide whether to obey the civil court or the Church court. That would put us back to the Ten Years' Conflict before the Disruption, when some ministers were deposed by the Assembly for obeying the Court of Session.

So we wait with interest to see what the Government's response to the General Assembly will be.

The second lesson for the future is that the Church must look to its own procedures, both as provided for in Church legislation, and as operated by Church courts. If, for example, it were to become clear that Church procedures were not in accordance with natural justice and basic human rights, pressure to change the legal position of the Church could grow, and could prove difficult to resist.

A point at issue here might be the practice of Church courts to meet in private for disciplinary cases, whereas in secular proceedings today the emphasis is much more on the need for cases to be heard in open court.

Another point to be considered is the availability of some equivalent of Legal Aid in Church courts, so that a person facing disciplinary proceedings is not at a disadvantage in mounting a defence.

In short, if we want to maintain our independence, we must make sure that our house is in order. We must be sure that, even if our procedures were scrutinised by a civil court, they would be found to be just and fair.

In this context, the fact that the Board of Practice and Procedure has set up a working group to consider disciplinary and judicial processes is to be welcomed.[2] On Wednesday, after the Assembly had affirmed its belief in human rights, it agreed to take steps to look at the question of incorporating the European Convention into Church law.

Nevertheless, even if the Church, by its legislation, and Church courts, by their practice, were to ensure that it would not lose any case taken to a civil court, the very fact that it got to a civil court would be contrary to the 1921 Act, and any legislation which made this possible would be a breach of faith on the part of the State.

On the broader issue of the relationship of the Church of Scotland to the Scottish Parliament, the initiatives reported by the Board of Practice and Procedure are also to be welcomed.

We do need to give careful attention to the working out, in this new context, of the statement in Article VI: 'The Church and State owe mutual duties to each other, and acting within their respective spheres may signally promote each other's welfare'.

---

[2] The working party's recommendations were implemented by Act III, 2001.

One of the difficult points today is the description in Article III of the Church of Scotland as a 'national Church representative of the Christian Faith of the Scottish people'.

I have written elsewhere that, even if a majority of citizens do not profess the Christian Faith today, it is still part and parcel of the history which has shaped Scotland, and the Church has an important role in representing it; but clearly there is room for debate about the extent to which Scotland may be regarded as a 'Christian country', and much depends on how that phrase is defined.

This leads to a consideration of the ecumenical dimension, and also to a consideration of the place of other faith communities.

It is certainly my view that the special position of the Church of Scotland is not one which we hold as one of privilege over other Christian Churches.

To the extent that the ecumenical movement is a movement towards Church unity, I believe that the Declaratory Articles are an important recognition of spiritual independence which we hold in trust for any larger united Church of which we may eventually become part.

Our legal status is not something we ought to give up for the sake of unity, but something to which we adhere for the sake of the enhancement of future unity.

It is also true, I believe, that this recognition of spiritual independence works in favour of other Churches, rather than against them; and I think it favours other faith communities as well. This is because, if secular authorities are going to talk more of a multi-faith culture, they are not going to be disposed to allow less spiritual freedom to other Churches and other faiths than the freedom enjoyed by the Church of Scotland.

It is interesting that the Chief Rabbi was recently reported as taking a view that the establishment of the Church of England is good for the Jewish community, because it recognises the importance of religion in national life.

I have not attempted to produce any blueprint for the Church in the future in this matter of relationships between Church and State. I have however tried to indicate at least some of the principles involved, and some of the factors about which the Church ought to be concerned. I hope that, in so doing, I have at least indicated the importance of this matter.

The final point I want to make is that the Declaratory Articles were approved by the Church, before they received recognition by the State. They were not imposed on the Church by the State, or even graciously given to the Church by the State. That is to say, our spiritual independence is derived from Christ, and not from the civil law.

Christ, the King and Head of the Church, is the ultimate authority, whom the State cannot replace and the Church cannot deny; but the satisfactory evolution of a continuing, relevant, and positive relationship with the State requires vigilance and imagination on the part of the Church. We cannot simply assume that the legal position will remain static.

In this area we are very much concerned with Thomas Chalmers' concept of the Church acting for the Christian good of Scotland. The institution of a Scottish Parliament offers opportunities which the Church must not miss. In the end of the day the Church's own commitment to Christ is more important than the State's recognition of the Church's independence.

# The Relentless Search for Christian Unity[1]

*Tom A Davidson Kelly*

**Presidential Address to the Scottish Church Society, 2008**

**Looking at ourselves**

This is neither a theological treatise nor a discussion of ecumenical mechanics, but a study of individuals engaged in the search for Christian unity. In his closing Presidential Address to the third annual meeting of the Scottish Church Society on Tuesday 28 May 1895 the Very Reverend Dr Thomas Leishman[2] referred to the conference held by the Society,[3] whose papers would be published as *The Divine Life in the Church*:[4]

> I believe that we all returned from the Conference to our homes under a deeper impression of our duties and our privileges, every heart fortified by good counsel, and filled with new matter for thought, not one saddened by recollections of discord. And we might look for such fruits in a Society formed rather for self-discipline than for assault. Ours is not a federation, gathered out of rival communions, drawn together for the time by the attractive force of a common dislike, ready when their end has been gained, or been found hopeless, to resume their competition with each other as before. Rather are we children of one house, uniting our efforts to preserve what is left of our common heritage of truth, and reclaim what has been wasted. Our only emulation among ourselves is how best to provoke one another unto love and to good works. And when we take up debateable ground, it is in the hope that those who are already one in Christian fellowship may become one in action and belief.

---

[1] This paper was read to the Scottish Church Society, 19 May 2008 and published in the *Report*, 2008.
[2] Also President 1901-02.
[3] Held in Edinburgh during February 1895.
[4] Scottish Church Society, *Annual Report, Third Year, 1894-95*, 11-12.

## Looking at rivals
Two years later[5] Dr John Macleod of Govan spoke at the semi-jubilee celebrations of St Mary's Free Church at Govan Cross[6]

> The chairman [Dr Robert Howie] referred to their old association as college friends ... Ecclesiastical questions drew them apart in unhappy times but congregational life, if spiritual and evangelical, were powerful helps to take these out, and if nothing else was genuine but the congregational life in the country he believed that in God's good time this would bring them to see eye to eye. But the things dividing them were great and deep, and he would not say more upon this; differences of this kind, if they followed their own convictions in their own way, should never be allowed to interfere with the courtesies and amenities of social life. He sympathised as heartily as any here present in wishing the congregation increased blessing in future and for Mr Howie length of years and increasing happiness in the great work which prospered and was carried on according to their convictions, and which he hoped would prosper still more to the end.

## Looking at the Church
This year of grace is the 60th anniversary of the birth of the World Council of Churches. No doubt each of us will have some quibble, issues with past or current thoughts and actions of the World Council of Churches, but all of us are committed to search for unity. It is my conviction that unity is an expression of the very life of God, a visible demonstration of the working of his Spirit in and among us, a divine action that begins in the human heart.

---

[5] 24 March 1897, towards the end of his Presidential year.
[6] Special Collections, Glasgow University Library, A13/H17, *Free St. Mary's Church, Govan. Origin of the congregation and its history until semi-jubilee year 1897*. Govan: John Cossar, 27th March 1897, 15-6.

In 1911 Arthur W Wotherspoon[7] began his Presidential Address by referring to the constitution:[8]

> When our Constitution first was published in 1892, an Edinburgh paper (the *Evening News*) said in comment that if the Church of Scotland as a whole was not working for the ends aimed at by the new Society, that Church ought to be swept away. We do not say so. We only say that in the essential purpose of our association, we are true to the foundational constitution of the Church of GOD, and of this Church as a particular member thereof.

The revised and shortened constitution published in 1998 in the centenary booklet retains unity as part of our view of the Church:[9]

> It [the Society] affirms ... her [Church] essential unity under the Holy Spirit. ... It is this [historical] continuity [of the Church] that ensures a lively awareness of the Communion of Saints, and that the Faith once delivered to the Saints is maintained and promoted; forbidding any secular, sectarian or individual view of the Church.

Our original constitution had twenty two special objects. The final pair concerned the unity of Christ's Church:

> **21** The deepening of a penitential sense of the sin and peril of schism.
> **22** The furtherance of Catholic unity in every way consistent with true loyalty to the Church of Scotland.

This helps to clarify our view: that there is something unacceptable, indeed deeply sinful about the present position; and that our concern for unity is not for a warm fellowship at any price. In this Society

---

[7] minister at Oatlands, Govan, 1883-1923.
[8] Scottish Church Society, *Annual Report, Nineteenth Year*, 1910-1911 (1911), 16.
[9] Centenary Publication, *Scottish Church Society*, 1998, (hereafter *SCS*), 69.

our concern is for catholic unity: in other words for the wider coming together of Christian people and for the universal historic continuity of the Church.

## The priority of Unity

At the 1992 centenary conference the Very Reverend Professor John McIntyre[10] defined the aims of our founding fathers 'in terms of promoting holiness, truth and unity within the Church.'[11] 'In a word, I have to conclude that the founders of the Society offered us a vision sufficient not only to take us into one century, but imaginatively to take us into two.'[12]

## Nathan Söderblom, Nobel Peace Laureate 1930[13]

A tombstone in Sweden's metropolitan cathedral at Upsala bears a simple design:[14] a circular clasp, crozier behind, and below the name Nathan Söderblom a pectoral cross with the resurrection rays between the dates 1866 and 1931. Centrally positioned the words of a scriptural text, St Luke 17. 10: 'So you also, when you have done all that you were ordered to do, say, "We are worthless slaves; we have done only what we ought to have done!"'[15] What an epitaph for the man awarded the 1930 Nobel Prize for Peace, the year before he delivered the Gifford Lectures in Edinburgh.

---

[10] President 1959-65.
[11] *SCS*, 32.
[12] *SCS*, 43.
[13] http://nobelprize.org/nobel_prizes/peace/laureates/1930/söderblom-bio.html
[14] Bengt GM Sundkler, *Nathan Söderblom: His Life and Work*. London: Lutterworth, 1968 (hereafter *Sundkler*), 429.
[15] *New RSV*, 1993.

George Bell, Bishop of Chichester from 1929, attended the meetings[16] which marked the tenth anniversary of the World Council of Churches in Nyborg, Denmark:[17]

> He preached from one of his favourite texts – St. Luke 17. 10, 'So, likewise ye, when ye shall have done all those things which are commanded you, say, We are unprofitable servants: we have done that which it was our duty to do.' It was a text which closely associated him with two of his great friends in the Ecumenical Movement. Bonhoeffer had chosen it for his first sermon as a young student for the ministry; while Archbishop Söderblom had used it constantly and it was engraved on his tomb in Upsala Cathedral. Bell preached a powerful and vigorous sermon, calling for faith and obedience in the quest for peace and unity; and it was described by those who heard it as 'Bell at his best.' ... It was fitting that he should also quote some words from Soderblom.
>
> When God's rule has penetrated man's heart and life so that the divine love and righteousness becomes the main factor, we speak of a saint. A saint is one who reveals God's might. Saints are such as show clearly and plainly in their lives and deeds and in their very being, that God lives.

Appointed to a chair at Upsala University in 1901, the Swede also held from 1912-14 the chair of the History of Religion at pre-war Leipzig, famous for its international horizons. Leipzig also afforded 'invaluable personal contacts with German theology, in those years of uncontested German domination in the field of theological research'.[18] It seems that Söderblom was the one theologian historian Karl Lamprecht could understand and appreciate. Lamprecht's 'whole message was the universal aspect of history ... He had established a Seminar for 'the universal history of culture''.[19]

---

[16] August 1958.
[17] Ronald CD Jasper, *George Bell, Bishop of Chichester*. London: OUP, 1967 (hereafter *Bell*), 385.
[18] *Sundkler*, 84.
[19] *Sundkler*, 85.

It is hard for us to grasp the extraordinary achievement of Söderblom's provision of a forum in the closing stages of the first world war for churchmen from all over Europe to visit Sweden and deliver lectures through the Olaus Petri Foundation he had established in 1908. In 1916 Leipzig Professor Albert Hauck had given Olaus Petri lectures on 'Germany and England and their mutual Church relations',[20] quoting Goethe's reworking of an assertion of Sophocles: 'not to hate, but to love do I exist'. Söderblom introduced the 1918 series with an exposition of his theme 'Evangelical Catholicity'.[21] There were four lecturers from Sweden, four each from other northern countries, Germany and Great Britain. There were two lecturers from Hungary, and one from France, Holland, Russia and Switzerland. 'The Olaus Petri lectures at Uppsala University from the autumn of 1918 were characteristic of Söderblom's approach. No one but Söderblom ... would have thought of using an academic foundation as a tool for furthering ecumenical contacts. Week after week, leading international churchmen and theologians found their way to Uppsala, in spite of visa difficulties and the other vicissitudes of the times. Söderblom showed that he possessed the magic wand to turn these academic occasions into something exciting and stimulating. The University, the Archbishop's house, and the Cathedral became a centre where people felt something of the reality of the Universal Church.'[22]

George Bell considered that the 1919 ecumenical conference at Oud Wassenaar near the Hague:[23]

> 'was the decisive event of those early days. ...Here Söderblom was able to secure

---

[20] *Sundkler*, 138.
[21] Söderblom also spoke in the series on the peace efforts of the Church. *Sundkler*, 215.
[22] *Sundkler*, 216.
[23] The first post-war meeting of the International Committee of the World Alliance for promoting International Friendship through the Churches was held from 30 September to 4 October 1919. *Bell*, 57-9.

weighty endorsement for his approach to Christian unity - the method of love and Christian co-operation: and it was a method which Bell made essentially his own. Preaching on the tenth anniversary of Söderblom's death in 1941, he said, 'It is, I think, pretty clear that this method of achieving Christian unity, the method of love, besides avoiding all problems of a purely ecclesiastical kind, offers a motive for Christian unity which is higher than any other motive, and has the capacity for marshalling all Christian forces, irrespective of denomination, as one body crusading against the cruelties and corruptions, the hatreds and wars of the world.'

## In Söderblom's own words:[24]

The nearest universal task of the Church may be formulated as follows: *The unity of nations must become religion or part of our religion.* The uniting element among nations is already religion. In the service of the Church we are regularly reminded of the coming of universal peace through right and justice. We hear the angelic message of peace on earth. And in these times millions of souls have clung to this thought of a community of mankind in justice as to a plank of safety on a sea of despair. Such a hope, and that alone, has for innumerable human beings been the means of saving their faith in the future, and in a justification, an ultimate purpose, behind the ghastly confusion of the world. Now the supernational code of justice is being warped by weakness and passion, and by the power of Mammon. .. Disregarding all minor differences of creed, Christianity must, as far as it is inspired by the spirit of Christ, unite in common prayer, teaching, exhortation and effort towards the strengthening of brotherhood and unity among nations.

Has the Church no need to be reminded of the Gospel of Christ? The brotherhood of mankind and the equal rights of peoples should be drawn from the Gospel itself. The ideal will remain vague, and without prospect of

---

[24] 'The Church and international goodwill' in *The Contemporary Review* CXVI, Jul-Dec 1919, quoted W A Visser 't Hooft, *The Genesis and Formation of the World Council of Churches*. Geneva: WCC, 1982, Appendix II, 98-9.

realization, if it be not supported in its faith by recognition of God's fatherly care, and the conviction of Christian charity that divine mercy exists, and that God's will manifests itself throughout mankind. Neither the false pathos of an arid, bureaucratic state religion, trusting ultimately to unaided human power, nor the self-satisfied egoism of piety in restricted circles can alone avail, whether the unit concerned be small or the most magnificent clerical institution ever seen.

Bell describes the impact made by the Swedish archbishop on first acquaintance:[25]

> 'a totally different person from what we had expected – very vivacious, alert, full of knowledge. He caught everyone, addressed them, was here and there and everywhere; not a dignified and distant figure, but in the stir and turmoil of everything and everybody.'

## Söderblom looking at George Bell (1883-1958), Bishop of Chichester 1929-57

Söderblom considered Bell to be a great asset to the nascent ecumenical movement:[26]

> He hardly said anything except when he was asked. Then, after consideration, he gave a thoughtful answer which always proved to be reliable. The face is dominated by two large, round eyes, which shine with the life and soul behind and indicate a rich inner life. In my opinion, no man means more for the ecumenical awakening than this silent Bell. This Bell never rings unnecessarily. But when it sounds, the tone is silvery clear. It is heard. It penetrates more than many boisterous voices. He does not speak without having something to say. The strong spirituality of his personality marks everything that he does.

---

[25] *Bell*, 59-60.
[26] quoted *Bell*, 60.

The 1998 version of our constitution reminds us that 'The Society encourages a higher spiritual life among all God's people'.[27]

### Söderblom (1866-1931) looking at James Cooper (1846-1922)

It has been suggested that 'Geneva 1920 [Life and Work Conference] was the climax of Söderblom's ecumenical efforts until that time.'[28] One of the four planks of support for the archbishop was the Scottish Church representatives. 'In his estimation of the conference, Söderblom felt that together with the three already mentioned delegations there was at Geneva a further, fourth 'point of support' in the group of Scots representatives, James Cooper, J A McClymont and J D MacGilp.'[29] Cooper and Söderblom[30] were kindred spirits: both stressed the catholic and evangelical nature of the Christian Church.

Unity between Christian denominations had occupied Cooper's mind since he was a boy at school in Elgin,[31] and his whole life was spent in the search for deeper unity among the churches. A product of the Ecclesiological Societies[32] had been greater understanding, respect, friendship and co-operation between members of the three Presbyterian Churches and the Episcopalian and Roman Catholic

---

[27] *SCS*, 71.

[28] *Sundkler*, 239.

[29] *Sundkler*, 241.

[30] *Visser 't Hooft*, 13 and 100: 'There remains, then, an evangelical catholicity, one that should allow the various religious communities to retain their creeds and organizations undisturbed, and continue their accustomed manner of divine service, but at the same time serve and strengthen the cause of spiritual unity, realizing that each one of the different sections of Christianity has its own gift of grace in the common heritage of faith, its contribution to worship, to the ideal of life and the future. An evangelical catholicity is imperative, or division will end in helpless weakness.'

[31] Cooper quoted in a cutting from the *Guardian*, pasted into his 1919 diary. Historic Collections, Aberdeen University Library, MS2283/41, 31.

[32] The Aberdeen (1886) and Glasgow (1893) Ecclesiological Societies were merged in 1903 into The Scottish Ecclesiological Society.

hurches. A constant feature of Cooper's diaries is the work of the Scottish Association for the Promotion of Christian Unity.[33]

Early in the last year of the war Cooper had delivered two addresses in London on the theme of Reunion.[34] At King's College on 7 February 1918 Cooper discussed the brief Scottish 17th century experiment combining Bishops, Presbyteries and General Assembly, what he termed 'The Scottish Precedent of 1610':[35]

> a memorable *Precedent for a combination of the main features alike of the Presbyterian and Episcopal systems*: a combination which as effected, if without popular enthusiasm yet without disaster or disruption, without the secession of so much as a single member from either the Church of England or the Church of Scotland; which lasted eight-and-twenty years, producing in the course of them conspicuous and admirable fruits of peace and godliness, of sacred learning, of intellectual and social progress, of church extension; and which would have produced much more but for certain intrusions of the Civil Power, which in Scotland have wholly ceased – ceased, it is but right to say, largely through the valiant efforts of those who in 1638 combined to overthrow it, and of their successors and imitators in 1843.

In the crypt of St Paul's Cathedral on 19 April 1918[36] Cooper approached 'the subject from the point of view suggested by the circumstances of the present day.'[37] The following year Cooper was in Sweden lecturing on the Church of Scotland[38] as part of a series promoted by Archbishop Söderblom through the Olaus Petri Foundation: 'Söderblom decided to invite a number of lecturers,

---

[33] Founded 1904 (mostly C of S, UFC and Scot Episc), it survived into 1950s, but only 19 members in 1956.
[34] *Reunion: A voice from Scotland*. London: Robert Scott, 1918 (hereafter *Reunion*).
[35] *Reunion*, v, 5.
[36] *Reunion*, vii.
[37] *Reunion* vi, vii.
[38] James Cooper, 'Ecclesiological Notes of a Visit to Sweden, September 1919' in *Transactions of the Scottish Ecclesiological Society* 6, Part 3 (1920-21) 1921, 125 and *Sundkler*, 215.

practical churchmen and academic theologians, to Uppsala at the end of 1918 to lecture on their own Churches, thus presenting a broad picture of the European church situation in the last months of the War.'[39]

Cooper would record:[40]

> Of late this foundation, ... has been devoted to the exposition of the different National Churches of Christendom, with the special view of preparing them for that mutual recognition, consent, and co-operation which the Archbishop rightly sees to be essential if they are ever to fulfil their high duty of bringing, with the power of a united voice, the testimony and law of our LORD JESUS CHRIST to bear on the International Relations of mankind. In pursuance of this scheme the National Churches of Denmark, Norway, Sweden and Finland have already been treated by representative divines of these countries, the Church of Russia has been described by a Russian bishop, and the Church of England by the Rev. Dr. A.J. Carlyle of University College, Oxford. To me fell the unexpected honour of being asked to speak of the Church of Scotland.

Söderblom had hoped that his long standing Scottish friend Professor David S Cairns of the UF College in Aberdeen would have given the Scottish lectures,[41] and yet they were delivered by Cooper. Was this because of Cairns' schedule and involvement with the wartime enquiry into the religious life of the nation published in 1919 as *The Army and Religion*?[42] Or was

---

[39] *Sundkler*, 213.
[40] Cooper, *TSES* 6, Part 3 (1920-21) 1921, 125.
[41] *Sundkler*, 212.
[42] Cairns was joint convener with the E S Talbot, Bishop of Winchester. "The Report is, in general character, and in its literary form, Dr. Cairns's work. ... Twice after the Hatfield meeting [4 days in August 1917] the whole Committee met for several days, at Lady Margret Hall, Oxford, in December, 1917, and as guests at Farnham in the autumn of 1918. Several whole-day meetings were also held in London. On all these occasions the Committee had before them printed memoranda supplied by Dr. Cairns." E S Talbot, 'Preface' in David S Cairns, ed, *The Army and Religion*. London: Macmillan, 1919, vii.

it because of Cooper's being so well known in Anglican circles?

The Swedish jaunt came at the close of a very busy two year period, including Moderatorship of the 1917 General Assembly. On 22 May 1919 Cooper addressed the annual breakfast of the Scottish Church Society:[43]

> Two years ago, when I laid down my office as Moderator, I told the General Assembly that I had given twelve addresses in England on the subject of Reunion. Since then I have been at Cambridge University, and my address there has been published. I have been over again in Ireland this spring, and have given addresses to people of whom previously I knew nothing. In England – at Chester, Northampton, and Newcastle – I addressed audiences keenly interested in reunion, and longing, as parts of the National Church of England, to be in full and active fellowship with us in the National Church of Scotland.

Söderblom wrote to Cooper on 9 August 1921, thanking him for the gift of his article on his time visiting and lecturing in Sweden. He addresses Cooper as "Wonderful man and friend":[44]

> I am very ashamed of the too kind words You have written about my humble sincerity in our common task for Christian Unity ... Personally I owe too much to Your kindness. ... Miss Söderblom, who expects to stay at Durham during the winter, asks her mother and myself eagerly if she cannot go to Glasgow once to see the great champion of Christian Unity, who at once became a paternal and venerated friend of our family.

## George Anderson looking at Nathan Söderblom

I would like to conclude with part of an 1970s Easter thought broadcast by BBC Radio - words penned by one of my teachers, that most elegant Methodist teacher and student of the Old Testament,

---

[43] Scottish Church Society, *Annual Report, Twenty-seventh Report*, 1918-1919 (1919), 20.
[44] Historic Collections, Aberdeen University Library, MS2283/43 dated 9th August 1921.

## George W Anderson:[45]

I do not suppose that in the present century any man (not even Pope John XXIII) has done more to promote understanding and co-operation between the various branches of the Christian Church than the great Swedish archbishop, Nathan Söderblom. He was a man of exceptional and many-sided gifts, a scholar, an ecclesiastical statesman endowed with vision and courage, a musician, and, not least, a character. He had a deep sense of the dignity of worship, and of ecclesiastical office, and yet brought freshness and vitality to all that he did. He combined great personal authority with overflowing personal charm. On one occasion when, as archbishop, he went to rededicate a church in his native province of Hälsingland, his golden crozier was, by an oversight, left behind in Uppsala. He got up early on the Sunday morning, went out into the woods, and cut down and trimmed a young birch.[46] Then, when the service was due to begin, he went into the Church in all the splendour of his ecclesiastical vestments, carrying the young birch as a crozier and announced, 'It is spring that I let into your Church and parish.'

That, surely, expresses one of the dominant notes in any Easter service, at least in the northern hemisphere. There is the sense of the stirring of life and new hope, and of days ahead which, at least in a physical sense, will be brighter. But, of course, there is a great deal more. For many who have experienced bereavement, the Christian resurrection faith brings a renewed consolation. And the Christian resurrection hope is inseparably linked with the resurrection of Christ.

**Behind it all is love: love for God and love expressed in service of fellow human beings. May we embrace those words of the Lord remembered by St Luke as distinctly as Dietrich Bonhoeffer, George Bell and Nathan Söderblom. May we spend our lives in the relentless search for Christian peace and unity, following the example of our first Secretary, James Cooper.**

---

[45] Unpublished typed script sent by George W Anderson to Tom Davidson Kelly.
[46] Söderblom's biographer adds the detail 'keeping the leaves only on top', *Sundkler*, 136.

"... So you also, when you have done all that you were ordered to do, say, 'We are worthless slaves; we have done only what we ought to have done!'"

Let us pray:[47]

Creator of all,
by your Holy Spirit
you have made a diversity of peoples one
in the confession of your name.
Lead them, by the same Spirit,
to show to the whole earth
one mind in belief
and one passion for righteousness;
through Jesus Christ our Lord. **AMEN.**

---

[47] Collect for Christian Unity, *Book of Common Order of the Church of Scotland*. Edinburgh: St Andrew Press, 1994; 2nd edn 1996, 688.

# Creed and Confession: Their Relations to One Another and to the Church
*Henry J Wotherspoon*

## The Macleod Memorial Lecture 1905[1]

I have thought that this topic might be appropriate for a lecture which is intended to be a tribute to the ever-honoured memory of your late pastor, Dr John Macleod. There was none readier than he to appreciate the distinction which I wish to make clear; no one was more anxious than he to recognise that while there are matters of faith, there are also matters of opinion; no one was more charitable to all difference in those things which are non-essential, or more insistent on fidelity in those which are fundamental.

The incidents of the past year have directed attention to the question of the relation of ecclesiastical communions to their official standards of belief, - of their right and power to revise and alter these, and of the expedience of their undertaking that task as occasion may arise. One point of view on the subject has, for example, been stated by an eminent divine[2] of one of the separated Presbyterian communions with expressions which form a convenient point of departure for the considerations which I wish to submit. The report of the address to which I refer bears that 'a Church is bound to maintain her right to alter her Confession. ... The Confession, in short, must be the Confession of the Church, and not the Church the Church of the Confession. She must make it, and not it her.... She must assert her entire and

---

[1] The distinction between Creed and Confession insisted on in this lecture is a perennial issue in the Church of Scotland. The lecture was republished in 1931 because debate in the 1930 General Assembly had treated Creed and Confession as one category. The matter is still under discussion.
[2] Dr Marcus Dods, *Scotsman* 29 June 1904.

constant right to amend, add to, or entirely reject her Confession.' The speaker went on to discuss the advantages and disadvantages of 'an unchangeable Creed,' 'a fixed Creed,' and then to speak of the marks of time upon 'our Creed'; and then again (using the terms apparently as interchangeable) to claim the Church's right 'wholly to recast or materially to alter her Confession.' I instance these passages, not for the purpose of contesting their sentiment, but merely to illustrate a use of words which is probably very common, but which I think tends to confuse the ordinary reader.

Undoubtedly there is much in them, if terms are duly defined and the scope of language is understood, with which it is natural to sympathise; and beyond question the expressions Creed and Confession have often in popular use been used, as they are here, without clear distinction. But the absence of distinction is unfortunate. It disturbs discussion of a matter in which mutual comprehension is urgently important. A great deal, for example, of what is claimed by the speaker above quoted might be heartily conceded, if it were made plain that he is speaking throughout of Confessions (as I think he is, for he speaks also of 'ascertained eternal truth' as the only true stimulus to life), and that he uses the word Creed inexactly; while if Creed in its proper sense were meant, every phrase might need to be contested.

The distinction, in fact, is real and goes far: we require to recognise it explicitly. There is a primary deposit of faith, 'the faith which was once for all delivered unto the saints.'[3] There is a trust committed by Christ to the apostles, and by the apostles transmitted to the Church. There is the faith[4] concerning which Christ asked whether, at His coming, He should find it in the earth. That there is such a deposit is the postulate of Christianity. Whether it exists or does not exist is a question at issue, not between Christian and Christian, but between

---

[3] Jude 3, Revised Version.
[4] St Luke 18:8, *tēn pistin*.

the Christian and the non-Christian. Christianity asserts that it does exist, and stakes its own existence on the assertion. There is, that is to say, something which is definitely 'the Gospel,' - a tidings, a knowledge converting the soul and working in man a supernatural and heavenly transformation; a Gospel taught by our Lord, not in words only, but by life and death, resurrection and ascension, and by the Holy Ghost from heaven; taught to this end, that it might save; where taught and believed, there effectually saving, vivifying, renewing, as only the divine, the eternal, the true can conceivably do. 'I have finished the work which Thou gavest Me to do,' Christ said; 'I have manifested Thy Name, ... these have known that Thou didst send Me ... Holy Father, keep them, ... sanctify them by Thy truth.'[5] It is inconceivable either that there should be more such truths than one, or that the divine of the first age should be the obsolete of ours. In relation to this deposit, the function of succeeding generations of Christianity must be to receive and to keep and to transmit it, whole and undefiled.

And, again by the nature of the case, Christianity being a historical religion based upon the life and activity of a Person, the elements of this faith are in the main historical: they are not principles, but facts. 'I declare unto you,' says, for example, St Paul, 'the Gospel'; and proceeds to enumerate certain occurrences, the narrative of which constitutes the Gospel in relation to the matters with which for the moment he is dealing,[6] - they are, that Christ died for our sins, according to the Scriptures, and that He was buried, and that He rose again the third day, according to the Scriptures, and that He was seen by persons enumerated.

The significance of such facts depends, however, upon the nature of the Person in whom they are accomplished. Apart from that, the rest may assert nothing to the purpose: many have died and have

---

[5] St John 17:4b -17.
[6] 1 Corinthians 15:1-8.

been buried, and of some we believe that they have revived from death, who yet are not objects of faith to us. The Incarnation is involved, and must be defined. The doctrinal element cannot be excluded even from the bare statement of fact; the Deity of Him of whom we speak is the principal fact of the whole statement. The Gospel cannot begin from the birth which it declares–its essence is the declaration that thus God enters human life. Its point of departure is in eternity: 'In the beginning was the Word; and the Word was with God; and the Word was God.' The Incarnation is thus itself also a historical event, and becomes part of a narrative–tidings that certain things, of significance and effect which faith must measure, have come to pass; and this narrative, completed to the intelligence by definition of the Person with whom it deals, and by assurance of the result potentially contained in what has been already wrought through Him, may be taken to constitute the essential Gospel. Everything else of doctrine or of ethic is inferred from these primary statements of event. All Christian teaching, all Christian precept, reasons from them. All Christian thought develops out of them. Whatever is to be said in Christ's name bases itself either immediately or mediately upon them. We have seen, therefore we believe; we believe, therefore we speak and act and feel after such and such a manner. The doctrine is an inference from the faith; the morality is an inference from the doctrine. The apostles of Christ were not teachers of abstract truth, they were witnesses to event; they did not live or die for principles (every religion has its martyrs, and martyrdom proves nothing but the sincerity and courage of the sufferer), they lived and died for testimony to what they had seen with their eyes and had looked upon and their hands had handled of the Word of Life,–testimony which involves mere veracity, and in regard to which martyrdom proves much. Christian teaching of dogma or of conduct prefaces itself with a 'therefore,' the premiss lying in the faith; the faith itself being in form historical–the statement of what has happened.

Therefore (once more, by the nature of the case) the faith, in this proper and ultimate sense, is unchangeable: because the past does not change. If a thing has been, that remains; nothing subsequent can affect the fact. If it has happened, we have still to ascertain its meaning and to pursue its inference and to work out its application to present emergency. If it has not happened - *cadit quæstio,* - there is nothing to discuss. The truth of Christianity, if it be true, is truth of fact. As a faith it is based not upon a theory of existence or on any system of thought, but upon a Person and a life. As for ideas, they have their time. They are the product of conditions, and belong to the general social condition of which they are begotten, and which they in turn help to shape. As that changes, they change. It is perfectly true, as it is certainly often enough said, that no two generations can see life or any part of its content from the same angle, and that each age must speak its own thought and in its own language. A religion, therefore, which is merely an expression of truth can express it only for its epoch; the next epoch must find an expression suitable to itself. If Christianity were only a religion, a doctrine of God and humanity, or if it were only a scheme of conduct and morals, it would necessarily have its day, and when the day passed, pass with it. Being what it is, whatever validity it possesses or has at any time possessed is essentially permanent, because its validity depends upon a past which cannot alter, and upon a present which exists above the sphere of change. Successive periods may utter, each as it can, the inference from these, may reason from them to its own conclusions, and may clothe in the garb of its own custom the social body which is animated by credence in them; the foundation abides the same, yesterday and today. To ourselves it is as much as to the men of a thousand years ago, and must remain as much to men a thousand years hence, if the world still stand, that the Word was made flesh and dwelt among us,–that God was in Christ reconciling the world to Himself, and being manifested in the flesh lived and suffered and died and is risen for us. No shifting of the conditions under which men live out their threescore years and ten can rob this of its significance; the supreme question will always be, whether these things have or have not taken place. So long as men are born and sin and die, this, if it be true, will still be the vital truth– that Manhood, being taken into Deity, has victoriously passed through death and is exalted to the right hand of God. And for every man of every time who receives it, the power of this faith is the same, - to lift his desire to the heavenly and eternal things, and to bring him out of his world and out of himself to God.

It is then to this nucleus of belief, and at most to a limited number of statements which are directly involved in it, or are demanded for its intelligibility and consistence - as, for example, the Trinity and Unity of the Deity, the Divine Fatherhood, the single personality and dual nature of the Christ, the descent into Hades (which is only a repetition on the side of the invisible of the statement of His death), the forgiveness of sins (as the intent and consequence of His sacrifice), the creation of the Church, and the Communion of Saints (as the external and internal results of the Mission of the Holy Ghost), - it is to this that the term Creed may be with precision applied. If there is anything that may justly be called ' the Faith,' anything elemental, essential, or necessary, any trust of doctrine to be preserved by the Church, and for which she must at the last account before her Judge; any truth in which resides the supernatural efficiency which converts and vivifies and sanctifies the soul, - which, because it has the testimony of the Holy Ghost, is discerned by the sheep of Christ as the voice of Christ, and is the common treasure of Christian hearts; if there is anything which, because it is vitally Christian, is credible to the human spirit, itself 'naturally Christian'; if there is anything which flesh and blood does not reveal, but the Father which is in heaven; if there is anything such that it can be believed only by the gift of God, or such that, believing it, a man passes from death into life; if, in fact, there is anything without which Christianity is not Christian: then that falls under the category of Creed; such things, and only such, the Church has desired to embody in her primary symbol; it is this necessary and saving faith, and that alone, which she has, with whatever success, designed to place there.

Obviously, however, the Christian mind cannot limit, and has never limited, its activity to the apprehension of the Gospel in this sense. Receiving that as the premiss of its thought, it proceeds to reason over an almost infinite range of questions which it cannot but encounter, and to which it must endeavour to find a solution. Our Lord does not explain–He announces; the Gospel does not explain–it proclaims. Christian theology is *our* attempt to explain upon the basis of the Gospel,– to correlate its factual truth with intuition and experience, to deduce from it a theory of God and of human life, to interpret by it the Divine purpose in Creation and the Divine method in Redemption, so making faith systematic and intelligent. In this process, which is a process of the human reason (quickened by the Holy Spirit, but not mechanically determined), no absolute identity of action or of result can be expected. It is a process necessarily conditioned by the individual types of mind which pursue it, by the philosophical apparatus at their command, by the characteristics of the society of which they form part, by the ethical standards of which they are conscious, and so on. Relatively to non-Christian thought, the range of deviation is narrow; since whatever the theology of the Christian be, it must be Christian–it must be rational inference from one and the same series of revealing and redemptive events. But, as regarded from within those limits which are demarcated by acceptance of that series of events, the scope for play of opinion and for the influence of idiosyncrasy, environment, historical evolution, racial characteristics, contemporary conditions, and the like, is wide. All Christians must believe that God is love–but Christians have understood in very different senses what Divine love may imply. All believe in the Atonement–but theories of the Atonement are far from identical. All believe in the existence of the Church–but Canon Liddon and Mr Spurgeon, both orthodox, conceived in widely opposed senses of the nature of the Church. All confess Christ as the Exemplar of conduct–but Count Tolstoi and Lord Roberts, both devout believers, deduce absolutely divergent canons of conduct in important particulars.

It is within the region of belief of this secondary and inferential nature that occasion for Confessional statements (as distinguished from Creed) has in the distracted state of the Church arisen. I submit the extreme desirability of observing a terminology which shall avoid confusing things so different as belief of the primary and essential type with beliefs of the secondary and derivative type. If, in reasoning of these matters, men are to understand one another, Creed and Confession must be studiously distinguished. For men may be in full agreement of principle, and even of conclusion, where the advisability of Confessional revision is in question, but may differ by whole horizons of thought if the suggestion of Creed revision be mooted. One may be asked to change a garment; to change one's skin is another matter.

Creed and Confession are, then, not identical; they are rather antithetic. Creed is the statement of essential belief - of what makes a Christian; that is to say, of Christianity itself - and is thus the bond of Christian men. Confessions, on the other hand, embody their differences. Creed unites; Confessions distinguish. Creed expresses the consensus of the flock of God and exhibits its fundamental unity, however divided. A Confession, on the other hand, belongs to a several communion and defines it, not from the world, but from other communions; not from unbelievers, but from brethren who agree in the faith, but do not argue identically to all inferences – as Lutherans have the Augsburg Confession, Anglicans their Thirty-Nine Articles, and we our Westminster Standard; while as to Creed, they and we are entirely at one with each other and with the Church universal of this and of other ages. Creed is catholic – Confessions are local and particular. Creed is from of old – Confessions are from the sixteenth or seventeenth century. Creed is in a true sense one[7] – Confessions are unhappily numerous. Creed is brief; for it intends to state only the absolute Gospel–Confessions are lengthy and detailed; for they contain as well the views of schools and the contentions of parties on subsidiary points. Creed is evangelical – Confessions are theological. Creed is positive – it is framed to declare verity. Confessions are largely negative and controversial. Confessions are accepted - they are 'terms of peace'; they are formulas of the harmony of certain persons as to things on which Christians may differ, yet remain orthodox and Catholic Christians. Creed is embraced; it is hailed; it is proclaimed to the glory of God and for the joy of men; it is an act of worship, a hymn of praise.[8] A Confession sets forth a distinctive theology - Creed states that which is the starting-point of Christian theology, the factual basis which, like other sciences, theology requires in order to exist. It gives those things with which the spiritual reason has to deal.

The distinction seems a real one; and if so, some care may be thought due to make it plain, when we have occasion to speak of these matters, whether it is the one or the other of which we speak. The relation which any section of the Church occupies to the universal Creed of Christians is quite different from the relation which it occupies to an exposition of its own special attitude in deduced theology, which it has itself for its own purposes constructed. It is one thing for a particular communion, national or separatist (if for lack of better I may use the word inoffensively), to modify the Confession which itself has framed and adopted, not as adopting Christianity but to rectify its position among fellow-believers – and entirely another thing for it to depart in

---

[7] In a true sense – notwithstanding the many forms of the Baptismal symbol, its intercalation at Nicæa, and its expansion by the subsequent Councils.

[8] *Salutare Carmen … Coelestis sapientiæ vitale Carmen.* – Faustus (De Spir.) quoted by Zahn.

any point from the faith of all, which the Christian Creed, accepted of all, embodies. It may be true that a 'particular Church' makes its own Confession and is not made by the Confession; but can that be said of Creed? Does not Creed make the Church, as it makes the Christian? 'As many as believed were baptized'–such was the apostolic rule; still, and always, 'as many as believe' constitute the family of God, the household of Faith. We do not make the Gospel, but the Gospel is declared to us, and we believe, and are made new creatures. The Gospel is before the Christian: it is the cause –he is the effect. And in exactly the same sense, the Gospel is before the Church, and makes the Church; would any of us venture to say that 'the Church makes the Gospel'? The Gospel transforms man, but man cannot change the Gospel–the Word of the Lord abideth for ever.

But (it may be said) is the Creed in its historical sense, the Creed as we have it from the past, identical with the Gospel? I have been dealing with the proper use of terms, and in that aspect I think that I may venture to say that the Creed aims to be identical with the Gospel. It stands, the expression of the effort of the universal and continuous and undivided flock of God to state truth as to which the Spirit of God testifies that it is essential and necessary truth–the vitalising and sanctifying truth, to which the Church is God's witness in the world. The Creed represents a consensus from which there is no appeal; an authority which is on this side of time the highest to which God has given power of utterance–the authority, namely, of the Christian soul. Thus believing, men have received power to become the sons of God. Thus believing, men have been made partakers of the Divine nature. Thus believing, the Church has stood, 'holding for shield the Faith,' and, having done all, it stands. In that shape we have received the faith; this, at least, is not of our making – it has been delivered to us by those who in their day kept it well and were kept by it. No 'particular Church' may judge it; for it is by this that each particular Church must itself be judged, whether it has or has not kept the faith, and is or is not in communion with the Church Catholic of the long past as of today. Let it be granted (with whatever necessary qualification) that 'a Church' may alter her Confession, amend, or add to, or entirely reject it; *ex hypothesi* her Confession is her own handiwork; what she has made she may doubtless unmake; what only she has said she may unsay. But what Christ has committed to her, that let her guard; what God has spoken, let her reverence. For that is the rock upon which she is builded together with the whole living Temple, and she must either abide upon it or fall from it – no third alternative exists. What is the 'particular Church,' but at most one pinnacle of the age-long wall of the city of God? The Creeds of the Church the particular Church may neither take from nor add to nor change, and remain what she was. For if she does, she is judged by the fact, judged by the canon itself, and found wanting. She is no longer measured by the measuring-rod in the angel's hand; she no longer repeats the watchword by which the faithful are recognised. Men talk of 'outgrowing Creed'; the Church cannot outgrow hers. Confessions may be outgrown; they speak men's thoughts, and thought changes. But the Creed speaks, not our thoughts, but the facts which bid men think. As to them, they happened or did not happen; they are to be confessed or denied. Through the centuries the Church has testified to them; if now she must reconsider, it cannot be to alter or recast them– they are not opinions–but to retract. We are then found false witnesses. It is not a question of the Church modifying, but of its ceasing to exist. There is indeed a fallacy underlying language which speaks of the Church altering Creed; if that has to be done, there is no Church to do it, and there has never been. She must stand or fall by her testimony.

But, it may be said, the language of the Creeds, that is sufficiently human–it is the language of a period; so far as the Creed goes beyond the barest description of what has lain within the sphere of earthly knowledge, it must employ phrases which are insufficient because they are phrases of ours, and terms which doubtless met the thought of the time when they were selected, but might not be selected now. And that of course is so far true: all language must be an imperfect instrument for the communication of absolute truth. But the imperfect is not necessarily the inadequate; adequacy depends upon purpose, and the purpose is in this case to state human faith for human apprehension, for which human language may serve very well. And an imperfect instrument may be as adequate as another which is also imperfect; if you restate, you must still restate in human terms. Doubtless to call God 'Father' is but to shadow forth the Divine relationship, either to the Eternally Begotten and Eternally Beloved, or to the creature which bears the Divine image; but the reference to Fatherhood is reference to the highest symbol of those relationships of which the human is cognisant; it is imperfect statement, but it is statement of truth in the best and highest way accessible to us. The categories of the Christology of the Nicene Creed are necessarily those of the fourth century; but they may be as true to the truth which they attempt to formulate as any which the twentieth century could substitute, and they may convey as much of the truth to our minds. These have, at all events, maintained since they were adopted the fundamental dogmatic unity of Christendom, and for sixteen centuries have kept alive in men the supernatural life. To adhere to their use may be to confess that an absolute and sufficient utterance of the mystery of the Divine nature is unattainable; while to revise them in terms of current philosophy would (as has been somewhere pointed out) be to imply that it is attainable – that we can hope to search out the Almighty unto perfection. And it would, of course, mean the dissolution of the harmony of Christendom in its ultimate basis, which is the catholic doctrine of the Trinity. Consentaneous revision is under present circumstances inconceivable.

One hears it said that the Spirit of God always abides with the Church, and is as truly with ourselves as with the Church of any age; and it is asked whether that which the Church was continuously doing through those early centuries during which the Baptismal formula grew to completeness of article, or in the fourth and fifth centuries, when the great Councils expanded its Eastern form to definiteness, the Church may not do today? *'The Church'* – yes, perhaps: if appeal to that august tribunal were practicable. But no such question in practice arises; the existing question is of the action of local communions, and of their isolated sections. Are we of these islands, or we of this northern half of one of them, or we a broken remnant of our own handful,–are we the Church of God? Can we claim for ourselves the authority of that one Body of which Christ is Head? Can we propose ourselves in our isolation as the organ of that awful Presence which fills the Temple, or can we say 'It seems good to the Holy Ghost and to us'? Could it be for us to speak of right or power to break the agreement in faith which has stood until now? God forbid. Came the Gospel out from us? or came it unto us only? We are not without law to Christ; and the first of His laws is that of charity, which binds us to our brethren in Him, and delimits every right of ours by their right in us, and every power of ours by our debt to them.

Or again, one hears it said that 'the Church' must rely on Christ's promise to be with her always through the ages, His promise to guide her into all truth, His promise that the gates of hell shall not prevail against her; and that having these promises, she may be bold to face whatever problem and to enter upon whatever course the need of the day may indicate. And undoubtedly such promises are made – but to whom are they made? To the apostles, and to the universal and apostolic Church in them. Against that the gates of hell shall not prevail: our Lord will always have a Church in the earth. With that He will abide where it is found, were it but a remnant. And doubtless the Church has assurance, if not of preservation from error, at least of direction into truth. These are promises which have validity for (to take the obvious example) such universally accepted action as that which has given us the Catholic Creed. They are promises to the Church–they are not promises to each and every section of the Church; not to local churches or national churches, and still less to the several groups within a local church which has divided against itself, or where group is organised against group. There is no promise, for example, to the Church of Scotland, and still less to the Presbyterian element of it, and still less to the part of that element which continues to adhere to national establishment, that Christ will abide with it to the end of the world, or that He will guide it into all truth under all circumstances and whatever it may become or do. There is no promise of the sort to any particular Church. To that, on the contrary, Christ speaks with warning and threat; He will deal with each as each particular Church deserves,– one, the faithful, He will cherish; and another, the unfaithful, He will spew out of His mouth. What Christ has to say to the particular Church is, that it take heed lest He remove its candlestick out of its place. The shores of time are strewn with the wreck of churches in that sense. The gates of hell have prevailed against them once and again. Yet Christ's promise is not broken–the promise was not to them, but to the Church of God; when they fell from the truth to which the Universal Church is God's witness, He came upon them, as He had said, and fought against them with the sword out of His mouth–which is the Word of God.

There is, in fact, an unhappy ambiguity possible between such phrases as 'the Church' and 'this Church'; there is a fallacy which in the past has had currency and effect, and may again appear to confuse thought–that, namely, of postulating, for whatever independently organised body of Christians, rights and powers which are inherent, if anywhere, only in the universal Church as the supernatural Body of Christ. The custom of language permits the use of the word 'Church' in applications from which dogmatic inference would be rash. All that is true of the city of God which comes down from God out of heaven may not be predicable of each autocephalous group of believing people, whether it be of an ancient national Church that we speak or of some more recent formation. Neither of these is that 'Church' of which Scripture speaks –the Holy Vine, the Body of the Lord, the Living Temple of the Holy Ghost, Pillar and Ground of the Truth; each is but at most a branch of the Vine, a member of the Body, a single chamber of the Temple. One's little finger is not a homunculus with brain and volition and life-cycle of its own: it inheres in the body. Christ is the Head of the Church; He is the Head of the Church of England or of Scotland, or as it may be, only in virtue of the fact that the part is part of the whole. There are, in fact, limitations which must be kept in mind when one conceives of the particular Church as a microcosm of the Church itself; and these limitations are reached when the common standard of fundamental Christianity is reached. Sweeping things may be said of the rights and powers of the Church, which may need careful guarding when they come to be applied to the particular Church. Sweeping propositions of a theoretical kind might be legitimately advanced as to the right and power of churches in Confessional matters, which would nevertheless be open to misunderstanding and apt to create alarm, unless a purpose of adherence to the Creed of the whole Church were at least certainly implied.

And again, when we speak (as doubtless we must all speak) of rights and powers in these directions, it will go far toward mutual understanding if we make it clear whether we mean right and power so far as human and external interference is concerned, or right and power before heaven and in the form of Christendom, in view of moral sanctions and of the vital interrelations of that Body of Christ which, like every organism, has its own law of life. A man may behave very selfishly and unkindly in his home without the interference of civil law - the domicile is sacred; but it would be hazardous for the teacher of ethics to express that fact by saying that a man has the right and power to act in that fashion. Before God and in truth he has no such right. It is one thing to claim, as we do, a 'spiritual independence,' the sanctity of the spiritual domicile - it would be something wholly other to forget the interdependence of that brotherhood of faith which has hitherto throughout the world borne one and the same testimony to the Unity and Trinity of God, and to the perfect deity and complete humanity of the One Lord Jesus Christ. I do not for a moment suggest, or in any thought fear, that our beloved Church is in peril of unfaithfulness in her testimony to that faith. But because language is educative, and because we are much at the mercy of phrase, and because in discussion of revision Creed and Confession seem to me to be often confused, I have wished to emphasise the distinction. It is Confession, not Creed, that I believe men have in view when they speak–as from all quarters men speak–of the right or need to alter or amend; and I submit the great practical convenience which will accrue, and the needless concern which may be avoided, if that is made evident by a careful use of words.

Creed cannot pass. If it is true, it remains true. It expresses the Church's essential testimony. Testimony to factual truth does not admit of revision; the Witness stands or falls by it. Even in the Church's perfected and ideal state her Creed will still remain her glory,–'Thou art worthy, for thou wast slain and hast redeemed us.' Confession, on the other hand, might in an ideal condition become unnecessary. We, however, are not in an ideal condition; and I for one can scarcely think it practicable (if there are any who think so) to dispense with Confession and to be content with only the Creeds of the Church for doctrinal standard. No Christian communion finds that possible. The Eastern Church knows only one Creed; but, along with the Nicene Creed, uses an extensive and detailed catechism, and possesses besides a liturgical apparatus which largely serves the purpose of a Confession. A catechism (the necessity of any Church) is practically a Confession. For ourselves (to instance a single reason), so long as the Roman claims stand, our protest must stand; and it must find voice in some Confessional form. But of the scope and detail of the particular Confession to be used by the particular Church (apart from legal questions, which apparently may arise, and apart from operations of the nature of concordat[9] – neither of which touch the abstract question, or call for consideration here), I venture for myself to believe that of such matters (loyalty to the essential faith being safeguarded and adherence to the Catholic standard of faith being explicit) the particular Church is the judge. There can be no surrender of spiritual independence on our part if, while thinking so, we yet own our debt to the greater fellowship in which by the act and grace of God we inhere, or in acknowledging that it is not for us – a part of that whole – to break unity with it; to acknowledge that every right of ours is delimited by the right which stands in the Church universal, and by the bond of charity to our fellows in the one Lord, one faith, one baptism.

In what has been said it is implied that, while there is antithesis of function between Creed and Confession, there is no clashing between their functions. Confessions were never meant to be substitutes for Creed, still less to supersede the Creeds. They supposed the Creeds as their background. Every Reformed communion proposed its Confession - often one Confession after another; every Reformed communion maintained at the same time unbroken and unchanged its former relation to the Creeds– maintained it jealously, boastfully, assertively.

---

[9] It is possible that for some minds among us, perfectly jealous for the truth, but rightly jealous for the Church's spiritual independence as well, there may have grown a feeling that there is some derogation from that independence in the fact of a statutory Confession. But that is the inevitable incident of establishment. The Church must at least condescend to say who she is, if she desires to be recognised by the State or by any one else. She confesses Christ before men; it is no derogation for her to do so.

The relation of our own national Church to the Creeds is absolutely regular and clear. One of the earliest acts of our General Assembly after the Reformation (1566) was to adhere, along with the Reformed of Hungary, Poland, France, Switzerland, and the Palatinate, to a joint Confession, which declares that

> we sincerely believe and loudly confess all that has been determined out of the Holy Scriptures concerning the mystery of the Incarnation of our Lord Jesus Christ, and is contained in the creeds and decrees of the first four Oecumenical Councils held in Nicaea, Constantinople, Ephesus, and Chalcedon, in the creed of St Athanasius, and all similar creeds; and we reject all contrary to the same. In this manner we retain, unchanged and entire, the Christian orthodox and Catholic faith, knowing that nothing is contained in the aforesaid creeds which does not correspond with the Word of God and aid in setting forth the true faith;

and to this the Scottish reformers personally subscribed,[10] the reservation of a single point (the observance of the greater festivals) making, as Dr Leishman has pointed out, their assent to the rest the more emphatic. The Apostles' Creed was repeated in every service so long as the Book of Common Order was maintained (till 1645); and in the Baptismal service, by the sponsor (the Scottish commissioners to the Westminster Assembly obtained a modification of the questions to be addressed to him in order to allow this practice to continue). The catechism (Calvin's) used in the Reformed Church of Scotland is, in its doctrinal section, based article by article upon the same Creed. At the Westminster revision it was placed with the catechism, and the whole doctrine and much of the language of the Nicene Creed was embodied in the Confession. No candid person can, I think, question that, whatever else may be contained in that 'sum and substance of

---

[10] *'Subscripsimus omnes, qui in hoc coetu interfuimus.'* The signatures of Knox, Craig, Wynram, Spottiswood, Row, Pont, Erskine of Dun, Douglas and thirty-three others follow.

the doctrine of the Reformed Churches' of which we hear, the entire doctrine of the Creeds of the Church is included in it. In its liturgical work of later years the Church continues to give the Creeds to her people for their place in public worship. Thus we maintain our part in the inheritance of the saints and our fellowship with all who in every place call upon the Name of the Lord Jesus, both their Lord and ours.

And to Him with the Father and the Holy Ghost, eternally One, eternally God, be glory in the Church throughout all ages. Amen.

# The Architectural Setting
## *George Hay*

Though modest compared with that of some other European countries the architectural heritage of the Church of Scotland is both wide and diverse. To those who find themselves its present day custodians it is at once a high privilege and a heavy responsibility. To maintain our historic churches unimpaired and in use it is necessary to apprehend their authentic character and appreciate the modes of worship for which they were designed.

The development of an effective ecclesiastical architecture in any age presupposes the existence of generally accepted standards of theology and liturgical practice. There is little doubt that in medieval times the virtual uniformity of faith and order of the western Church provided a constant and consistent theme around which to develop. The design of the early Romanesque churches no less than that of monasteries, cathedrals and the great town kirks developed by rich burghers and confraternities clearly demonstrate the prevailing aesthetic and liturgical outlook of the times in which they were built. The same might be said of the more modest buildings of early Reformed times. With the Reformation and the adoption of the theology and worship of Calvin and Geneva there passed out of use much of the liturgical structure and architectural apparatus of medieval worship hitherto characteristic of western Christendom. Contrary to the journalistic 'blight of Calvinism' myth, most of Scotland's pre-Reformation parish churches were retained and adapted for Reformed worship, albeit sometimes in rather utilitarian fashion. Architectural essentials were - and still are - facilities for the administration of the sacraments of Baptism and the Lord's Supper according to the Reformed rites and for the preaching of the Word, with physical conditions whereby the people might see, see, hear and participate. These in fact anticipate the so-called 'auditory' principles later propounded by Wren when he was designing the city churches of London after the great fire. The dominant factor in the layout of Scottish churches down to at least the third decade of the 19th century, even in times of infrequent celebration, was the disposition of the long tables at which the communicants sat in relays. It is interesting to reflect that this austerely impressive arrangement was probably the closest approximation to the Upper Room ever achieved by the Christian Church.

The mode of administering the sacrament of Baptism had little impact upon the architectural setting. Nevertheless it followed an orderly Reformed pattern which required it to be associated with an act of public worship and to take place in the presence of a congregation. This traditional reformed attitude was re-affirmed in 1645 by the *Westminster Directory of Public Worship* which declared

> Nor is it (baptism) to be administered in private places or privately, but in the place of public worship, and in the face of the congregation, where the people may most conveniently see and hear ...

Hence the normal practice of bracketing the basin to the side of the pulpit, which itself would occupy a fairly central position, often within a balustraded or panelled enclosure, known in the Netherlands as the *doophek* ('baptismal corner'). Many wrought iron brackets of good design survive, some still in use, while the basins, usually of silver but sometimes of pewter, conform to the high standards of design and craftsmanship which characterise Scotland's communion plate.

The existence of medieval parish churches available for adaptation and continued use along with a stringent ecclesiastical economy resulted in an almost complete cessation of church building during the first half century after the Reformation. As in most other Protestant and Reformed countries church building tended to become a minor branch of architectural activity. About two-thirds of Scotland's medieval parish churches were modest gabled structures of rectangular plan devoid of structural chancels. They were often of attenuated proportions and were originally thatched. The presence of a transeptal aisle of secondary date usually but not invariably on the north side and perhaps in origin a chantry chapel produced a T-plan structure - a classic Scottish type which was widely used as a model for later new churches. Such buildings were admirably suited for Reformed worship. The pulpit, usually a comely structure with back-board and sounding board and reader's *lattron* or desk, was set against the middle of the south wall. The space in front was at communion services occupied by the long tables set out along the east-west axis of the church. Additional seating was provided by lofts in the three wings. In one of them, usually the north, was the laird's loft, which had retiring rooms and the family burial place was below. Alternatively this complex was sometimes at the chancel end, the family probably already having burial rights there.

By its very nature the larger medieval church was a compartmented building divided by a system of screens and partitions into a number of different liturgical centres - a veritable 'house of many mansions'. In addition to the main structural elements of *kirk, queir* and *cross-kirk* (nave, choir and transept) space had to be provided for numerous chantry altars which were variously dedicated. With the Reformation such altarages were removed but in the adaptation of such buildings the early Reformers, both Scots and Continental, apprehended and retained the main structural elements. The nave was generally set out with pulpit and seating for preaching and daily services (*predigtkirche*) while the choir behind its screen furnished with long tables and benches was used for communion (*abendmahlkirche*) and known in Scotland as the 'communion aisle'. As time went on, however, the trend both architectural and liturgical was towards unicellular and even centrally planned buildings.

When new churches came to be built, many hardly differed from their medieval predecessors. They exhibited conservative masonry traditions sometimes combined with considerable ingenuity and diversity in planning. In addition to rectangular and T-plan buildings there were several centrally planned structures. The first was the 1592 church of Burntisland, which was planned around a square tower with lofts against the external walls and a wide central space for the communion tables. The 17th century churches of Fenwick, Kirkintilloch, Thurso and Lauder are of Greek cross form. In Edinburgh, Greyfriars (1620) is a Gothic aisled and arcaded building almost identical in plan to the nave of Glasgow Cathedral. It originally had a square west tower. Canongate (c.1690) was designed by James Smith as a remarkable cruciform Baroque building with side aisles and an apse, more suited to counter-Reformation use than 17th century Reformed worship. The strange little church of Dairsie (1621) in an odd revived Gothic idiom was designed by Archbishop Spottiswoode as a model parish church with a chancel screen and other fittings, no doubt intended as an appropriate setting for the Anglican practices initiated by the 1618 Articles of Perth.

The 18th and early 19th centuries witnessed a fairly extensive programme of rebuilding of parish churches to replace decaying and inadequate medieval ones. In general the new churches followed the earlier well-tried rectangular and T-plan formulae but employed a modest Georgian idiom which in due course succumbed to the allure of the early Gothic Revival. Instead of the normal gable belfry some were dignified with a tower either at the west end or against the middle of the south wall. This was an effective focal feature especially in an urban setting into which the church was often integrated. The internal arrangements followed earlier practice though by this time the churches were fully seated with fixed pews and the long tables were a permanent feature convertible into a series of box pews at times other than communion. They were usually allocated to the poor of the parish. An alternative 19th century expedient sometimes adopted was to provide at the front of the church a block of seats with hinged backs and moveable benches to alternate rows. They were so devised that by the adjustment of a few bolts a number of long tables and flanking benches was quickly achieved. Roof spans were greater than formerly and east, west and north lofts were often linked to present a continuous panelled breast of semi-octagon or horse-shoe plan.

During this period several centrally planned churches of more than ordinary interest were built. Some were octagonal as at Kelso (1773), Dreghorn (1780), St Paul's, Perth (1807), Glenorchy (1811), Kilmorich (1816) and St Stephens, Edinburgh (1828), with Killin (1744) as a variation on that theme. Kilarrow (1769) is circular with a squat tower dominating the main street of Bowmore, while at Hamilton William Adam's church of 1732 has a circular core and an overall plan of Celtic cross outline. St Andrew's, Edinburgh (1785) is oval, fronted by a pedimented portico and an elegant spire of classical design.

The Gothic Revival first manifested itself in decorative details which insinuated themselves into churches of traditional Reformed plan but some buildings of medieval form with aisles and arcades made their appearance towards the end of the 18th century. In general their Gothic is of a rococo decorative order, paper-conceived and devoid of serious ecclesiological intent. Typical examples are those of Craig (1799), Kincardine-in-Menteith (1816), Inverkeithing (1826) and Kilmartin (1835). In Edinburgh two notable arcaded churches, St John's (1876) and St Paul's (1816) were erected by the Scottish Episcopal Church. Both now have chancels of later date. The Roman Catholic Cathedral of Glasgow (1816) was for long the largest of such arcaded churches in the kingdom. Like those of other denominations, it was furnished to suit its own liturgical requirements and it also had galleries in the side aisles.

During late Georgian and early Victorian times probably the most numerous type of church building was the galleried hall church, comprising a rectangular hall with a gallery encircling three sides, a pulpit at one end and an entrance vestibule and stairs at the other. In many ways a convenient type of building with good acoustics it was employed by nearly every religious denomination, one of the earliest being Wren's St James's, Piccadilly. In Scotland the central pulpit with combined reader's and precentor's desk was the dominant focal feature at the liturgical east end with the communion table pews stretching down the main axis of the church. The layout of Anglican churches did not differ greatly. The two-or-three-decker pulpit stood either against the east wall or some distance forward. In the case of the former the altar stood in front of the pulpit and in the latter it was set within a railed space between the pulpit and the east wall.

The first quarter of the 19th century saw far reaching changes in the method of administering the Lord's Supper in Scotland. Hitherto the infrequent celebrations attracted large congregations who listened to sermons preached in the kirkyard from a portable pulpit known as the 'tent'. The sacrament itself was received in the church by relays of communicants. Such an occasion was noted by Robert Southey in his Journal and was depicted by Alexander Carse in his painting of Holy Fair. Few of the new urban *quoad sacra* churches or chapels-of-ease had a kirkyard to satisfy the logistics of earlier practice so the custom of communicating in the ordinary pews was adopted. It is said to have been previously employed by the Zwinglians and by 17th century English Independents. It was roundly condemned by the General Assembly in 1825 but once adopted it came to stay.

Few factors had more devastating effect upon the internal arrangements and appearance of Scottish churches than the advent of organs, after their use was sanctioned by a General Assembly ruling of 1866. Unlike Continental churches or the city churches of London, where, enclosed within fine casework, they generally occupy a rear gallery, most Scottish organs were given pride of place to dominate all else. Normally the original pulpit was replaced by a great upholstered rostrum, often with double stairs, attached to the organ front and before this strange ensemble an enclosed dais was contrived, cluttered with 'communion chairs' and other pieces of church furnisher's 'orra gear' as well as a communion table and organ console. In some instances the last has been known to serve as both. To complete this religious concert hall congestion chairs were provided for a choir which might sing to, for or at the congregation. Such architectural and liturgical bedlam was clearly the product of late 19th century *laissez faire* attitudes and standards, strangely combined at times with architectural idioms and craftsmanship of no mean order.

Despite the generally dismal standards then prevailing, some churches of real merit were designed by scholarly architects like Alexander (Greek) Thomson, Frederick Pilkington, Hippolyte J Blanc, Rowand Anderson, Marshall Mackenzie and Macgregor Chalmers. The founding of the Church Service Society in 1865 and the Aberdeen (later Scottish) Ecclesiological Society in 1886 stimulated interest in liturgical studies and in ecclesiastical architecture and its preservation. On the other hand new churches were mainly in eclectic renderings of English, medieval styles intended to satisfy the predilections of romantic clerics to whom 'the beauty of holiness' meant a Gothic Anglican church planned to accord with Victorian precepts current some seventy years earlier. It was as though the Kirk had turned its back on Geneva and its Reformed and European affiliations. Influenced by the ecclesiological and Tractarian movements some creditable restorations were carried out like John Kinross's Greyfriars, Elgin or Rowand Anderson's Dunblane Cathedral but the general standard of such work left much to be desired. A great amount of unintelligent mutilation was passed off under the specious label of 'restoration'.

Post-Reformation churches of douce Georgian design were savagely Gothicised by uncomprehending architects and ministers, who added irrelevant chancels, installed leaded glass in place of wood sashes and clear panes, destroyed authentic furniture and fittings and replaced them with items of church-furnisher's Gothic in 'natural Oak' - this and much more - in a frantic effort to achieve what may be termed the Victorian Anglican approximation.

The inter-war period (1918-39) witnessed in 1925 the Church of Scotland (Property and Endowments) Act by which the *quoad omnia* parish churches were transferred from the heritors to a new body, the Church of Scotland General Trustees. This was a prelude to the union in 1929 of the Established and United Free Churches and as a necessary consequence there was initiated a vast scheme of local unions and readjustments. As a result many parish churches of good design were abandoned, short term ecclesiastical expediency being preferred to historical interest or architectural merit. At the same time the Home Board embarked upon an ambitious church extension programme to provide churches in the new suburban areas of state-aided housing which had been built to take the place of the congested and sub-standard dwellings of the older town centres. Many of these churches were buildings of some quality and varied design but their plan forms and internal arrangement tended to follow the Victorian Anglican line. After the Second World War (1939-45) stringent building controls permitted of severely limited church extension activity. The Church of Scotland policy was to build what was known as a hall-church or dual-purpose building which would become a church hall when improved circumstances would permit of the erection of a church. The working formula for a hall-church appears to have been: a badminton court = 300 seats = a hall-church +/- a diminutive chancel. Fortunately, despite inflation and soaring building costs it has been possible in more recent times to erect proper churches of varied plan form and architectural idiom.

The architectural remit for the renovation of an historic church should include a structural survey and an analysis of the building, an appreciation of its original form and later modifications. It is all too easy to be caught up in the trivia of architectural confectionery and lose sight of basic maintenance and liturgical function. Needless to say, the work should be under skilled and experienced professional direction and both architect and clients should avoid stylistic predilections, the temptation to reduce all to an arbitrary one-period uniformity and slavish conformity with current ecclesiological trends. On grounds of mere prejudice many churches of good traditional design have been reduced to barn-like structures of grotesque proportions by the drastic removal of galleries and the addition of chancels. What has been termed the 'dominant note' of the building must be apprehended as the basis of operations. Where there has been a loss of authentic character a measure of 'de-restoration' might be justified. For example, where the injudicious removal of harling or plaster has reduced the building to a stark stoney cavern the recovery of the original wall finishes would be a legitimate item of restoration.

The principal liturgical centres should be clearly defined and adequate space provided about them. A well-proportioned Holy Table should be central to all else, sited either on a dais before the pulpit in churches of Reformed type, or on an advanced stance in a structural chancel where there is one. The surrounding floor space should be clear of steps and nothing interposed between the table and the congregation. Unlike the domestic dining table the communion table is seen not from above but on elevation and should therefore have a measure of bulk about it either with a panelled front or with an overall cover of damask or other fabric. Again unlike the standard 30 inches height of the dining table, the communion table should be about 3 feet 2 inches high to suit the standing posture of the minister behind it - the so-called 'basilican posture', long ago adopted by the Reformed Churches but now being taken up by the Roman Catholic and Anglican communions.

The table top should have a fair projection to emphasise its role as a table rather than an altar or cenotaph. Throne-like 'communion chairs' as invented by church furnishers should be avoided and seating for serving elders should be in the form of simple benches or stalls against the side walls of the chancel or flanking the dais.

In accordance with Reformed and Lutheran practice the baptismal font, sited in medieval churches near the west or south-west door, is now likely to be near the front of the dais or chancel 'in the face of the congregation' but all too frequently is perched precariously on the chancel steps. In certain of Macgregor Chalmers' attractive churches in a highly personal style of Neo-Celtic-Romanesque the font is set within a small apse terminating the east end of a north or south aisle - an attractive and functional solution.

The traditional pulpit sites, as earlier described, are unlikely to be bettered. Nevertheless ecclesiologically-minded ministers and architects have not hesitated to destroy original pulpits or to mutilate them by removing their back-boards and sounding-boards and to wrap the meagre remains around the north or south abutment of a chancel arch. Needless to say, all original pulpits should be preserved in their completeness, including the reader's or precentor's desk, which can take the place of a lectern.

For some time after the Reformation Scottish churches remained as devoid of seating as they previously had been but gradually private pews and desks were set up by individuals or by corporate bodies until there was quite a wealth of vernacular woodwork to be seen in Scottish churches. Logan in his *Collections*[1] records and illustrates what was still extant in the early years of the 19th century in Aberdeenshire and the north-east. There were seats with carved backs and ornamental canopies like the great patrician pews

---

[1] J Cruickshank (ed) *Logan's Collections* (Third Spalding Club: Aberdeen, 1941).

of the Netherlands and heraldic displays and craft symbolism richly tinctured. In due course it became a legal obligation of the heritors to provide seating for two-thirds of the 'examinable persons' of each parish - i.e. those of twelve years of age and over - as well as the communion tables, pulpit, elders' pew and manse pew, the last two usually flanking the pulpit. There were also in the vicinity of the pulpit a baptismal pew and a marriage pew and often the seats within a *doophek* enclosure were used for these purposes.

Only a few fugitive pieces now survive to remind us of what once adorned the interiors of our churches so thorough have been the activities of latter day 'restorers' and 'improvers' following the short-lived vagaries of ecclesiastical fashions. Since the 1925 Church of Scotland (Property & Endowments) Act the seating of churches has been the direct responsibility of the individual congregation. It may take the form of fixed pews or chairs or a combination of both. During the 18th century the seating allocated to the various heritors was in landward parishes divided among the tenants of the country houses and farms and the names of those were painted on the pew ends. Normally there were several box pews and the remainder being straight benches, all somewhat congested but tidily closed with doors. Where there are pews they should be reasonably spaced, arranged in tidy blocks and separated by generous gangways. Pews are more restful in appearance than chairs though the latter lend themselves to alternative arrangements, especially in the larger churches and in those of modern date.

As earlier indicated dignified functional arrangements to satisfy the liturgical needs of a church must take precedence over subordinate matters such as choir and organ. No amount of extraneous embellishment will compensate for an unworkable plan. Neither choir nor organ should be interposed between the congregation and a remote communion table whether arranged in concert hall fashion or following the Victorian Anglican formula. Acoustically and aesthetically there is much to be said for the traditional continental place in a west gallery. Here enclosed in well-designed case-work it can be a fine architectural feature. Alternative places, depending upon the plan of the church, are transepts or side aisles, with or without galleries with the choir seats adjacent. Specialist opinion should be sought regarding the scope and nature of a suitable instrument. For a small country church a modest chamber organ of good tone should suffice.

Drabness is neither a characteristic or tenet of the Christian faith nor are predilections for stripped rubble walls, 'natural' oak or bare pine woodwork derived from the authentic design of either medieval or Reformed church buildings. Internal rubble walls were almost invariably plastered and lime-washed and in medieval times provided a ground for decorative and didactic painting. The commoner timbers were usually painted, as is still the custom in Scandinavian churches, with details picked out in gold leaf and contrasting tints. Stained glass is not an essential and in most Renaissance and Georgian churches clear glass in original sashes is to be preferred. Where stained and leaded glass is appropriate it should accord with the architectural setting.

# Scottish Church Furnishings[1]
## *Henry R Sefton*

Church furnishings tell much about those who design and use them. This is illustrated by the furnishings of two places of worship in Aberdeen - King's College Chapel and the West Church of St Nicholas. The former dates from 1500 and was designed for the offering of Mass and the singing of the Daily Offices. The members of the College would spend many hours of each day in the Chapel and so seats are provided for them. These canopied stalls are one of the great treasures of Scotland. A screen separates the college community from the general public and no seating was provided in the ante-chapel. A small balcony projected from the screen on the outer face and from this the visitors could be addressed. The West Church of St Nicholas dates from 1755 and replaces the nave of the medieval Kirk of St Nicholas. It was designed for the preaching of the Word of God and the interior is dominated by a huge pulpit with a sounding board. Every available space was filled with box pews with doors so that the maximum number of people could hear and understand what was being said from the pulpit. The West Church is separated by a permanent wall from the surviving medieval transepts to provide a space in which the preacher could be seen and heard. The quire of the medieval kirk was similarly separated from the transepts for the same reason. Aberdeen thus has the finest medieval seating and the most complete 18th century seating in Scotland.

**Seating**

In an article contributed to *History*, the journal of the Historical Association, Mr Andrew Spicer concludes : 'Perhaps it is appropriate

---

[1] Originally published with illustration and references in Colin MacLean and Kenneth Veitch, eds, *Scottish Life and Society: A Compendium of Scottish Ethnology*, vol. 12, *Religion*. Edinburgh: John Donald etc., 2006, 616-28.

to see the provision of some form of seating after 1560 as being as essential as the pulpit for Reformed worship'. He takes issue with the view expressed by the architectural historian George Hay that 'For some time after the Reformation Scottish kirks remained as devoid of seating as they had been earlier'. Both refer to an order made in 1560 by the Town Council of Edinburgh for 'saittis, furmes and stullis... for the people to syt upoun the tyme of the sermoun and prayarris within the Kirk'. Hay claims that this was not accomplished until much later but Spicer questions the accuracy of this assessment as it depends on the surviving physical evidence of church furnishings. It is therefore not clear whether Jenny Geddes threw her own stool at Dean Hannay or a moveable one provided by the Town Council! The seating was obviously of varying quality and those who could afford to do so set up their own pews and corporate bodies installed private seated galleries.

There were two reasons why seating was necessary after the Reformation. John Knox and the other Reformers insisted that communicants should receive the sacrament seated at a table so seating had to be available. The transition from mere presence at Mass, lasting usually less than an hour, to lengthy preaching services during which the congregation was expected to hear and understand what was being said from the pulpit also made some form of seating necessary.

It became the obligation of heritors (landowners) and town councils to provide in each church sufficient seating for two thirds of the 'examinable persons' in the parish, i.e. those of twelve years of age and over, as well as an elders' pew and manse pew. The dimensions were to be 29 inches wide with seats of 18 inches in breadth. The extent of each heritor's responsibility was determined by the value of his property and the area of the church was divided up on this basis. The heritor then erected pews on his allocated space for himself, his family and tenants and he remained entitled to this seating as long as he held land in the parish. When the church of Kinneff was rebuilt in 1738 and space allocated, one heritor considered that his space had been encroached upon and he took an axe to his neighbour's pew! In the towns the seats were not associated with lands and allocation was made by the town council with preference for magistrates. In addition to the general seating there were often a baptismal pew, a marriage pew and a 'cutty stool' or place of public repentance which was usually on a platform in the middle of the church. There is some evidence that men and women were separately seated for some time after the Reformation. In some places the practice died out in the 17th century, in others in the 18th, but as late as 1827 the women sat by themselves in the Church of St Giles in Elgin.

Baptism, marriage and penitential seats have disappeared but the manse pew and the elders' pew survive in the old church at Newbattle. Magistrates' pews are to be seen at Burntisland and in the West Church of St Nicholas in Aberdeen. Elaborate laird's lofts are to be found at the old churches at Pitsligo and Kilbirnie. Pews consisting of long seats and book-boards are still the most common form of church seating but in many churches pews have been replaced with chairs. In a defence of such a replacement in Queen's Cross Church, Aberdeen, the minister Rev R F Brown has written 'Pews have no theological or ecclesiastical significance. They were simply a cheap and efficient, and often uncomfortable, way of seating people in a previous age... they have no special place in churches'. When the north transept of the Kirk of St Nicholas was re-furnished in 1990 chairs were designed by Tim Stead which fit the curvature of the human back. By using the initial letters of different kinds of wood the message 'We remember you' was incorporated in each piece of furniture in memory of the victims of the Piper Alpha oil platform disaster.

## Bells

The first *Book of Discipline* does not specifically mention seating as indispensable in every parish church but it does list the following requirements: 'Every Kirk must have dores, close windowes of glasse, thack able to withhold raine, a bell to convocate the people together, a pulpet, a basen for baptizing, and tables for ministration of the Lord's Supper'. A judicial decision of 1777 established that a steeple is not a necessary part of a church but that a bell is. A later decision in 1835 maintained that only the Established Church was entitled 'to assemble her members for public worship by the sound of a bell'. The Town Council or heritors were obliged to provide a bell but the Kirk Session had the right to decide when it was to be rung. The normal practice was for the bell to be rung three times on a Sunday morning. The first bell was rung at an early hour to prepare the people for setting out, the second at the commencement of the Reader's service, the third to mark the beginning of the Minister's service. The writer can recall the ringing of the early bell at Careston in the 1930s. The bell was usually hung in a belfry but hand bells were also used especially at funerals. This was known as the 'mort' bell. Many of the bells were of Continental origin but late in the 17th century bells were made in Scotland following Continental patterns. Bells have been imported from England from the 18th century until the present day. Change ringing is rare in Scotland but in Aberdeen a carillon in the tower of St Nicholas Kirk is played before the service on Sunday morning and so can be said to 'convocate' the people.

**Pulpits**

The emphasis on preaching the Word of God in Reformed worship made the provision of a pulpit necessary. This was not an innovation. There is a fine pulpit made for St Machar's Cathedral, but now in King's College Chapel, Aberdeen which dates from 1531-45. A pulpit said to have been used by John Knox stands in St Salvator's Chapel in St Andrews but was originally in the parish church. This is a two-decker pulpit, the upper stage for the Minister and the lower for the Reader and this is the normal style of pulpit until the middle of the 19th century. Only one or two examples of three-decker pulpits occur in Scotland though common in England. A canopy to act as a sounding board was an aid to audibility in the days before microphones but many have disappeared. Another feature which has almost entirely disappeared is an enclosure round the pulpit to be the place of baptism. The baptismal basin was held in a bracket on the side of the pulpit. Several of these brackets survive but the only baptismal enclosure is at the Auld Kirk of Ayr. Some pulpits also have a holder for a sand-glass which measured sermons by the hour. Clocks are often placed opposite the pulpit in view of the preacher but not of most of the congregation.

The pulpit was intended to be a fixed and permanent feature of the furnishing of the church. Moveable pulpits are to be found in some modern re-arrangements, as at Sherbrooke St Gilbert's Church in Glasgow. In some cases the pulpit has been removed altogether, as at Queen's Cross Church in Aberdeen.

Theological justification for this can be found in the writings of Karl Barth. For him the ideal solution is a simple wooden table to serve at one and the same time for pulpit, communion table and baptismal font. He comments: 'No matter how it is done, the separation of pulpit, communion table and baptismal font can serve only to dissipate attention and create confusion; such separation could not be justified theologically'.

## Baptismal basins and fonts

The first *Book of Discipline* prescribes a 'a basen for baptizing' as a requisite for every Church and this took the place of the font which had been hitherto used for baptism. It seems that most of the medieval fonts were destroyed for very few have survived and these are often to be found in episcopal churches. Medieval fonts were positioned near the main door of the church to symbolise entrance into the church by baptism and this meant that they were usually at the back of the church. As well as objecting to 'superstitious figures' on fonts the Reformers considered that the position prevented baptism in the face of the congregation after the preaching of the Word. For this reason the baptismal basin was placed near the pulpit or in a bracket attached to it.

When the writer was baptized in 1931 his parents presented a baptismal basin for use in the Church of Pitsligo and in homes when baptism was given there. When a font was presented to the church the baptismal basin disappeared and only recently was discovered being used as a rose bowl. There are still churches, such as West St Nicholas, Aberdeen which do not have a font and the Communion table serves as the stand for the baptismal basin. Fonts in many cases have been privately given and are in some cases moveable but quite often fixed at the front of the church. In St Leonard's Church, St Andrews the font is located in its own apse. St Margaret's Church, Knightswood, Glasgow has a font located at the front of the church but also near a door.

**Communion Tables**
The first *Book of Discipline* prescribes 'tables for ministration of the Lord's Supper' as necessary in each parish church. These were not permanent fixtures. For many years it was customary to erect tables when they were required and take them to pieces after the observance of the Sacrament. In some places this continued up to the 18th century. The table was flanked with forms on which the communicants sat and the elements were passed along from one person to another. Sometimes there was only one long table, sometimes more than one. There was usually a 'head board' or cross table at which the minister and his assistants sat and on this table the elements were placed before distribution to the communicants. Frequently there was a temporary open fence enclosing the tables. This enabled elders to restrict admission to the tables to those deemed worthy to approach. Worthiness was determined by the possession of a Communion token which was presented on admission to the enclosure.

The Scots maintained the practice of sitting at the Communion table against King James VI who commanded communicants to kneel and the English Puritans who took the elements to communicants in their pews. During the 18th century when fixed seating was generally adopted long communion table pews became a central feature of the church building. Pews in the centre of the church were constructed in such a way that they could be converted into a long table with seats round it.

In 1824 an innovation in the manner of communicating was made in St John's Church in Glasgow. Instead of the people coming forward in relays to the Communion table the elements were taken by elders to communicants in their pews. This practice was condemned by the General Assembly of 1825 but has become the norm. The cross table became a permanent furnishing and at the time of Communion the table and pews were covered with white cloths. Pew cloths are now gradually being discontinued. Communion tables are usually made of wood and moveable but the communion table in Crathie Church is made of marble and is a fixture.

## Lecterns

During the 19th century two-decker pulpits largely went out of use and the 'lattron' or Reader's desk came to be replaced by a lectern. Most churches now have a lectern or reading desk apart from the pulpit. They are often made of brass and consist of an eagle bearing a book board for the Bible. The East Church of St Nicholas in Aberdeen is probably unique in having a pelican instead of an eagle.

Dr Stewart Todd has questioned whether the lectern should be a permanent item of church furniture: 'In many churches in Scotland it is scarcely ever used and simply adds to the general clutter... Why should the place for the reading of the word be two or three or more feet lower than the place for the preaching of the word?' In St Machar's Cathedral the word is now read and preached from the pulpit.

**Prayer Desks**
Prayer desks are a comparative novelty in Scottish parish churches and were introduced as a result of the concerns of members of the ecclesiological societies which were founded in the 19th century. They arose out of the feeling that the pulpit was not a suitable place for leading prayer as it was above the level of the people.

**Organs**
It was not until 1865 that the Church of Scotland General Assembly permitted the introduction of organs subject to the supervision of the presbytery concerned. By the following Assembly eighteen organs had been installed and by the end of 1867 at least thirty-one organs were in use. The United Presbyterian Church removed the ban on organs in 1872. The Free Church gave permission to congregations to install organs in 1883. From being absolutely prohibited the organ soon became the most prominent feature of many Scottish Presbyterian churches and still is today.

**Collection Ladles**
Collection ladles are still in use at Guthrie in Angus and at Balquhidder in Perthshire. These are boxes with a half lid fixed to a pole and are pushed along the pew for the offerings of the congregation. At Newbattle the practice was to have offering plates on stools outside the entrance to the church. This had disadvantages on a windy day as bank notes were apt to be blown away and it has been discontinued. Many churches have plates for the offerings as the worshippers enter but inside the vestibule. In a former day Kirk Sessions were their own bankers and the offerings were locked in the poor's box. These boxes had two or three different locks so that no one person could have access.

## Hearses

The hearse was originally a triangular frame for holding candles in a church but the term is also used of a hanging chandelier. There is particularly fine example in Brechin Cathedral which was presented by Bishop Lamb in 1615. It was later converted to take gas and later electricity but has been restored to take candles. The West Church of St Nicholas, Aberdeen has three fine hearses dating from 1755 and fitted to take electric light in 1939.

## Benefaction Boards

Benefaction boards were a common feature in Scottish post-Reformation churches. It was hoped that the recording of gifts and mortifications (or legacies) on a wooden board in the church would encourage others to follow the good example. Few of these boards survive but in the north transept of St Nicholas, Aberdeen there are boards recording mortifications between 1629 and 1799. In the vestibule of the West Church of St Nicholas there is a curious monument in the shape of a sail and anchor which records the benefactions of a shipmaster to individual charities and totals the amount.

## Mural fabrics

In a former day fabrics were used to decorate the church on great occasions. In 1688 a set of embroidered panels was sold to the Town Council of Aberdeen 'for the decorement of the King's loft in Nicholas kirk in dayes of Solemnitie'. Four of them are preserved in the vestibule of the West Church. They are thought have been the work of Mary Jamesone, the daughter of the painter George Jamesone, and depict the Finding of Moses, Jephthah and his daughter, Esther and Ahasuerus, and Susanna and the Elders.

# Church Furnishings[1]

## *A Stewart Todd*

**Flower stands**

The increased interest in floral art on the one hand and the increased professionalism and business acumen of florists on the other have greatly encouraged the provision of flowers in churches and especially in the sanctuary. Stands for flowers are now readily available 'off the peg' and are frequently the gift of modest benefactors. The style and quality of such artefacts will be discussed later.

The important point for this part of the chapter is the placing of such items. In general floral art should be subject to the same discipline as other arts: it should not obtrude. It is there in an ancillary capacity, like music, architecture, stained glass and the rest. Flowers and foliage have been the traditional inspiration of carving and decoration in churches and on church furnishings, but if a holy table is so encrusted with carving as to be primarily a showpiece of craftsmanship and only incidentally a flat surface which can serve as a table then the decoration, for all its splendour, is out of place. So if flower stands and what is placed on them are such as to compete for pride of place and importance with table and pulpit, indeed steal the sanctuary limelight, they do the Church and its liturgy a disservice.

Flowers are there to enhance the two focal points of the sanctuary, not to obscure them. Even at a wedding, where current fashion seems to take vast expenditure on flowers as a matter of course, the Church must retain the right to keep its ecclesiastical and liturgical geography clearly discernible, the lineaments of the sanctuary unobscured and

---

[1] Previously published in *The Record* of the Church Service Society, Spring 2001.

their witness unimpaired. A wedding service is not an occasion for creating a floral idyll to be the space for a bit of matrimonial theatre. On the contrary, the church as Church is the space.

The couple and their friends, whether they are formally the Church or simply associated with the Church on this occasion, identify with the Church and the Church gives thanks to God for the gift of marriage to humanity and for the providence which has brought the couple together. The Church also proclaims at a wedding service that the relationship of husband and wife, like every other relationship, can be enhanced if Christ is in it. Even if the pulpit is not used on these occasions that proclamation is a part of or a deduction from that word of God to which the pulpit in a church itself bears witness. Likewise it is Christian belief that all relationships find their true fulfilment in that most intimate identification with Christ and therefore with one another which is possible in the sacrament of Holy Communion, the action of which is centred on the table. That remains Christian faith, even if at any particular wedding the couple merely approach the table to kneel at its steps.

The flowers and their stands must be so arranged as to point up and enhance the silent witness of the sanctuary's principal furnishings, not to replace it with a romantic gush.

The flowers bear witness in their way to the glory of God and the beauty of his creation, 'for there is a language of flowers.' But the Church which speaks of the glory of creation speaks most authentically when it proclaims God versatile and inventive in creation and equally versatile and inventive in grace and salvation.

### The lectern
A lectern is a useful piece of furniture, especially if it is not too heavy and can be easily moved. Whether or not it should be present

permanently in the sanctuary is a real question. In many churches in Scotland it is scarcely ever used and simply adds to the general clutter. Where it is used for the reading of scripture its distinction from the pulpit, especially its lesser height and more modest appearance, has a weakening effect on the whole visual impact of the sanctuary and may represent a distortion of the silent witness of its principal furnishings. Why should the place for the reading of the word be two or three or more feet lower than the place for the preaching of the word? The reading of scripture may have been entrusted to lectors from earliest times, and they may have been a 'minor order', but there can be little doubt that the importance of their service was appreciated. The ambo that was provided for them was wheeled out to give greater proximity to the worshippers. The sermon was preached from a sitting position behind the table until, around the fourth century, the complaint was heard that preaching from behind a distant table was too much of a strain on the preacher's voice in the larger basilicas. The preacher then came forward to preach from the platform from which the scriptures were read.

The reader of scripture today may sometimes be someone other than an ordained minister but, as in early centuries, the ecclesiastical status of the reader is not the important thing: the important thing is the function performed. The importance of the function sadly is not always appreciated. Readers could learn from the reply of a professional actor to an invitation to read lessons in a certain Aberdeen church. Would he be able to have the lessons in time to give himself three or four hours for preparation? He did not intend to memorize them! For the reading of scripture the place also deserves consideration. More and more writers, not least Roman Catholic writers (with Vatican Council encouragement) are stating plainly that careful consideration of the matter points to the desirability of reading and preaching the word from the same place. Among other things it underlines the mutual need of the word read and the word preached.

## The prayer desk

The principal furnishings of a sanctuary are pulpit and table: we are concerned with a ministry of word and sacrament. Let it be assumed that the ministry of the word, reading of scripture and preaching, is concentrated in the pulpit: we have dispensed with a lectern. We have therefore two focal points in the sanctuary in some sort of relationship to one another. Do we need anything else? *The Book of Common Order (1979)* and *The Church Hymnary: Third Edition* both provided orders for morning worship and both recognized three main parts in the order: APPROACH TO GOD; THE WORD OF GOD; RESPONSE TO THE WORD OF GOD. Both spoke of the eucharistic pattern of worship even where Holy Communion is not celebrated.

The section APPROACH TO GOD includes praise; call to prayer; prayers of approach, confession, absolution, supplication etc. This part, coming before the beginning of the action proper in the reading of scripture, seems to ask for a minister identified spatially with his people in an intermediate place, not addressing them, facing ecclesiastically north or south. It should be a modest place, at the sanctuary's edge, a place where the minister will kneel and the desk will be at the appropriate height. The 'word function' is thereby enhanced, because this approach, this preparation, has been made. The climbing of steps into a pulpit is now for the purpose for which the pulpit was intended. Now there is proper eye contact. Now there is proclamation, the congregation begins to be addressed with a new intensity.

The minister may return to the prayer desk to make prayers of intercession before going to the table, unless intercessions are to be made along with thanksgiving at the table. A prayer desk in the position recommended seems particularly appropriate for biddings, intimations and explanations of any part of worship, if such be required.

## The font

There is no *one* right place for the font in a church any more than there is any one right plan for the church building itself. There is no *one* enlightened, early church practice to be restored but only a history of development and a multiplicity of models. For some the Reformed insistence that baptism be in the face of the congregation will be guideline sufficient and without further question they will place the font in the sanctuary.

While, however, the guideline need not be questioned, the location of the font certainly should. The vast theological interest in baptism in our day, the liturgies rich in baptismal images, the prominent and promising part baptism plays in the ecumenical debate, the tightening of Church law anent baptism in our own Church - all of these have restored a dignity and significance to the sacrament of baptism which deserves to be expressed visually and spatially.

In many churches in Scotland the visitor could scarcely doubt the importance of preaching, so impressive is the pulpit and so prominent is its position. In others the lines of the building may draw the eye primarily to the table. The sacrament of baptism is of such fundamental importance that the font deserves to be similarly impressive. But if this is to be done in the sanctuary surely it will detract from the two liturgically monumental furnishings of the area - the table and the pulpit. Their relationship can be readily represented and registered. There may be also liturgical progression and regular movement from one to the other Sunday by Sunday to drive the point home. It is questionable whether there is any one theological relationship between font and table or between font and pulpit which is so simple and obvious as to permit of being represented spatially. Certainly there is nothing as simple as the message conveyed by the font at the west end that baptism is entrance to the Christian life.

This model has much to commend it, provided space enough is afforded for an adequate amount of baptismal symbolism. Such an arrangement depends of course either on the congregational seating permitting the worshippers to turn 180 degrees comfortably or alternatively on the congregation's leaving their seats to gather round the font. The latter may require a large space. Given that for many congregations movement out of pews (except to go home) would be troublesome this may not be popular or even possible. Spatially, however, it is a model which makes sense.

It may be equally satisfactory to give the font its own space, its own architectural setting, with accompanying window or wall hanging or other representation of baptismal motifs, in an area north or south of the sanctuary or of the approach to it, provided the sight lines are reasonably good. The fact that the odd person cannot see the affusion because of a pillar in the way scarcely invalidates this solution. Such a baptistry may indeed be the preferable way of creating that sacrarium which truly befits the font and more particularly the sacrament with which it is associated.

## The pulpit and the table

The decision to leave discussion of pulpit and table to this point was taken in the belief that points raised in discussion of other furnishings would contribute cumulatively towards identifying the really important things that had to be said about pulpit and table. The reason for treating these two together under one heading is that it is the relationship of the two that presents the biggest challenge both to those privileged to build a new church and to those given the opportunity to effect some reordering within existing churches.

The picture that has emerged from the preceding sections is of a sanctuary having no font in it, no lectern in it, only a pulpit, a table, a prayer desk at its outer edge and a discreet flower stand or stands. Flowers will not be on the table: rather they will be part of the adornment of the setting along with lighting and fabric. Such a simplification of furnishings reads clearly word and sacrament. Such an arrangement reflects simple obedience to two dominical commands: 'Go ye therefore and teach all nations ... teaching them to observe all things whatsoever I have commanded you' and 'Do this in remembrance of me'.

So in the sanctuary there is a pulpit and a table and they bear faithful witness to the principal functions around which all other constituents of regular worship gather. This table is a table and not an altar, though it is a place where the overtones of sacrifice will often be heard - our sacrifice of prayer and praise: of ourselves or of our gifts, always in response to the one true, pure, immortal sacrifice. It is pre-eminently a table, though it should not be a table at which the celebrant or celebrant and elders sit. Symbolically all sit at this table. The celebrant stands. Chairs immediately behind the table may blur the symbolism. If space permits they should be set considerably further back. In a chancel or in an apse they may indeed be sedilia on the outer edge. The celebrant can easily walk a few paces to take the elements to elders or elders standing to right and to left may perform the task. Where space does not permit, a bench on which the celebrant may sit, say during the distribution of the elements, is preferable. The 'presidential' chair belongs in a different scenario: in the early Church, as we saw above, it was the place from which came preaching and teaching and the preacher sat in it to preach. The chair was made to look important because the function was important. Now that that function is performed in a pulpit, the 'presidential' chair is confusing and tends to lead us into the personal status trap, which is to be avoided.

Establishing a visual and spatial relationship between pulpit and table is, however, the greater problem to be faced. It is particularly acute in some inherited situations. The medieval cathedral makes marvellous architectural provision for the table but may have a pulpit as merely an appendage to a pillar, with no architectural setting of its own. The simpler chancelled church may bring the pulpit into somewhat closer relationship to the table but the pulpit may still require embellishment – a tester, antependium, superimposed liturgical colours, lighting etc.– to give it any kind of equivalence of importance with the table.

Time and again the situation will be reversed: the pulpit will dominate architecturally. The table below will have to be rescued from a jungle of chairs and other items, be given space, perhaps be covered with a rich cloth. An organ console may have to be removed so that the table may be seen properly by the congregation!

These matters deserve to be given our best thought. Theological effort is required certainly in looking into the implications of the faith for liturgy and for liturgical space. But liturgy and the doing of it involve more than precision of rationality and criticism. Liturgy is the celebration of the mystery of Christ: it will express that in its own way, in an evocative, poetic, symbolic way. We are concerned here more with art than with science, and the best art, certainly in the service of the church and the faith, points beyond itself to eternal truth. The disposition of church furnishings is part of that distinctive endeavour.

# The Individual Cup: Its Use at Holy Communion[1]

*Alastair K Robertson*

**Presidential Address to the Church Service Society, 1978**

The earliest record I can find of the use of the Individual Cup is in the USA in the last decade of last century. It was introduced purely on grounds of hygiene at a time when public health and the combating of infectious diseases had come to the forefront. Its use was developed in a new country where men as yet set more store by things new and modern than by things ancient and traditional. In bringing in this innovation no one apparently argued that the use of small cups was nearer to the Passover usage or that it expressed a fundamental doctrine of the Faith or might be construed to do so. The innovation was based on hygiene.

Even in the USA, but much more in Scotland, the innovation made slow progress. Most people saw in it a serious departure from the use and wont of the Catholic Church. Many who were unable to formulate doctrinal objections were offended by the substitution of a rather irreverent, new fangled method in place of what, to put it at its lowest, was a beautiful piece of symbolism, rendered the more sacred by memories of services of the Lord's Supper held often in the open air, often in quiet country kirks, often in great town churches and cathedrals throughout the land, where the worshippers received the wine in cups from which generations of worshippers had received Holy Communion. In the Church of Scotland matters came to a head in 1906 when the Presbytery of Glasgow overtured the General Assembly for a ruling on the use of the Individual Cup.

---

[1] Originally published in *Liturgical Review*, viii.2 (1978).

The practice had been adopted by three congregations in Glasgow and the Presbytery wished to know the legal position. In 1878 the General Assembly had allowed ministers discretion in the use of unfermented wine. The Presbytery wondered if a similar discretionary use would be permitted in the use of the Individual Cup. The General Assembly appointed a special committee which reported in 1908, but its report was not unanimous. A minority report was given in by Professor Cooper.

The report showed that 21 parishes had to date adopted the Individual Cup, while three were using spoons. The reasons for these departures from use and wont were 'the desire to avoid the risk of infection and a wish to spare the feelings of those who shrink from a promiscuous use of the same cup by 50 or 60, or possibly more people'. The general feeling was that seemliness was being preserved and that the innovation did away with the habit of 'passing the cup'. Only in one case did the committee report disharmony and displeasure and absenting oneself from the Lord's Supper because of the introduction of the Individual Cup. The committee could see no objection to the Individual Cup in principle or in the law of the Church of Scotland and therefore urged a permissive use. The committee recommended that the method of administering the wine be left to the discretion of the minister, provided the harmony and peace of the congregation be not disturbed, and always subject to the control of the Presbytery.

The Minority Report, however, saw in this innovation a departure from the original institution of the sacrament, and this throughout the ensuing debate remained the chief argument used by opponents of the Individual Cup. Christ, it was argued, used one cup after the meal and handed it to the apostles to drink from. Cyprian and Calvin were quoted to stress that we must adhere strictly to our Lord's command and example.

It was pointed out that the innovation had no precedent in the history of the whole Church. As early as 110 AD the symbolism of the Common Cup was emphasised by Ignatius who said, 'for one is the flesh of our Lord Jesus Christ, and one the chalice in unity of his Blood'. Uninterruptedly throughout Christendom the Communion of the Blood of Christ was ministered in a large cup, usually by the deacon. The Minority Report saw this innovation as a departure from the law of the Church of Scotland, noting that in the Westminster Confession Christ's 'ministers are to pray and bless the elements of Bread and Wine, and thereby to set them apart from a common to a holy use, and they (communicating also themselves) to give both to the communicants'[2] and the Directory which requires that the wine be 'set on the Table in large cups'.[3] It was illegal to have introduced the Individual Cup without having previously received the permission of the church courts. The permission to use unfermented wine could not be extended to cover an innovation affecting a fundamental element of the sacramental action . . . taking, blessing and giving and receiving. The innovation, it was argued, would destroy the unity of observance throughout the Church and spoil what should be a feast of Christian brotherhood. 'It is not good that one should fear another. It is worse if a poor brother is made to feel that a richer one fears his presence and his sharing the cup of brotherhood'.

The alleged danger to health, the Minority Report said, had never been proved and appears to be greatly exaggerated. The Bishop of London said the other day that 'after careful consultation with the best doctors, he found the danger is regarded as absolutely infinitesimal, and no one ought to allow any such fear to prevent him from coming'.[4] Moreover, such danger as there is meets one daily in almost every action of social

---

[2] Westminster Confession of Faith, chapter 29, paragraph 3.
[3] *Directory of Public Worship*, Of the Celebration of the Communion, or Sacrament of the Lord's Supper.
[4] *Church Times*, 10 April 1908.

life – in the passing of coin and bank notes, and even in the grasp of a friend's hand. Much of what the innovation sought to achieve could be achieved by more frequent celebrations of the Lord's Supper as has been recommended over and over again by the General Assembly; by ministers and elders taking good heed and care that such sick persons as come to receive this sacrament . . . communicate last ... or by communicating sick persons in their own homes or in times of plague or infection by the General Assembly authorising Communion by intinction or by the spoon, or tube, for all which practices there are precedents in the early Church'.

Professor Cooper and his followers also feared that the introduction of the Individual Cup might lead to 'tampering' with the sacrament. The case of the Barclay UF Church, Edinburgh, was cited where simultaneous Communion had been introduced, the elements being set out in individual containers in the pews before the service commenced.

The General Assembly of 1908 received the Report, but in view of the 'limited' nature of the inquiry made by the committee decided to remit the whole question to an enlarged committee of 56 members for fuller investigation and subsequent report under four heads, viz; 1. The Critical, Doctrinal and Historical Aspects of the Question. 2. The Legal Aspect. 3. A Medical Report. 4. The General Feeling of the Church. In 1909 this enlarged committee brought forward its report which proved to be a very full document.

Once again there was a Minority Report which was characterised by a scholarly approach.

The Report itself argued that St Matthew 26: 27 should according to the oldest manuscripts read 'Having taken a cup' and that 'drink of it' could well refer to the wine and not the cup. It argued that in

I Corinthians 11: 25 'as oft as ye drink it' should read 'as oft as ye drink'. The NT text gave no indication as to the mode of drinking the wine. The title 'cup of blessing' showed that the sacramental cup was either the third or fourth cup of the Passover at which small cups, one for each person, were used. However at the Kiddush it was definitely the custom for all to drink from the same cup. The committee felt that the change from individual cups to a common cup was possibly made during the second century AD when concern began to appear lest any of the consecrated elements be spilt. They admitted that the common cup creates a deep sense of brotherhood but felt that this is equally well expressed by all eating of the one consecrated bread.

On the legal aspect the committee decided that there is no authoritative ruling in the matter. Past usage does not constitute church law to the extent of excluding modifications such as the individual cup. The Church may make rules as to the manner of administering the wine as seems good to her.

In the light of conflicting medical evidence submitted the committee decided that there is danger to health from the use of the common cup and do not accept the view that the risk of infection is negligible. They emphasised the medico-psychological aspect of the question as being of great importance ... many communicants are affected by only temporary antipathy to the sacrament, but in every congregation there are those especially women of sensitive natures to whom the common cup is painful. A census of church opinion showed that 28 parishes felt the need for departure from the use of the common cup. 776 wanted no change. In answer to the question, 'Do you think that the individual cup should be permitted in congregations that desire it?' 500 answered in the affirmative; 155 in the negative and 155 gave no reply.

Summing up, the committee concluded that there was no evidence to justify the prohibition of the individual cup, but they emphasised that dangers to health from the use of the common cup were often exaggerated. They regretted any occasion of departing from the beautiful, ancient and seemly custom of administering the wine and recommended that before the individual cup is resorted to, every effort should be first made to remove cause for offence. The Report said the individual cup at least allows a sick person to communicate with others with a clear conscience. The mode of distributing the elements falls to the minister subject to the control of the presbytery.

A Minority Report, again presented by Professor Cooper, claimed that the Report's exegesis of NT passages was forced and erroneous and was in opposition to the interpretation of them held sacred by centuries of Christian scholarship and devotion. Its main argument was that definitely after the Supper or Passover our Lord took one cup and caused the apostles to drink from it. St Mark makes it perfectly clear that they all drank from one cup (14: 23) and I Corinthians 11: 21 is specific by repeating three times the phrase '*touto to potérion*'. The Church has no right to weaken the symbolism which Christ commanded. She needs more than ever to be reminded of Christ's words at the institution 'that ye love one another' (St John 15: 12).

The suggestion that the individual cup was used during the first three centuries AD was felt to be purely conjectural. The pictures in the Catacombs show large cups and communicants drinking from one cup. In all churches the common cup has been in use for centuries; the earliest known use of the individual cup being 1896.

With regard to the legal aspect, the fact that the statutes of the Church contain no direction prohibiting the individual cup does not sanction the innovation but rather forbids it, because it was obviously always assumed that there was only one way of administering the wine, namely in large cups.

This Minority Report condemned the Report because it sanctioned division in the Church and even within a single congregation in the matter which stands at the heart of the church's life. It dismissed the medical evidence as inconclusive and rejected the census of church opinion as a method of reaching a decision concerning this innovation. In the General Assembly of 1909 the question was hotly debated. Finally 145 voted in favour of the Minority Report, 240 in favour of a compromise motion which stood half way between the Committee's Report and the Minority Report, but gave no cordial welcome to the individual cup. It read:

> The General Assembly see no sufficient reason for departing from the ancient and uniform practice of the Church in the administration of the Lord's Supper – so expressive and solemn and endeared by hallowed associations of centuries; but in view of the information on various aspects of the subject submitted in the Report, they do not feel justified in forbidding the individual cup, much as they regret the introduction of a practice so novel and in many respects so undesirable. The General Assembly at the same time charge ministers and presbyteries to see that the harmony and peace of congregations are not disturbed over this holy ordinance and that those who desire it shall always have as convenient means and opportunity of partaking in the manner heretofore in use.

The Procurator ruled that the individual cup was illegal according to church law, but his ruling was ignored and the foregoing motion became the deliverance of the General Assembly on the use of the individual cup.

We note that expediency and compromise guided the fathers and brethren to a decision which they accepted certainly without enthusiasm and perhaps not with intense conviction. In the intervening years the use of the individual cup has made widespread progress, thanks largely to unremitting commercial advertising and the timely or untimely actions of do-gooding donors who up and down the country presented congregations with individual communion cups usually designed in utilitarian rather than artistic manner. Thousands of communicants have never known any other mode of distribution of the wine and some moving to another parish would be so put off by the prospect of receiving from the common cup that they might choose to travel some distance to another church where the individual cup is in use. To many younger people the whole question of individual or common cup seems irrelevant now. For them the manner in which the wine is administered is a completely secondary matter which does not affect the validity of the sacrament. The intention to fulfil Christ's command in celebrating the Lord's Supper, personal faith and the real presence of Christ in the sacrament are what matter. There can be different ways of distributing the wine. Others would argue that the use of the individual cup is a natural development in the social history of our people. Hygiene has altered many aspects of cooking and retailing food. Medical research has isolated many germs and viruses. We have moved a long way from Reformation times when people normally drank from the same banqueting cup or humbler people ate from a common dish of meat without using cutlery.

At the same time there have always been those who disapprove of and dislike the individual cup and these are by no means confined to the stupidly conservative or unrealistically aesthetic. A reasoned and consistent stand was taken by the Scottish Church Society which until the 1930s excluded from its membership any minister who used the individual cup. The Society's theology of the common cup was defined by the publication of Dr Cromarty Smith's booklet: *The Cup of Blessing*. According to this view the use of the individual cup is a breach of Christ's command at the institution of the Supper and it divides men instead of uniting them. The fear of contagion is unworthy in a faithful communicant. 'If we trust God for eternity, can we not trust Him for His present care? If for our souls, can we not for our poor bodies? How could the Lord in His own sacrament do us harm? Our opportunities to be lowly with Christ are not over many. Let us do joyfully what He bade, He who for our sakes became poor and sat at meat with publicans and sinners.'[5]

The reiteration of the words 'the cup' in the Scriptural accounts of the institution are significant. *The blood is the life* in Hebrew thought and in setting forth the cup as He has commanded the Church sets forth the memorial of His sacrificial death. There is one sacrifice for sin. There is one Lord. There is one cup. All the faithful are made to drink of one Spirit. 'Dare we shatter this sacred symbolism? The cup signifies for us that Christ is the only Author of life. From Him alone flows the life blood which cleanses from sin, dare we break it into a crowd of vessels which signify nothing intelligible? To change the symbol is to change the sense.'[6]

We now review this controversy at some distance in time. We must try to look objectively at the question whether the use of the individual cup is permissible and if permissible desirable. The individual cup has created a division within the Church of God and even within particular congregations. The General Assemblies of 1908 and 1909 in a sense kept the peace but shattered the unity of the Church in its rulings with regard to the administration of Holy Communion. Some will say there can be unity without uniformity. This is true, but not surely in the context of how the wine is administered. Christ did not leave us completely free with regard to sacramental practice. He said, THIS DO. He gave a command and instituted a sacrament whose symbolism is very simple, but basically unalterable because given by Him. In the words of the poet John Donne,

> He was the Word that spake it.
> He took the bread and brake it.
> And what that word did make it,
> I do believe and take it.

---

[5] *The Cup of Blessing*, p. 16.
[6] op. cit., p. 14.

Our primary concern then must be not with hygiene but to ask what exactly Christ commands us to do with regard to the wine in the Lord's Supper. This is decisive. If, following Jeremias, we accept that the Lord's Supper was instituted at a celebration of the Passover and that Christ blessed and handed to His apostles a common cup, bidding them all drink from the one cup: we see that drinking from the same cup and breaking the same loaf are fundamental eucharistic actions which cannot be departed from without failing to fulfil our Lord's command THIS DO. Jeremias has shown that the use of individual cups at the Passover was introduced on grounds of hygiene after Christ's time, but that on festal occasions the cup, over which grace after the meal had been said, was handed round to let everyone share in the benediction. This view is supported by the analogous treatment of the bread: the bread over which the blessing had been said was broken so that every guest could share in the blessing by eating a piece.[7]

This would suggest that in order to be the Eucharist, at least the minister and elders who are assisting him must receive from the common cup, even if the congregation receives from individual cups. This seems to rule out celebrations where even the presiding minister and assisting elders receive from individual cups. It also rules out celebrations where individual pieces of bread and cups are set out in the pews before the service and Christ's command to take, bless and share is disobeyed. The celebration of the Passover at which the Lord's Supper was instituted averaged ten persons.[8] It was a simple matter for a small group to share the one cup. Celebration of the Lord's Supper in small groups is likely to increase among us and is most meaningful. Here the common cup symbolism is most effective. The trouble arises when many persons have to be communicated and all cannot drink from the same cup. The Scottish Reformers do

---

[7] J Jeremias, *The Eucharistic Words of Jesus (SCM, 1966)*, p. 69.
[8] op. cit., p. 47.

not seem to have had any difficulty in the matter. Knox is credited with celebrating at Kilmacolm with a pair of inverted candlesticks as chalices.[9] Certainly no care was taken to preserve and continue in use the mediaeval chalices which met strange fates. Stirling sold two to repair the streets and Aberdeen sold a quantity of church plates to the highest bidder.[10] The oldest communion cups we have are *mazers* which were formerly used as grace cups. Each College, Corporation, Guild or notable family possessed at least one. These were handed round social gatherings each guest drinking out of the same cup to symbolise the family feeling of brotherly love and goodwill.[11]

Thus Scottish people of the 16th century found it perfectly natural to receive the wine in a common cup and saw in so doing a close bond of fellowship with Christ and with other believers. This all fitted the times and their understanding of the manner of Christ's presence in the sacrament. There was no harking back to the practice of receiving the wine from the chalice by means of a tube or spilling a little of the consecrated wine into a chalice of unconsecrated wine to give the people communion or of using a spoon to communicate or of withholding the cup from the laity, all of which had been practised somewhere at some time in the Universal Church. Christ's command THIS DO must be fulfilled. All must receive in both kinds and the common cup, even if several such were needed, seemed the obvious way. It had not been hygiene but fear of spilling the Precious Blood which had dictated past evasions of giving the cup to everyone and now that it was understood that worthy believers received the Blood after a spiritual manner this difficulty was overcome. For long enough many parishes did not possess any cups and had to

---

[9] G B Burnet, *The Holy Communion in the Reformed Church of Scotland, 1560-1960* (Oliver & Boyd, 1960), p. 3.
[10] W McMillan, *The Worship of the Scottish Reformed Church, 1550-1638* (James Clarke, 1931) p. 239.
[11] op. cit., p. 241.

borrow from others. For long periods the Lord's Supper was all too infrequently celebrated. Yet the Scottish Church was quite clear as to what the sacrament meant and the bare simplicity of the Calvinist rite, enriched by the finely designed silver cups which appeared in the 18th century, made the occasion liturgically memorable. Von Allmen says that 'a eucharistic liturgy which is not patently beautiful casts a kind of doubt on Christ's presence there.'[12] Individual cups can be used with reverence and dignity but alas the effect is often otherwise—tossing glasses, squeaking boots, clinking trays, and if children are to be admitted to communion further difficulty can be envisaged in handing round the trays. As celebrations become more frequent the Church may move away from the 'mass rally' type of service with cards, pens, cloths, elders' duties and formal dress to something more beautiful, quieter and deeply spiritual, where communicants sharing a common loaf and cup are brought into Holy Communion with Christ and with one another. Had the injunction of the General Assembly of 1825 forbidding the administration Holy Communion in the pews and insisting on the retention of the long tables been enforced then the individual cup would most likely never have found an entrance into the Church of Scotland, as the people continued to come up and sit at the table fulfilling as nearly as possible Christ's command THIS DO. Once communion was administered in the pews and the individual cup came in, receptionist views of the sacrament filtered in too, and Presbyterianism sailed near English Nonconformity, drifting away from her anchorage in what the Scots Confession said about the real presence of Christ's Body and Blood and viewed as an alien land the sacramental teaching of the Christian Church across the ages.

It is not too late to profit by mistakes. The individual cup remains an innovation – it is not part of the living body of the Christian Church.

---

[12] J-J von Allmen, *The Lord's Supper* (Lutterworth, 1969), 59.

Thus, assessing the controversy now, we cannot dismiss the whole question as irrelevant, for the use of the individual cup is too closely involved in the theology of the Eucharist and especially in the expression of that unity of which the participation in the Eucharist ought to be the most visible symbol.

Those who have advocated the use of the individual cup have for the most part failed to grasp the *anamnēsis* aspect of the Eucharist — the setting forth before God and men of the memorial which Christ has commanded. They have failed to understand the supreme spiritual significance of *the action*. They have stressed *the reception*, emphasising that each individual faithful communicant receives the communion of the Body and Blood of Christ (although not infrequently this may have been construed to mean just spiritual fellowship with a Risen Saviour). It is hard in retrospect to determine where fastidiousness ended and genuine concern about hygiene began. Certainly, as the General Assembly said, other remedies for hygiene could well have been tried instead of grudgingly adopting an innovation which for many disrupted the symbolism of the sacramental action and broke Christ's command. Today, if we still had only the common cup in use and strong agitation were to arise about hygiene, it is not likely that the individual glasses would be adopted. The use of drinking straws, tubes or spoons would probably be proposed.

On the other hand those who opposed the innovation were not quite honest in their stress on 'use and wont' in the post-Reformation Church of Scotland and on what usage is implied in the Church's Standards. There was no strenuous endeavour to fulfil Christ's institution to the letter regarding the wine. Things were much more casual and the large cups were in part at least suggested by the secular practice of the times. Nor did they face up to the fact that once more than one large cup is used, the symbolism of drinking from the one cup is impoverished.

Nevertheless, the important point in the whole dispute is surely that apart from all points of hygiene or of post-Reformation Church law, the present day Church is duty bound to endeavour to fulfil Christ's command. Neither the Bread nor the Wine nor both together is the Sacrament.

The whole eucharistic action is the sacrament. Therefore what we do with the elements and how we handle them is of crucial theological importance. Our actions here have to be dictated by Scripture, by the faith and practice of the Catholic Church and by a sincere desire to maintain the visible unity of the Church especially in the Eucharist, which by its very nature ought to be the chief visible expression of Christian unity and the chief means whereby the Church in her unity is renewed and recreated again and again.

In the contemporary situation we have to say to those who see no offence in the individual cup that the Eucharist is a mystery. The superstitious can be excluded from our interpretation of the rite but not the mystical. In the words of Dr H J Wotherspoon:

> The whole transaction of the Sacrament takes place, not as an episode of earthly event, but on the plane of our Lord's present existence: it is among the *epourania*, the Heavenlies, in which the conditions of our fleshly existence do not apply, and all is as Christ sees it and as Christ wills. It is not the Elements – it is we and the whole action and the Elements in the setting of that action which are taken into the atmosphere of the supernal: We are 'lifted into some apprehension of the Eternal': we taste the powers of the coming age and look upon the invisible. It is no objection that such a statement is mystical – if it were not, it could not hope to be true: the sacramental cannot be discussed in material terms — it is only in mystical apprehension that faith can approach some literality of understanding.[13]

---

[13] H J Wotherspoon, *Religious Values in the Sacraments (T&T Clark, 1928)*, p. 283.

Today we are grateful that the Church of Scotland has never tied herself down to Calvin's or anyone else's definition of how the Body and Blood of Jesus Christ are present in the Lord's Supper, but has repeatedly, simply and boldly said to her people: This is my Body . . . this cup is the new covenant in my Blood. Thereby she has left the flood-gates open for each communicant to explore for himself through faith and the power of the Holy Spirit, the height and depth and length and breadth of the glorious reality. Anything that would needlessly diminish or detract from that reality must be shunned. It seems to many of us that this is exactly what the individual cup does. It is in danger of reducing a mystery to something too near the level of the toast glasses handed round at the wedding reception or the tray of medicine glasses taken round the beds of the hospital ward.

In these latter years we have been reproaching ourselves with neglect of the doctrine of the Holy Spirit. As we study and pray about the Person and work of the Holy Spirit, we shall surely see that, leaving aside all questions of hygiene, textual criticism and church law, we must strive to grasp what the Holy Spirit does in the Administration of the Consecrated Bread and Wine. We are, or at least many of us still are, rightly proud of the ancient Scottish tradition of the *epiclesis* in the prayer of consecration at the Eucharist. Therefore, let us never write down to an earthly level what the discerning of all ages have termed a translation into the heavenly realm when the Holy Spirit has been called down upon us and upon God's own gifts of bread and wine.

# Christian Worship – An Introduction

## *Colin R Williamson*

Christian worship is the celebration of God the Creator by His people, through the priesthood of Jesus Christ, in the power of the Holy Spirit. There is no equivalent of worship in human relationships, for there is no parallel in human affairs to the covenant relationship between God and His people; and worship both arises from that relationship and gives expression to it. The opening chapter of the Bible affirms the special status and responsibility conferred upon mankind in the created scheme of things. Other creatures, and the structure of the universe, bear witness in their own way to the goodness and glory of God; but only human beings are capable of knowing their Maker, and of consciously enjoying a relationship with Him. At the other end of Scripture, looking as far forward to the future as Genesis looks back towards the past, constant worship is the destiny in store for glorified humanity when everything that is unworthy and ugly and evil has been purged. The enjoyment of God is mankind's supreme and ultimate fulfilment. We live in the world of the in-between and the not-yet: in a fallen world permeated by sin to such an extent that the species entrusted to look after it may blow it out of existence at the touch of a few buttons, yet at the same time a world still precious and loved by God, given a second chance and a new beginning through the incarnation, death and resurrection of God's only Son.

As the people of God in the age of the Spirit, it is now the Church's task and privilege to exercise a priestly function in creation - praising and adoring God for what He is, thanking Him for what He has done in the great acts of our salvation, growing towards a more mature obedience and devotion, interceding for a world still largely unaware of God's love and of His mercy. The 'chief end'[1] of the human

---

[1] *The Shorter Catechism*, 1648.

race is the glorification of God. The race as a whole may not yet recognise that basic truth, but the Church of Jesus Christ cannot afford ever to forget it. In a series of inspiring, humbling metaphors the New Testament sets forth the glorious vocation and the awesome responsibility entrusted to the Church. She is the bride of Christ, the body of Christ; she is light, salt, leaven; she is 'a chosen race, a royal priesthood, a dedicated nation, and a people claimed by God for his own, to proclaim the triumphs of him who has called you out of darkness into his marvellous light'.[2]

No-one claiming to perceive God's grace and truth in the incarnate life of Jesus could imagine for a moment that God is glorified only in our acts of worship. In the ongoing work of reconciliation, in the preaching of the Gospel to a world that does not yet see and believe, in right stewardship of time and talents and resources, in small deeds of kindness and of sacrifice, in work of teaching and of healing and the sharing of each other's burdens, Christians serve their Lord and glorify their Maker. We are well warned in the gospels of the dangers that arise when people seek to turn regular worship into a substitute for dedicated service. Much speaking and vain repetitions, detached from the decisions and the struggles and the opportunities of daily living, are not an expression of love towards God: they are an escapist self-indulgence. Discipleship involves our heart and soul and mind and strength; it has to find expression in the fruits of sacrificial living. Yet this in no way casts doubt on the primacy of worship as a Christian privilege and duty. It is true we cannot claim to love God and at the same time hate our brother; but it does not follow that by being well disposed towards our brother we have fulfilled our duty to God. Christianity may overlap at many points with humanism, but they are not the same thing. God is entitled to our worship just because He is God and we are totally dependent on Him for each breath we take.

---

[2] I Peter 2:9.

## Worship and Mission

To claim that the Church of Jesus Christ exists for mission is only a half truth. It is misleading if it is seen as a suggestion that the long-term aim of the Church is to work itself out of a job. Missionary outreach is undoubtedly a fundamental part of the Lord's purpose for His people. In an age of declining membership, when the Western Church seems to be making little headway compared to younger and more vital churches in other parts of the world, there is a special urgency about the need for a more dynamic missionary thrust. There is a difference though between the Church's celebration of the source of her existence and the Church's sharing of the gospel with the rest of the world. We can look forward and work towards the day when there will no longer be any need for mission; but when that day comes, there will be as much need as ever for worship. It is the enduring Christian task both in the world of time and in the world of eternity. It is a confusion to equate the Church's worship and her outreach to the uncommitted. Both are basic to the Church's calling, but they are not the same thing.

## Worship and Education

There has in recent years been a much needed revival of emphasis on the importance of Christian education for elders and other adult members of the Church. Yet the importance of our educational task should not mislead us into thinking that our congregations assemble for the principal purpose of instruction. Worship is the people's offering to God. It is a corporate activity. In the course of worship congregations have the right to expect help in the form of teaching. They also may legitimately hope, though, to be taken beyond information, to communication with the God who is the source and object of their worship. It is possible within the framework of the Christian Year to draw attention to specific needs or areas of church work while keeping the main emphasis of worship firmly on the mighty acts and the great love of God.

## Worship as a Gift of God

Worship is a universal human instinct, and can by no means be claimed as an exclusively Christian activity. But we believe that only Christians are enabled to worship in and through Jesus Christ, the High Priest who alone is entitled in His own right to approach God the Father.

Christian people are 'in Christ' by their incorporation into the people of God at Baptism. This is a truth deserving more serious interpretation than a sentimental assurance of Jesus' love which is probably what the phrase often suggests to congregations at an infant Baptism. Because we are in Christ, identified by grace with the death that Jesus died and with His resurrection life, our worship becomes His - or more truly, we are enabled to participate in His worship. Jesus as head of the Church is not a figurehead, nor a gracious patron who allows us to use his name on our notice-boards. He is a working president, who is the constant and indispensable intermediary between the Church and God. The phrase 'through Jesus Christ our Lord' is not a signal to the congregation that a prayer is drawing near to its close. It expresses a truth fundamental to all Christian worship: that our relationship with God depends entirely on the intermediary role of the living Christ.

Christian worship depends also on the power of the Holy Spirit. From a subjective viewpoint it is often difficult, especially for beginners in faith, to recognise the reality of the action of the Holy Spirit underlying their own struggles and efforts. This applies to every area of faith, because the guidance of the Spirit does not absolve Christians from effort. He works through us but He does not manipulate us. Thus, the Christian grappling with some difficult decision, uncertain of the course his life should take, may well feel that he has had to resolve the situation in his own strength. Only later, if at all, will he realize how great a part the Spirit played in leading him to his decision. The youngster who has felt uneasy over his right to become a communicant church member, decides to take the plunge and make his vows of membership. At the time he is unlikely to see any truth in the proposition that he has not chosen Christ, but Christ has chosen him. Only with a degree of spiritual maturity and growth in faith do we come to recognise that faith is itself a gift of God. It is the same with worship. Members in the pews will very likely regard a church service as the product of their minister's gifts and training. Ministers for their part may burn midnight oil by the gallon, toiling over sermons without any conscious sense of being assisted, let alone inspired, by the Holy Spirit. But it is easier for ministers than members to recognise and marvel at the role of the Spirit in worship; for they discover at an early stage that many of the efforts they were secretly most proud of strike no responsive chord in the worshippers, while other products which seemed poor and shoddy in the study are transformed on Sunday into precious and memorable experiences. St Paul assured us that the Spirit does come to the aid of our weakness and pleads for us even through our inarticulate groans; but the fulfilment of that promise never loses its power to surprise us. The first step for anyone preparing to lead worship should be earnest, hopeful prayer for the illumination of the Holy Spirit. Without that, worship will have no reality.

If we claim that worship must be processed through Christ and inspired by the Spirit given to the Church at Pentecost, what are we to say of those of other faiths who worship the Creator God by different names and do not recognise the Trinity? In an increasingly pluralist society, the question is not just academic, but it is not one to which we can give any firm and authoritative answer. We know that God's grace is always bigger than our understanding of it; at the same time we are committed to the revelation we have seen in Jesus Christ, committed to our faith in Him as the way and the truth and the life.

There can be no compromise with those who deny the lordship of Christ; but our duty to set forth the positive insights of Christian faith does not carry the right to evaluate or judge those of other faiths. In saying that worship must be offered through Christ in the Holy Spirit we are not entitled to announce on God's behalf that all other worship is valueless.

## The Individual Christian and the Worshipping Church

Worship is a privilege belonging to the Church, and by extension to the individual Christian man or woman. The essentially corporate nature of the Eucharist is a continual reminder, right at the centre of the Church's worship, that the Christian covenant is between God and 'a people' just as the old Hebrew covenant had been. This is a truth undervalued in some popular Protestant thinking, when a false distinction is drawn between the people of God in Old Testament times and the individual Christian's relationship with God in Christ. It is a misleading distinction, and it gives rise to the prevalent but quite unbiblical assertion that 'you don't have to go to church to be a Christian'. That assertion contains many false assumptions - (a) that worship is a chore (b) that it is an optional extra from which those who are sure of their own status can confidently claim exemption (c) that people go to church because they need to be made better people (d) that God is interested only in how we behave. The concept of Christian discipleship divorced from worship, and of individual Christians existing in a self-contained relationship with God, is totally unbiblical. It often exposes an unwarrantable pride on the part of those who distance themselves from their fellow-Christians, and it also reveals an inadequate doctrine of the Church. Christ died for a new humanity. He 'loved the Church and gave himself up for it'. It is the Church to which the Spirit is given, and the Church which is the worshipping community. The individual Christian at home or at work or wherever, worships as a representative of the Church, a member of the body of Christ.

## The Congregation and the Wider Church

There is great diversity within the worship offered in our churches up and down the country on the Lord's day: diversity of order, music, ritual, local custom. We of the Reformed tradition cherish this diversity. Yet no congregation, whether in a great cathedral or a tiny country kirk, worships as an isolated unit. Through Christ, in Christ, they are all participating in a common single act - the worship of the one Church catholic. That one Church transcends all boundaries of nationality, language and cultural forms. It transcends even the ultimate frontier of death, since worship is the one activity we are quite sure the saints are now engaged in. Every congregation worships as a part of the entire Church, in communion with the entire Church.

This should caution us against judging the value of a service by the numbers attending it. Psychologically it is a heartening experience to be in a church full of worshippers. Evangelically it is tragic if a huge majority in the community absent themselves from worship or have no sense of the claims of the living God upon their lives. To this extent we have to be concerned with numbers. But worship is being offered to God constantly. What we do is to join our praises to the praise that is continually going on. Worshippers in the pews may not be consciously aware of the great scale of the activity in which they are engaging. Leaders of worship must always be conscious of it. An awareness of the world-wide Church alongside us and of the great cloud of witnesses surrounding us, lifts worship from the setting of a little local happening and establishes it in its context as part of the offering of all creation to God the Creator.

## The Minister and the Congregation

Ministers are ordained explicitly to a ministry of Word and Sacrament; the conduct of the church's worship is the primary responsibility and privilege belonging to that office. It will often fall to other people to take services or lead devotions in particular situations - prayer meetings, house churches, school assemblies, Guild meetings, youth organisations, Sunday School departments. In areas where there are insufficient numbers of ordained ministers the Church is perennially indebted to the readers, deacons and lay missionaries who lead services Sunday by Sunday. The norm, however, is for worship to be led by men and women called and ordained by the Church to minister God's word and sacraments. No-one can feel wholly confident of his ability or worthiness to take on such an awesome task. We are called to lead them in an offering that is acceptable to God, and to make God real to His people. Who can consider himself worthy of that daunting task?

The very fact of ordination is a great help here: the fact of having been called and commissioned by the Church 'in the name of the Lord Jesus Christ, the King and Head of the Church'.

The minister has two roles to fulfil. On one hand he or she is called to interpret God's Word and God's will to His people through preaching and to minister God's gifts to the people through the sacraments and benediction. On the other hand he or she is also a spokesman for the people in the leading of prayer. In both cases, the significant parties in worship are not minister and congregation: they are God and the people of God.

The Reformers rejected the concept of worship as a sacrifice performed essentially by priests, with congregations relegated to the status of spectators. There is another and more subtle brand of sacerdotalism though, which is as much a distortion of the real place of the laity - and this is the tendency to regard the congregation as the minister's audience. This can be tempting for ministers because it is gratifying to their self-esteem to be thought of as charismatic and authoritative orators. It can be tempting too for congregations to collude in seeing worship as a ministerial performance. It distances them from what is actually going on, and allows them to focus on the medium while avoiding being confronted by the message. Going to church to hear the minister is as much of a distortion as going to church to watch the priest. In both cases the role given to the Church - the worshipping community, the royal priesthood - is being projected on to just one figure. The minister, instead of opening up communication between God and the people, ends up standing in the light and blocking the view.

Ministers not only hold a particular office: they also have the benefits of theological education, of constant involvement in spiritual issues, and of wider experience in the life of the Church than the vast majority of worshippers. The people who assemble in the pews on Sunday often have the benefit of no such reinforcement. They have the more difficult task of seeking evidence of God at work in industry or marketing or working for exams or looking for a job. The majority of those with whom they are in contact through the week are probably not practising church members, and among them will be many with no faith at all.

This affects the expectations of our people when they come to church. If members are ploughing a lonely furrow through the week it is the more important that they should be adequately nourished and built up in faith through worship. It also means that they are likely to come to church with a background of problems and preoccupations very different from the minister's; and part of the sensitivity required on the part of those leading worship is the ability to recognise that difference. Prayers that are familiar and precious to students of liturgies and which bear the hallowed respectability of centuries of use may not be the easiest devotional medium for a man worried about redundancy. Tightly argued sermons on fine points of doctrine, splendid in the context of a college theological society, are unlikely to give much help to the housewife whose responsibilities towards the young and the elderly leave her drained and depleted by the end of each week. A series of entirely unfamiliar hymns, which may have captured our attention in the study by the aptness of their words, can be an irritation to people craving some stability and reassurance from their faith. An experimental form of service which once made a great impression as the highlight of a residential conference may wither completely if transplanted to a parish setting where everyone is coming to it cold.

Theological scholarship, liturgical expertise, facility with words, a thorough knowledge of the church's music and devotional inheritance - all these are helpful to effective ministry, none so fundamental as a sense of God and sensitive awareness of God's people. When Christian people are brought by the action of the Holy Spirit into touch with God the Father, the Church worships: and in worshipping fulfils the purpose for which she was brought into being.

# The Word in Worship

## *Colin R Williamson*

Reformed churchmen have seen a distinction in form - the Word made Flesh, Jesus Christ himself; the written Word, Holy Scripture; and the Proclaimed Word, preaching. Clearly though Christ himself, *logos* in the midst of the people of God, is always pre-eminent. Christ himself must govern all our thinking even concerning Scripture itself. It was only in the 17th century under the sorry influence of high Calvinism that the Word was 'contained' in Scripture and Scripture came under bondage to the Confession. In more recent times there has been a recovery of the Reformed understanding of God's Word in its creating and redeeming freedom; of the realisation that in Christ's Person, Word and Act are inseparable. As John Calvin has it, 'Christ clothed with his Gospel and his saving act'. The Gospel is not a message about Christ but Christ Himself, no mere word concerning Jesus but the living Word of God present and active in time and space.

The following quotation from Calvin may serve to consolidate these introductory remarks: 'Among the many noble endowments with which God has adorned the human race, one of the most remarkable is that he deigns to consecrate the mouths and tongues of men to his service, making his own voice to be heard in them'.

From the beginning it was held that preaching along with the sacrament was an essential vehicle whereby the Word would come among his people. The mark of the true Church for the reformers was not the acceptance of Scripture as the rule of faith and life but the proclamation of the Gospel in Word and Sacrament.

As the Scots Confession of 1560 (a confession concerned as much with affirming catholicity as with marking out separate identity) has it:

> The notes of the true Kirk... we believe, confess, and avow to be: first the true preaching of the Word of God, in which God has revealed Himself to us, as the writings of the prophets and apostles declare; secondly the right administration of the sacraments of Christ Jesus, with which must be associated the Word and promise of God to seal and confirm them in our hearts; and lastly ecclesiastical discipline uprightly ministered, as God's Word prescribes.

This is no place to attempt a rehearsal of the reformation doctrine of the Word of God but this must always be in the background if we are not to be deceived by the plainness of much reformed worship. We should be aware that in the Divine Service the Word is received as one would receive the sacrament - the real presence of God in Christ.

We shall now look at the reformed pattern of worship with special regard to its treatment of the Word. At the risk of over simplifying the development of 450 years, it is fairly true to say that the Church of Scotland has seen three stages in its liturgical life: original intent, decay and gradual recovery.

There is ample proof that Calvin and Knox shared the conviction that it was the Eucharist which was normative of Christian worship on the Lord's Day. Thus when for three Sundays out of four popular reluctance and magisterial suspicion over the frequent reception on Holy Communion meant that the bread and wine were absent from the table, the service proceeded in the same form nevertheless. So it is today in the Church of Scotland that the recommended order of service where Holy Communion is not celebrated is eucharistic in form. It is not based upon the offices.

The Liturgy of the Word is thus followed by the Liturgy of the Upper Room - the response to the Word of God. Professor J J von Allmen helpfully speaks of the Galilean and the Jerusalemite phases. The Kingdom breaks in by proclamation; our Lord then moves towards his self-offering on the cross, his triumph and ascension. Where in the Scottish parish church the Great Entry has been preserved this movement is given dramatic presentation. The Word having been proclaimed and received by Scripture and preaching, the bread and wine are brought by the elders in solemn procession to the Holy Table (from Galilee to Jerusalem) where they may become to us the body and blood of our Lord, the only true offering to the Father in response to his Word to us. Similarly the sacrament of Holy Baptism is administered after the preaching of the Word of which it is the sign and seal.

The service will have begun with the Word. A Scripture sentence accompanies the call to prayer as an exhortation or a setting of the theme. *The Book of Common Order (1979)* (*BCO 79*) happily suggests a return to the practice of the apostolic greeting followed by the collect for purity and a processional hymn.

At this point it may be of interest to note three points in the service where the Word is manifest in a unique way: the Greeting; the Absolution; the Blessing.

That there should be an apostolic greeting at the threshold of the service is perhaps of doubtful liturgical pedigree but it does carry us immediately to the Word, not only to the epistles but to our risen Lord himself who greets his people with his peace. As the service begins the congregation is entitled to expect a word from God by the mouth of his minister, ensuring that from the outset the Word Himself who has gathered this people is present in power in their midst. 'Grace and peace to you from God the Father and our Lord Jesus Christ'.

Similarly in the absolution the Word of God is known to be active about the business of healing and reconciling. Those who question the place of a declaratory absolution in the reformed rite should be reminded of Knox's form:

> In the name and authority of Jesus Christ, I the minister of his blessed evangel, with consent of the whole Ministry and Church absolve thee N. from the sentence of excommunication, from the sin by thee committed and from all censures laid against thee for the same before according to thy repentance; and pronounce thy sin to be loosed in heaven and thee to be received again to the society of Jesus Christ, to his body the Church, to the participation of his sacraments and finally to the fruition of his benefits: In the name of the Father, the Son and the Holy Spirit. So be it.

An absolution was present in the Strasburg rites for Sunday service. Those Scottish ministers who, since the scruples of English non-conformity were imported in the 17th century, would merely pray for forgiveness have belied a low view of ordination. They have withheld an entitlement from the people and blocked a way by which the Word of God (and it is **God's** Word) comes to perform his work of healing. In modern days the American reformed Churches were amongst the first to restore the declaratory absolution to the liturgy, a practice hopefully gaining ground in Scotland under the influence of *BCO 79*.

A similar story attaches to the blessing. Calvin used the Aaronic Blessing. Knox commended an alternative trinitarian blessing. In more recent times however many reformed churchmen have been content with a conclusion to the service which entreats rather than declares: 'May the blessing of God …'. It is devoutly to be hoped that such an abdication of ministry and denial of the rights of the people is a short-lived aberration and that the traditional high view of ministry and the Word prevails. As the rubric in *BCO 79* has it, 'The minister shall bless the people from God'.

The gathering and Greeting; the Absolving; the dismissing and Blessing: these are vital activities if the Word is to be given His rightful place in the liturgy.

Now as to the Scriptures themselves. Before looking at the reading of Scripture lections it would be well to make two preliminary points. First the Reformed belief about Scripture and, second, the influence upon Reformed worship exercised by Scripture.

It could well be said that it was never reformed belief that the Scriptures are the Word of God. Calvin says, 'Holy Scripture is like a dead impotent thing to us until we have learned that God speaks and makes his will known to us there.'

In 1971 the Panel on Doctrine of the Church of Scotland produced a draft revision of the preamble, questions and formula used at ordination. The revised preamble began, 'The Church of Scotland is part of the one Holy Catholic and Apostolic Church, worshipping one God, Father, Son and Holy Spirit. It stands in the tradition of the Reformation and receives the Scriptures of the Old and New Testaments as the supremely authoritative witness to the revelation of God culminating in Jesus Christ who is himself the Word of God and the sovereign Lord of faith and life'.

This superbly reformed redrafting caught the imagination of many and was approved by the majority of presbyteries. Sadly the proposals were defeated in General Assembly by a determined lobby including Calvinists who preferred the existing statement, '… acknowledges the Word of God which is contained in the Scriptures of the Old and New Testaments to be the supreme rule of faith and life'.

Yet Scripture is not an incarnation. The reformers knew that the Word is Christ and that it is God in Christ through the Holy Spirit who speaks in Scripture and preaching, The second note in parenthesis is the degree to which Scripture has shaped the reformed service. Reference has already been made to the basic evangelical sequence of Word and Sacrament. The eucharistic order as the model for the service is, in other words, determined by the Gospel itself. Parish ministers who in the 19th century copied *Book of Common Prayer* matins in their frustration at the poverty of Scottish worship at that time made a radical mistake. Instead of the office of morning prayers concluding with sermon, they should have gone to their own heritage and recovered at least the *missa sicca*.[1] The repair is all the harder now.

We find also, when we look at the orders for the celebration of Holy Communion, that Scripture is quoted at several points other than the lessons themselves: the sentences at the beginning of the service, the ascription after sermon, the comfortable words of invitation, the Pauline words of institution and the Blessing.

The prayers too have traditionally been imbued with scriptural phrase. Whilst this is not a new style, the difference since the *Euchologion* of The Church Service Society (published 1867) began to show ministers how to pray is that prayers became dignified, doxological and recognisable to the rest of the Church Catholic. For too long God's folk in Scotland had been wearied by so-called extempore prayers which in fact fell into a rigid mould and which, although couched in Biblical or quasi-Biblical phraseology, were tedious and verbose rehearsals of the mighty acts. Many ministers of the earlier 19th century as Dr Lee of Greyfriars wrote, 'plunged on each occasion into a great wilderness of thought and language - like Abraham who went forth not knowing whither he went'.

---

[1] 'dry mass': a service following the classic order of the communion service with the consecration of the elements and the giving of communion omitted.

But with the publication of *Euchologion* and the official service-books which have followed upon it to the present day, we find at its best a model for public prayer which draws on the catholic treasury of the Church's prayer and breathes the air of Scripture for its concepts and its language.

As to the lections themselves, there is little doubt that Reformed Churches continued the old lectionary, but a new approach very quickly developed. At first in Strasburg Epistle and Gospel were read. By 1525 a whole chapter must be read and the sermon based thereon. A year later it was permitted to read the Law and the Prophets in place of the Epistle. By 1530 the Epistle as a distinct lection had disappeared and with it the last trace of the old lectionary. To this day in many parish churches the lessons are specified only as 'Old Testament' and 'New Testament'.

*The Westminster Directory for the Public Worship of God (1645)* specifies Old Testament and New Testament and proscribes the Apocrypha. The reading, which must be distinct, should be from the best allowed translation. Normally this will be one chapter each from the Old and New Testaments, more if the chapters be short or the meaning requires it. All canonical books should be read in sequence so that the people might become acquainted with the whole body of Scripture.

Some years before the Westminster Assembly when, under James VI, the General Assembly had set up a committee to revise Knox's *Book of Common Order,* an attempt was made to restore Epistle and Gospel, but there was little hope of this. Even the very reading of Scripture at all was at times under attack by extremists. A letter to Calvin from England complained of 'those who exclaim against the public reading of the Word of God as an irksome and unprofitable form'. And a hundred years later, Alan Ramsay, Moderator of the

General Assembly, protested that 'of late all public reading of the Scriptures in the Church is laid aside as dry and useless unless there be a minister to explain it'. Once again we sense the first cold tendrils of sectarian Brownist[2] influence which would blight Scottish worship for a couple of hundred years and more.

This is the point to note an imported aberration which would hardly have met with Knox's approval. In the early 17th century in English Reformed Churches where Calvin's *Form of Prayers* was used it became customary to preface the morning service proper with a 'Reader's Service'. The purpose presumably was that the people might have the Bible read at length in their hearing week by week. The Reader, not being ordained, was appointed by the elders. He led the Psalms and read not only Scripture but prayers from the service book. The source of this practice was probably Prayer Book matins, the morning office not special to Sunday nor to the ordained ministry. In practice the Reader's Service lasted from anything up to an hour in its early manifestation to 15 minutes or so later in the 17th century. Some parish churches built in days of puritan influence still have a two deck pulpit. The lower tier came to be known as the Precentor's Desk but before that it was undoubtedly the place from which the Reader led his service of prayers, readings and psalms, finishing when the minister himself arrived in church and entered the top pulpit.

This awkward cuckoo of the Reader's Service may not have continued long as such but it left two marks. The Third Edition of the *Church Hymnary* and *BCO 79* speak of Approach to God followed by The Word of God and Response to the Word of God, including the Sacraments. Is there here a feeling dating from the old Reader's Service that there should be some 'warm up' activity before the dual action proper of the rite begins?

---
[2] Robert Browne visited Scotland in 1583-4.

The second feature for which the Reader's Service may have been partly to blame was the scandalous treatment of Scripture in 18th century Scottish worship. It became common practice for the minister not to read Scripture but to have the 'lecture' - a homiletical reading verse by verse interspersed with commentary. This 15 minute so-called 'lecture' was not the sermon, which was to follow. It would be difficult to prove but it may be that this state of affairs arose because it was assumed that Scripture reading *simpliciter* had taken place in the pre-service office.

The 19th century liturgical movement recovered the discipline of lectionary. *Euchologion* produced the first lectionary since the reformation in Scotland and with it of course acknowledged the principal feasts of the calendar. The *Book of Common Order (1940)* offered its own two year lectionary for morning and evening services with a full calendar. The present age has seen the reformed Churches participating in ecumenical lectionary projects. The Church of Scotland has adopted the Joint Liturgical Group two year cycle. The American Presbyterian Church has provided pioneering work on the 'Common Lectionary', an adaptation of the Roman Lectionary which, it is hoped, will have profound ecumenical consequences.[3]

It would be wrong not to point out that for some members of the Reformed family the ideas of lectionary and indeed of the Christian Year are totally alien. In Scotland one would think of the Free Church of Scotland, the Free Presbyterian Church and the Reformed Presbyterian Church. Similarly the Reformed Churches in Ireland. These bodies are of course calvinist in a sense that the Church of Scotland is not and they are anti-Roman which the Church of Scotland is not, so that one suspects that they preserve identity by what they object to and their objections have as much to do with culture as they have with theology. And even within the Church of Scotland,

---

[3] Since this was written, *Common Order* adopted the Revised Common Lectionary.

what point is there in adopting a lectionary if there is no obligation to follow it?

Of course, there are many ministers, in the main conservative evangelicals, who will never have regard to the lectionary. They think of it as an unwarranted imposition and prefer to pursue themes, series or the consecutive reading of books. Other ministers will have recourse to the lectionary at the principal seasons of the Christian Year but will sit light to it, for example during the long post-Pentecost weeks.

The former Panel on Worship was, however, encouraged firstly by the use which **is** made of lectionary in parish churches, and secondly by the recognition it receives in official circles such as other General Assembly Boards in planning special Sundays to highlight their activities. That the Calendar and Lectionary should have become a point of first reference is achievement indeed given the historical record. The lectionary is consistently held up as the recommended model, allying the national Church with the Church Catholic and bringing her people under discipline to the word thus liberating them from themselves and their limitations.

A brief word now about the physical attitude to the Word in liturgy. It was long the almost exclusive practice to conduct the entire service from the pulpit in reformed churches and to move to the table only for the celebration of the Eucharist. In buildings constructed in the calvinistic era with their lofts on three sides the pulpit was the only place where the minister could be seen and heard by all the worshippers.

Indeed there was often a bracket fixed to the pulpit where the baptismal bowl would be placed, enabling the minister to baptize a child whilst still in the pulpit. The liturgical movement had a profound effect upon churches built from the latter part of the last century and on the refurbishment of older buildings. Chancels began to appear with the symbolism and furnishing normal in western Christendom.

Almost all churches are now equipped with a lectern where the reading of Scripture as such can be given its distinct place.

An almost universal and worthy practice is the carrying in of the Bible by the Beadle (the Kirk Session Officer) who precedes the minister. There are still traces in Scottish parishes of the old practice of following the passage in one's own Bible as it is being read. Some congregations provide pew Bibles. In most parishes however all that remains is the occasional rustling of pages here and there as some elderly parishioner finds the place. Evangelical parishes, of course, consider this following of the reading important. Other ministers find it irrelevant if not distracting. There is much to be said for the belief that in the liturgy Scripture is to be **heard** by the people.

In some churches a lectern stands upon the Holy Table with an open Bible facing the congregation. No explanation can be offered for this irrelevance save perhaps the sheer embarrassment of a Table which is bare for much of the year lacking the very things which are appropriate there, the bread and wine of the Eucharist. The Word has its place in the reformed churches and needs no open Bibles lying about. It is the Body and Blood of Christ which must be given room.

A very significant aspect of the Word in liturgy for reformed Churches is of course the metrical psalters. The history of the metrical psalms is a detailed and specialist study. Suffice it to say that the essential place of the psalms in Christian worship is axiomatic. By the time of the Reformation, however, the psalms, sung in Latin and to elaborate musical settings had become the exclusive property of the choir. It was partly to give the psalms back to the people that the reformers produced metrical versions to be sung in the vernacular and to singable tunes. Of all the reformed family it was in Scotland that the metrical psalms established themselves most firmly, becoming interwoven with the nation's history and culture for over 300 years. For most of that time they furnished Scots with the only medium of their praise. The Free Church of Scotland minister still promises at his ordination that he will allow nothing to be sung other than the psalms.

Of course it is easy to criticise the metrical psalms for their paraphrasing which distances them that bit further from the text, for their occasional infelicity of language and so on. But by the same token they can rise to the spiritual heights coupled with rugged tunes in which one can hear the wind upon the moor and the cry of the curlew.

Their use has diminished gradually over a century and the number in regular use has been small for generations now. Yet when the *Church Hymnary, Third Edition* was published in 1972 without the 1929 *Scottish Psalter* in its binding there was a storm of protest from those who wished to preserve it (compare the defenders of the 1662 Prayer Book). In the opinion of the former Panel on Worship such protagonists confused the Psalms with the Metrical Psalter. They ignored the fact for instance that since 1898 there had been an authorised version of the Psalms and Scriptural Canticles, pointed for chanting. They refused to see that by selecting psalm portions in a variety of forms (prose, chant, Gelineau as well as metrical) and placing these throughout the liturgical framework of the new hymnbook the compilers were in fact seeking to revive interest in the psalms in worship. The Panel's publication, 'The Year's Psalms', suggested psalm selections to complement the JLG Lectionary and also psalms appropriate to the various points in the order of worship. For the psalms in metre should never be mere punctuations in the reformed service, as the people's confession, adoration and thanksgiving they are integral to it.

Work began in the 1740s on the production of metrical paraphrases of Scripture passages. 67 were published with the Church's approval in 1781 and are normally bound up with *The Scottish Psalter 1929*. Some of these paraphrases are very fine renderings and several have been given honoured place in the hymn books of the Churches.

Although the **Gloria Patri** in appropriate metres was used from the beginning and has appeared in all editions of the metrical psalter, the practice of concluding a psalm or portion with such a doxology fell away until it was revived by *Church Hymnary: Third Edition* which places the *Gloria Patri* in the form of a concluding verse.

Finally, a word about preaching. The second Helvetic Confession in its first chapter says,

> When this Word of God is now preached, in church by preachers lawfully called, we believe that the very Word of God is preached and received of the faithful and that neither any other word of God is to be invented nor is to be expected from heaven.

A certain mythology has been created around Scottish preaching. One has heard this voiced in the United States for example. Yet the Scottish preacher can be no more intelligent, no more spiritually endowed, no more surely called to God that any of his brethren in the catholic Church of Christ. Certainly there has been an emphasis which has raised up preaching in his understanding of ministry, that high doctrinal position which makes him see 'preaching in an almost sacramental sense as a means whereby the Church knows God in Christ to be truly present in her midst.'

It is still understood that the reformed minister will spend considerable time in preparation for preaching although the pattern of modern ministry has routed the old assumption of 'every morning in the study from 9 until 1'. Traditionally at any rate, theological education in the four Scottish faculties of Divinity had preaching very much in mind, not only homiletics but a whole range of disciplines. Unfortunately this has been greatly weakened recently by university policy of widening the appeal of the degree course and so diluting the element of commitment to ordination in the student today.

Through preaching it is believed that God's Word comes to challenge, to judge, to assure, to cast down and build up. Properly understood, preaching is not an educational exercise nor even a missionary one; and it is certainly not to be prostituted for the opinions of the minister or for chatty pep-talks. Preaching is doxological - it is worship. So there is probably still less embarrassment in the reformed tradition about preaching, more resistance to so-called dialogue sermons and the like. It is laid upon the minister to break the Word; it is the people's part to receive it.

The Church is rightly jealous of those who may preach. The *Westminster Directory of Public Worship* permitted only the ministers and ordinands to preach, the latter with Presbytery's permission. The current Church of Scotland regulations continue to specifiy who may conduct public worhip. Some years ago an ecumenical discussion document circulated in Scotland by the Multilateral Church Conversation suggested that a preliminary step in mutual recognition of ministry might be an increase in pulpit exchanges. Apparently a worthy sentiment but was this to say that proclamation of the Word is a lesser thing than celebration of the Eucharist? That any Tom, Dick or Harry can mount the pulpit steps but let him not approach the Table? The reformed tradition will refuse to permit any wedge between these for they are inseparable. We are ordained into the fulness of Christ's ministry of Word and Sacrament.

That must be the note upon which this paper concludes; the inseparability of Word and Sacrament. For the Sacrament without the Word proclaimed is robbed of its context - that of which it is a sign is not there - that which it would seal is absent.

But equally, and here is our need for reform, when the Word is proclaimed and does not immediately find its consummation in the Eucharist, it is to that extent frustrated, and truncated worship must wait for its fulfilment.

'Remember your word to your servant: on which you have built my hope. This has been my comfort in my affliction for your word has brought me life.' *Psalm 119: 49-50*

'How shall I repay the Lord for all his benefits to me?
I will take the cup of salvation and call upon the name of the Lord.'
*Psalm 116: 11-12*

# The Divine Service and Morning Service: Their Common Structure
## *A Stewart Todd*

In the 20th century winds of change swept through many parts of the Christian Church and liturgical renewal was an objective ardently pursued by all but the most conservative. The Reformed Church was party to many of the changes and Scotland boasted its own measured progress. It was a century marked by a blossoming of theological study, not least of the theology of worship. In the Reformed Church in Germany, Switzerland, in the United States, and to a modest extent here in Scotland, writers strove to create frameworks of thought within which the Church's liturgical heritage could be understood and evaluated and to identify principles by which liturgical renewal might be governed. I think it is fair to say that those responsible for producing our books of Common Order and other worship books were strongly influenced by these writings. William D Maxwell of course was the Scottish guru in the earlier part of the century but later he was somewhat eclipsed by the Swiss J-J von Allmen and by the host of contributors to liturgical journals. What follows here in this paper owes much to the thinking of Reformed writers in the post-war decades of last century and to the work that was done by successive worship committees of our Church and in the two Societies, the Church Service Society and the Scottish Church Society.

**Basic Elements**
The title of this paper associates the structure of Morning Service with the structure of the Divine Service or Holy Communion. The particular form of Morning Service under discussion will be that presented in outline on page 43 of the *Book of Common Order 1979 (BCO 79)* and presented *in extenso* as First Morning Service in

*Common Order 1996.* This service is described in the introduction to BCO 79 as being 'ordered according to the eucharistic pattern, that is to say where the reading and preaching of the word lead to prayers of thanksgiving and intercession and all the fullness of eucharistic devotion save the partaking of bread and wine'. This was the earlier tradition of the Reformed Church in Scotland. And the grand simplification which will direct the thrust of this discussion can be neatly stated: there are two basic elements in the structure of Morning Service as in the structure of the Divine Service or Holy Communion, only two, word of God and eucharist. Word of God is to be understood to include the reading and hearing of scripture, the preaching and hearing of sermons and the hymns and psalms that may act as comment upon these exercises. For the purpose of this paper the word eucharist is not going to be limited to a Holy Communion context, it is also going to be used as a convenient term for the prayers of thanksgiving and derivatives therefrom in a Morning Service.

This idiosyncratic use of the word eucharist needs to be explained. Indeed the use of the word eucharist at all in a Church of Scotland context needs to be defended. Though it is used widely in the world Church it is not often used in this Church to define Holy Communion: the term most often used here is The Lord's Supper. That name occurs only once in the New Testament[1] and appears to have been coined accidentally by Paul in the heat of his fierce denunciation of Corinthian malpractice. He heartily disapproves of their overriding concern with their own supper at their gatherings and deplores the disrespect they show thereby for the Lord's. The New Testament designation for Holy Communion would appear to have been 'Breaking of Bread' but that term did not persist in the Church and is found only rarely outwith the New Testament. The word that took over and became established

---

[1] 1 Corinthians 11:17-22.

was eucharist (Greek *eucharistia*, a giving of thanks from the Greek verb *eucharisteo*, I give thanks). The prayer of thanksgiving, being a very significant element of Holy Communion, gave its name to the whole and, since Holy Communion seems to have been the norm of Christian worship and celebrated whenever the Christian community met, by the beginning of the second century eucharist was the name for Christian worship.

The original and more specific reference of the word eucharist should not be forgotten however. The record of Our Lord's institution of the Sacrament in 1 Corinthians 11 reads 'and when he had given thanks (*eucharistesas*) he broke it (the bread) …' Eucharist here is prayer. There can be little doubt, that when Our Lord said 'Do this in remembrance of me' he will have been understood to mean the giving of thanks was to be 'done' as well as the breaking of bread and sharing of the cup. Paul likewise describes prayer when he says in 1 Corinthians 14:16*ff*: 'Else when thou shalt bless with the Spirit, how shall he that occupies the room of the unlearned say Amen at thy giving of thanks' (*eucharistia*).

## A Framework of Thought

The word eucharist is a significant and useful word. It is even the subject of dominical command! The same might be claimed for everything subsumed under the 'word of God' in our structure. 'Go ye therefore and teach all nations' sounds as direct as 'this do'. But with or without proof texts no one can really doubt that imperatives about speaking and hearing the word of God spring automatically out of the indicatives of the Gospel. The preaching and teaching mission of the Church was embarked upon only after controversy but once begun the entire propriety and inevitability of it was never really in doubt. For the witnesses of the resurrection it was implicit in their whole remarkable

Easter experience from the start.[2] And as for sustained teaching and preaching as distinct from a missionary proclamation Matthew in particular foresees this and mentions it specifically: 'teaching them to observe all things whatsoever I have commanded you.'

Given the Christ-event and the New Testament witness to it there are things to be said and things to he heard, momentous and glorious things to be said urgently and with all the eloquence and versatility of communication at our command and to be heard intently and with all the sensitivity with which we are endowed. Christians owe it to God and to their souls and to the souls of all humanity to say these things and to hear them - word of God. Given the Christ event and the New Testament witness to it Christians cannot but lift up their hearts: thanksgiving will be their most natural reaction, optimism their most characteristic mood. Given also the quite explicit command of the Lord: 'Do this' (which includes, as we have seen, thanksgiving as well as sharing bread and wine) surely Christians ought to obey - eucharist. Here in the logic of the Gospel is the origin and basis of the structure of the Divine Service or of Morning Service and were there no history of liturgy to guide us, were the liturgical slate to be wiped clean and we were devising a liturgy for our times *de novo* we should still conclude that the basic elements are word of God and eucharist.

We are constructing an evangelic framework of thought to help us speak reliably about the structure of the Divine Service and the Morning Service. Developing that structure or renewing it or innovating in any way with the structure (as distinct from the contents of the parts) will have much more to do with obedience to those implicit imperatives and explicit commands we have identified than with aesthetic considerations, human predilection or whim. The

---

[2] See, for example, Eduard Schweizer, *The Good News According to Matthew* (London, 1976) 529; cf. Galatians 1:16; 1 Timothy 3:16; Romans 18:26 etc.

main question always must be whether this or that way of structuring the service permits the word of God to be spoken more eloquently and heard more authentically and whether there are arrangements of eucharistic prayer and communion that will make adequate provision for the profound emotions and desires the Gospel evokes and for the reception and sharing of the gifts of grace and peace which communion promises and imparts.

## Practical Considerations

What has been constructed in this paper is only one possible framework of thought. There are others. But if this emphasis on two main elements in the structure of Divine Service or Morning Service is valid (and the history of liturgy does in fact validate it) then we can make some observations on our practice. For example it can be argued, in defence of the Morning Service ordered according to the eucharistic pattern, that it is simpler and more logical to have a sequence rather than a mixing of the two basic elements. Again, if it is right to say that essentially these are the things we have come to do then it will be sensible to address ourselves to them without too much time being spent in preparation for them and we shall return also to this point. Likewise it will be important, to ensure a proper balance between the two main elements, A full celebration of eucharist must not overshadow the word of God. Neither must the treatment of the word of God be so expansive that eucharist feels like an anticlimax. This is especially a danger in Morning Service where only eucharist in our narrower sense follows the word of God.

Again bearing in mind that we are structuring the service primarily in obedience to implicit imperatives and explicit dominical commands, the quality of obedience we render as clergy in our part in the word of God and eucharist respectively needs to be examined and a balance here achieved. A prayer-book approach to a Book of Common Order may be tolerable where eucharist is being celebrated only two or three times per year but if eucharist is to be celebrated frequently then our traditional dislike of a prayer book surely demands preparation of some new prayer material at least at regular intervals. Equally however where our eucharist is confined to prayers in Morning Service it is important for the proper structuring of the service that the prayer-material of the second element be as well prepared as the sermon material of the first element.

**Word of God**
Clearly we shall read the scriptures and preach. Concerning scripture the question immediately arises: how much and on what principle shall we choose it. The answer to the first part of our question will depend upon our evaluation of the reading of scripture. If the reading of scripture has no intrinsic value, if the view is taken that it has to be preached on before it comes alive, then a minimum of scripture will be required. One reading from the Old Testament and one from the New will be deemed adequate or indeed any two readings from any part of the Bible may be selected, as a prelude to preaching. If however the other view is taken that by the action of the Holy Spirit the reading of scripture can be as efficacious for proclamation as the expounding and applying of it in preaching then scripture will be honoured and there will seem to be no reason to doubt the wisdom of the traditional answer to the question how much by providing in the structure of the Divine Service and Morning Service readings from Old Testament, Epistle and Gospel.

The other part of the question concerns the use of lectionaries or choice of readings by the preacher, again with an eye on his sermon. A disciplined preacher following the course of the Christian year may manage perfectly well without a lectionary. Many preachers however, lacking a sufficient degree of self-discipline, do need a lectionary if they are to avoid arbitrariness. The ideal for our own situation is probably a judicious mixture of the two: a basic loyalty to a lectionary coupled with a feeling of freedom to depart from it whenever, with the newspaper in one hand and the Bible in the other (to use a Barthian image), we preachers know beyond a peradventure that a particular text is the text from which we must preach and the passage from which it comes one of the passages we must read.

Who should read the scriptures in the service? Discussion of this question is proper here only in so far as it might affect the structure of the service. Whoever reads must he able to perform competently the very considerable task involved. If the scriptures are inaudibly or badly read, if moreover this happens with any regularity and the reading of scripture becomes a 'throw-away' then the structure of the service is seriously weakened. The invitation to persons to read scripture must be made not in terms of courtesy or democracy but unashamedly in terms of ability.

As for preaching, as it affects the structure of the service, the concern will be as mentioned above that the sermon is not so expansive that eucharist feels like a perfunctory extra or an anticlimax. The danger arises particularly in a Morning Service. Our tradition of preaching in the Church of Scotland is something for which we have all been grateful but it is not without taint of sin. The most obvious temptation has been to suppose that the sermon is an end in itself. Recalling however our evangelic framework of thought we have to resist that. Preaching is either addressed to all nations in order to bring them to baptism or it is addressed to the faithful in order to deepen their faith, refine their spirituality, rekindle the flame of their optimism, lift up their hearts and bring them into an ever closer relationship with a living Lord and through him with God. If Christ is present in the word we may take it for granted that he will not be content merely to help us meditate, it will be his aim, as it ever was, to establish relationship and to take us with him into the holiest of all, hallowing God's name as we go. A sermon may be in its way a minor miracle. We should nevertheless remember that it was of the essence of Our Lord's miracles that they should not draw attention to themselves, that they should contribute with faith, to the achievement of wholeness and bring men and women into encounter with God in such a way that they would feel themselves addressed, moved, set on a new and hopeful path to human maturity and happiness and fulfilment. And when the early Church thought about the greatest miracle of all they thought about it too as one that pointed beyond itself.

There is an art of preaching but every art-form has to be disciplined in the Church, whether it is architecture or music or the contribution of the florist. It can be argued that, even in the world outside, the true contribution of art is not to commandeer our attention for a thing of beauty encapsulated, say, in a small canvas but to be transparent, to carry our thoughts beyond the confines of the canvas and the frame. Certainly the latter is the true function of art in the Church. A preacher may be electric in a sermon but if he has not tuned his hearers' lips to praise of God, to buoyancy of faith and a zeal for the companionship of Christ it must seriously be questioned whether he has really preached the Gospel.

## Eucharist

Recalling the origin of the word eucharist, recalling the logic of the Gospel which demands that Christians lift up their heart and give thanks, recalling also the simple command of the Lord 'this do' which we have understood to include giving thanks, what follows? Certainly as in the freedom of the Spirit we are at liberty to develop the word of God element in worship in all kinds of imaginative ways provided always that the structure remains secure, so also the Church in the freedom of the Spirit has developed the eucharist element in worship, especially in Holy Communion, and we are likely to be bewildered by the multiplicity of motifs and the tangle of technical terms not to mention rationale after rationale offered to explain every detail of it. Even where there is no communion, eucharist is complex - prayers of thanksgiving of all kinds but also prayers of intercession, self-dedication, thanksgiving for the faithful departed, which are derivatives therefrom.

When Holy Communion is celebrated, what are we to say about structure? For many in Scotland last century the analysis recognised was that provided by Maxwell or by Gregory Dix and now some of the conclusions of these scholars have been discredited. Dix spoke confidently about a four-action shape[3]: 'he took'; 'he gave thanks and blessed'; 'he brake'; 'he gave'. 'He took' was thereafter identified with the action in the offertory; offertory was also equated with collection and presentation of offerings including money at the Table. The distinguished liturgical scholar A H Couratin wrote an essay[4] however in which he reduced the offertory and the fraction to a subordinate status and showed that the only indispensable elements of the action are prayer and communion.

It is worth considering some of the consequences of this shift in liturgical thinking as they affect our own practice. In particular I think the subordination of the offertory is an important corrective. There is a danger especially at Morning Service that offertory arrangements are so impressive as to exaggerate the importance of our offering and to create here an emotional high-point where it does not belong. We may be so eloquent in offertory prayers about the offerings **we** make and the quality of **our** self-dedication and so reticent in thanksgiving for Christ's sacrifice as almost to sound Pelagian. The emotional centre of gravity belongs theologically to eucharistic prayer.

---

[3] Gregory Dix, *The Shape of the Liturgy* (Dacre Press, 1952).
[4] Unpublished but referred to on page 19 of *The Sacrifice of Praise* edited by Bryan D Spinks (Rome, 1981).

Our Lord 'blessed and gave thanks'. Scholars are fairly confident that they can reproduce what he said and that early eucharistic prayers are derived from Jewish blessings. These blessings are a blend of thanksgiving to or celebration of God and anamnesis or remembrance of his mighty acts in creation and in salvation, all expressed with confessional directness. In other words they are saying in effect: 'we bless thee for what thou art, we remember what thou hast done for us, we put our whole trust and confidence in thee; blessed be God'. Louis Ligier demonstrates[5] how even the most complex of later eucharistic prayers have developed from this original, simple blend of celebration and anamnesis, the one sometimes differentiated from the other, sometimes not; the one sometimes more amply expressed than the other but nearly always both motifs present. If the logic is to be faithfully worked out and the progress of the service is to reach a fitting climax these spacious themes need to be heard: in all eucharistic prayer whether in the context of Morning Service or of the Divine Service the ancient models probably teach us a sound lesson.

## The Preparation

This heading refers to the part of the service which precedes the reading of scripture, with which the earliest services probably began. The emphasis here on confession of sin, which we owe to Calvin, would not be necessary were there some other way of practising penitence and of obtaining absolution. However since there is not we must treat it seriously but not too seriously. As J-J von Allmen remarks[6]: 'Christian worship is normally celebrated in a banqueting hall rather than in a laundry'. The situation requires a proper balance between the seriousness of confession and the faithfulness of anticipation.

---

[5] Louis Ligier, *Eucharisties d'Orient et d'Occident* (Paris, 1970) Vol. 2: 139.
[6] J-J von Allmen, *Worship* (London, 1965) 165.

The greatest disservice to the structure common to the Divine Service and Morning Service which we have identified is often offered by the content of the prayer which precedes the aforesaid confession. Our books of Common Order call this prayer adoration, which is a misnomer: a prayer of approach is a more accurate title. Brief words of acknowledgement of the Trinity to complement what has probably been expressed in the opening item of praise are in place but the full-scale recitation of all God's attributes and all his works that is often heard at this point, by inept anticipation, robs the service of its proper climax in eucharist. On festivals of the Christian year the theme of the day will be celebrated from the opening words of salutation or call to prayer but even then the theme will only be announced, to be developed in the word of God section of the service and to undergo a grand restatement and lyrical elaboration much later.

'Preparation' and 'Approach to God' are odd subjects with which to conclude this paper but introduce an eschatological perspective and they recall John Donne's lines which do form a fitting conclusion:[7]

> Since I am coming to that Holy room,
> Where, with thy Quire of Saints for evermore,
> I shall be made thy Music; As I come
> I tune the Instrument here at the door,
> And what I must do then, think here before.

---

[7] Hymne to God my God.

# The Book of *Common Order* of the Church of Scotland[1]
## *A Stewart Todd*

### I A General Overview of the Contents

The first and most remarkable feature of *Common Order*[2] *(CO)* is the amplitude of the provision. Indeed, to handle the book is to be aware of its considerable bulk: it contains seven hundred pages. Prayers are set out, not in prose paragraphs, but in short lines like verse. The layout becomes an art form, in this case a thing of beauty, facilitating and enhancing the speaking and hearing of the prayer.

The amplitude of material in this new book stands in stark contrast to what now seems the meagreness of its predecessor, the *Book of Common Order (1979)*[3] *(BCO* 79), even with its companion volume.[4] The comparison is even more striking when one knows that where choice was offered in *BCO 79* it was often between a service in traditional prayer language and one in modern speech, since the committee of that day fondly believed that traditional prayer language would have a continuing role in liturgy. The two books differ, however, in more significant ways. *BCO 79* gave primacy of place to orders for Holy Communion under the heading The Divine Service. Provision for Morning Service without Holy Communion followed. In this way the committee believed clear expression was being given to the normative character of the service of word and sacrament, which character had been recognized by the Reformers (not least John Knox), as it had been down the centuries by the

---

[1] Previously published in *Studia Liturgica*, 2001.
[2] *Common Order* (Edinburgh: Saint Andrew Press, 1994; 2nd edn 1996).
[3] *The Book of Common Order 1979* (Edinburgh: Saint Andrew Press, 1979).
[4] *Prayers for Sunday Services* (Edinburgh: Saint Andrew Press, 1980). This book contained prayers for sixteen morning services, prayers for the Christian year, etc.

universal Church. In 1987 the General Assembly, without making any judgment on the merits or demerits of the 1979 book, simply called for a new Book of Common Order to be produced. As Charles Robertson reports,[5] in the discussion which preceded the formulation of the motion to proceed, it was made clear that the new book should take as its model the 1940 *Book of Common Order*[6] *(BCO 40)* rather than the 1979. That the new committee did. No doubt it was felt that the identity of the Church of Scotland was not properly reflected in the arrangement of *BCO 79* and its companion volume. Nor by any means was the committee's eagerness to press towards greater frequency of celebration of Holy Communion shared by the whole Church.

## II The Order of Public Worship

For the vast majority of churches in the Church of Scotland, the main diet of worship on a Sunday is a morning service which includes basically prayers, lections, and sermon, with psalms and hymns, sometimes arranged in a 'eucharistic' order with prayers of thanksgiving and intercession after the sermon, and sometimes with the sermon dislocated from its natural position following lections and placed at the end of the service. Holy Communion is celebrated every Sunday in only a handful of churches, though monthly celebrations are more common than they were twenty years ago.

The few who may regret defects in these Church of Scotland worship patterns will almost certainly acknowledge two consoling features: first, a serious and sometimes scholarly engagement with scripture in preaching, prepared for often with the Bible in one hand and the newspaper in the other as Karl Barth recommended long ago; and second, celebrations of Holy Communion, which because they are infrequent, gain in importance and in sense of occasion. Where

---

[5] *CO,* xiii; and *To Glorify God: Essays on Modern Reformed Liturgy,* ed Bryan Spinks and Iain Torrance (Edinburgh: T. & T. Clark, 1999), 2.
[6] *Book of Common Order* ( Oxford: Oxford University Press, 1940).

the movement of minister and elders is sensitively choreographed, where the book-boards of pews are covered with white linen cloths (to symbolize extension of the holy table), where silence is kept during the distribution of elements to the people, where the riches of hymnody and psalmody in the Church of Scotland's Hymnary[7] are exploited imaginatively to give eloquence to appropriate words and dignity to processional entries and exits, and where, moreover, felicity of language in prayers is more or less guaranteed because on these infrequent occasions prayer material in *CO* is used verbatim– here you may have the context for an interpenetration of the divine and the human of singular intensity. 'The sacraments are an essential part of ecclesial aesthetics.'[8] In a Church of Scotland communion service at its best can be found witness to the splendour of grace that still observes a decent reserve in the presence of the Christ from whom that grace is derived.

The order of contents of *CO*, following the design of *BCO 40*, has as its first main section five orders for Morning Service and five for Evening Service. In the shape of the first of these Morning Services a salute has been made to the Scottish Reformation tradition, mentioned above and reflected in the 1979 book, and the order is 'eucharistic.' The second order for Morning Service portrays the other practice, still widespread in Scotland, of placing the sermon at the end of the service.

The first order for Morning Service is a rich and noble vehicle for the mystery of worship. Psalmody and hymnody feature prominently in Church of Scotland services: they are very much the people's part. In this service hymns are recommended in four positions, as are a psalm between the Old Testament and the epistle, and an Alleluia between

---

[7] *The Church Hymnary: Third Edition* (London: Oxford University Press, 1973).
[8] Hans Urs von Balthasar, *The Glory of the Lord* 1 (Edinburgh: T & T Clark, 1982), 582.

the gospel and the Prayer for Illumination that immediately precedes the sermon. Additionally, the people are invited to say the Apostles' Creed and the Lord's Prayer. Responses are confined to the *Kyries* and Amen.

As indicated above, the second Morning Service places the sermon at the end of the service. The only response made by the people to this preaching of the word is the offering, a prayer of dedication, and a hymn. The number of readings from scripture is not specified in this service and no psalm or alleluia is suggested. There is likewise no creed. In all other respects this service resembles the first. The third, fourth and fifth so-called Morning Services are really sets of prayers that may be used following either of the two preceding orders.

It is not to be supposed that because five orders are provided for Evening Service the people of the Church of Scotland are unusually pious, attending worship twice on a Sunday. In fact, weekly evening worship is found in only a few churches; in the main, if there is evening worship at all, it is monthly. Furthermore, what is being offered in these services is an alternative hour of worship. The first order of Evening Service almost replicates that of the first Morning Service, except that the scripture readings are reduced in number and the gradual psalm, alleluia, and creed are omitted. The second Evening Service provides sets of prayers only. The others, while innovating, still offer a full service of the word. The third comes closest to being a complement to a Morning Service.

## III Holy Communion

For the purpose of this essay, it will be convenient to deal next with the eucharist or, as it is called in the table of contents, Holy Communion. Despite modest advances in ecumenism generally in Scotland in the last twenty years, the compilers of *CO* clearly thought the Church of Scotland was not yet ready to adopt the word 'eucharist.' In the first order, as is to be expected, the liturgy of the word is a variant of the first order for Morning Service. As in *BCO 40* and again in *BCO 79*, the first prayer begins with the Collect for Purity and includes the modern version of the *Book of Common Prayer* collect for the sixth Sunday after Trinity. The *Gloria in Excelsis*, said or sung, occupies the slot for what in Morning Service would be the second hymn. After the sermon the Nicene Creed is said instead of the Apostles' Creed, and intercessions with thanksgiving for the blessed departed come before the eucharist proper. Words of invitation follow, together with a choice of 'comfortable words,' but then, curiously, the offering interrupts the natural progression of the service. Even in the slickest scenario the collecting of money from a congregation takes time: it is therefore difficult to justify this intrusion.

In a procession designated the Great Entrance (as in *BCO 79*) the elements of bread and wine along with the money offerings are brought to the holy table, and during this a psalm or hymn is sung. Then follows the Grace; a prayer during which the minister unveils the elements; an offertory prayer; and the Narrative of the Institution (although a note states that the narrative may instead be incorporated within the eucharistic prayer). The remainder of the service has a shape that is for the most part common to many traditions: the taking of the bread and wine; the eucharistic prayer;[9] Lord's Prayer; fraction; *Agnus Dei;* communion;[10] the peace; post-communion prayer of thanksgiving with extended *Gloria;* a hymn; and the dismissal and blessing.

---

[9] Within this first order for Holy Communion three forms of the eucharistic prayer are offered, though it has to be said that the traditional lineaments are not easily discerned in the second.

[10] Either the elders take the elements to the people in their seats or the people may gather round the holy table.

A second order is described in the Introduction to *CO* as reflecting 'the Celtic tradition'; the third is shorter; the fourth is for use at a service when children communicate; and the fifth is for use at home or in hospital.

One comment must be made before leaving this section of the book concerning the theology underlying the offertory prayer and kindred prayers. In some of these otherwise splendid communion services there is a tendency to refer so frequently to the offerings we make, of bread and wine, of worship, of ourselves, as to detract from Christ's offering of himself, though the phrase 'pleading his eternal sacrifice' does happily occur. One looks back also to the prayers of dedication and self-offering in the orders for Morning Service and also those for Evening Service. Add to this the status of the prayer of dedication in the second order for Morning Service where, along with one hymn, it represents the response to the preaching of the word, a response which the logic of the gospel would suggest ought always to be thanksgiving for the supreme offering of which our human offering is a derivative, and one detects surely a hint of Pelagianism.

## IV Christian Initiation

It may seem arbitrary to use the term 'Christian initiation' as a heading when it occurs nowhere in *CO*. Nevertheless, since there is provided an order of baptism for a child, another for an adult (with confirmation and possibly Holy Communion), and another described as an Order for the Public Profession of Faith, Confirmation, and Admission to the Lord's Supper with the Sacrament of Holy Baptism (and possibly with Holy Communion), Christian initiation is a proper designation. Of course in Scotland, as in so many other places, we live with the fragmentation of Christian initiation: yet shyly, indeed as an afterthought, *CO* does recover the possibility of Christian initiation in the words of a rubric after the services of confirmation which indicates that Holy Communion *may* follow.[11]

A rubric at the beginning of these services states, 'Normally, the Sacrament is administered during Sunday Worship, usually after the sermon.' The first part of this rubric is intended to discourage private administrations and the second to register gentle disapproval of the arrangement in many churches where the sacrament is administered at an early point in morning service so that children can be present before going off to Sunday School. Of much greater significance, however, is a comparison of the two editions of *CO* in their treatment of the beginning of the baptismal service. Understandably, prominence is given to dominical institution, and in the first edition the first heading is Words of Institution. The lesson from Matt 28:18-20 is then read by the minister, followed by Acts 2:38-39. The second edition makes what many will see as a proper and enlightened improvement on this, replacing 'Words of Institution' with 'Institution' and placing as the first reading the record of Jesus' baptism in Mark 1:9-11.[12] This substitution is in line with the caution that is urged by modern New Testament scholarship on the life and ministry of Jesus, in particular with the question mark that is placed over the authenticity of the Matthean text as *ipsissima verba*. There follows a selection of short passages, one or more of which may additionally be read. The ensuing Statement, amended in the second edition, makes brief mention of Jesus' baptism but passes quickly to say that his baptism was completed through his dying and rising again.

A question is now put to the parents. They are asked whether they 'receive the teaching of the Christian faith which we confess in the Apostles' Creed.' The context of faith is then further established by all saying the Creed. Prayer follows, using language rich in biblical

---
[11] This rubric did not appear in the first edition of *CO*, though it did appear in *BCO 79*.
[12] Omitted entirely in the first edition, though present in *BCO 79*.

water images connected with Noah, Moses, and Jesus at Jordan (reminiscent of Luther's *Sindflutgebet* or Flood Prayer), and ending with another reference to the baptism of his death and resurrection and the way being opened to eternal life. The prayer continues with an invocation of the Holy Spirit: 'Send your Holy Spirit upon us and upon this water …'

Then follows a Declaration, used words adapted from the French Reformed Church's liturgy:

'N…,
for you Jesus Christ came into the world:
for you he lived and showed God's love;
for you he suffered the darkness of Calvary
and cried at the last, 'It is accomplished';
for you he triumphed over death
and rose in newness of life;
for you he ascended to reign at God's right hand.
All this he did for you, N.,
though you do not know it yet.
And so the word of Scripture is fulfilled:
'We love because God loved us first.'

Here are lines of pure kerygma beautifully and movingly apposite. Not everyone will agree with the rubric that indicates the words should be spoken for each child or candidate. As a declaration the words are splendid; as an incantation their effect would be diminished, there being too many.

Into all of the material up to this point there is interwoven good baptismal theology. The priority of the love of God and his gracious initiative in baptism are made clear, as are Christ's part as the baptizer and the one who calls us to share his ministry in the world. The theology of Romans 6 is well to the fore. One can imagine that in the next Book of Common Order an alternative order for baptism will be offered in which greater prominence will be given to Jesus' own baptism in Jordan on our behalf and to associated images as well as to John 3 rebirth imagery. Also in the future the idea of the communal priesthood of the baptized will probably be elaborated, but the inclusion of 1 Peter 2:9 (a royal priesthood) as a possible reading and the reference to sharing Christ's ministry in the world is a welcome pointer in that direction.

After the baptism itself, accompanied by the traditional Trinitarian formula, words of blessing follow, and then the minister on behalf of all welcomes the newly baptized 'as a member of the one holy catholic and apostolic Church.'

Under the heading of Promise is included a brief charge leading into a vow the parents are required to take: that they will teach the child the truths and duties of the Christian faith, and by prayer and example they will bring the child up in the life and worship of the Church. This vow, in previous baptismal services coming before baptism, is more happily placed here, where it is less a precondition of baptism and more an imperative arising from the indicatives of the gospel which have been proclaimed. The vow taken by the parents is complemented by a vow of commitment taken by the congregation. One fears that in the context of a large congregation where baptisms may take place at frequent intervals, perhaps monthly, this renewal of commitment would soon become meaningless. Nor is it the only act of recommitment that is recommended in the book. Recommitment occurs in the confirmation service, in the order for the ordination and admission of elders, and in the covenant service. Repetition on this scale within the worship of a congregation would be intolerable.[13]

---

[13] See also Torrance in *To Glorify God*, 171ff.

The order for the baptism of a child is repeated with the necessary changes in text and rubric to make it serviceable where the candidate is an adult. The order envisages the possibility of a candidate's not wishing to proceed to confirmation and first communion. In northern and northwestern parts of Scotland, there is a tradition, still observed by many, of not being confirmed on the grounds of unworthiness to take communion.

The confirmation part of the service involves the making of numerous vows concerning worship, Bible reading, prayer, stewardship of time, talents and money, and witness. Thereafter, with the confirmand kneeling, the minister lays hands on her and prays that she may daily increase in God's Holy Spirit. Using a formula beginning 'In the name of the Lord Jesus Christ, the King and Head of the Church, and by the authority of this Kirk Session,' he then welcomes and admits the confirmed 'to the full privileges of the children of God'. After the congregational vow of recommitment and prayers, the order reverts to that for Morning Service with or without Holy Communion.

**V Marriage**

Provided in *CO* are three orders for marriage,[14] an Order for the Blessing of a Civil Marriage, and an Order for Thanksgiving for Marriage (With the Renewal of Marriage Vows). There is also found, under a separate heading, a generous selection of scriptural passages.[15] There are also options within the services, more than ever before. Homage has been paid to political correctness, more precisely to gender equality, and wherever in the past there has been a hint of male precedence, for example in making the vows or in giving the ring, the choice of order now is to be made by the couple. Views will differ as to whether this multiple choice is helpful or whether it introduces an element

---

[14] There was only one in 1940, and although two were offered in 1979, the choice was really between traditional and modern language.

[15] Thirty in fact! Sixteen are printed in full.

of instability in a rite where simplicity, familiarity and a degree of uniformity were appreciated (and loved) by congregations—and by guests, very many of whom would have no church connection.[16]

In all three of the marriage rites the main emphasis is on the exchange of vows, as is the case in most western rites, this exchange being the seal of the marriage. Orders one and three follow the pattern of earlier rites and have readings and an address after the marriage vows; order two innovates by having the readings and address before the vows. The case for this latter 'eucharistic' order[17] would be stronger if the Bible, or any part of it, were a marriage manual, which patently is not the case: Jesus says little about marriage; the Epistles show some apparent inconsistencies. The function of readings is therefore to celebrate God's gift of marriage and the potential beauties of it, and to bear witness to the enhancement and enrichment which Christ can bring to a marriage. In association with prayers of thanksgiving, as in the first and third rites, readings and the address following vows may really be preferable. The second order is impressive in its treatment of the covenant theme. God's covenant love is a paradigm for the marriage relationship in terms of God's total faithfulness and constancy, though it is less appropriate in terms of our modern understanding of marriage as a relationship between two equal partners.

A Statement follows the first hymn in each of the rites. The first rite, alone among the three, mentions procreation. The first and the third include reference to the welfare of human society. All stress the commitment of husband and wife to each other. All begin by acknowledging marriage as part of God's loving purpose for humanity.

---

[16] It has to be remembered moreover that the Church of Scotland is a 'national' Church, with 'established' status.

[17] There is, however, no provision for Holy Communion in any of the rites.

The Order for the Blessing of a Civil Marriage is exactly what it says it is. The Statement spells it out: 'A... and B... have been married according to the law of the land. They have pledged their love and loyalty to each other. Now, in faith, they come before God and his Church to acknowledge their covenant of marriage.' By contrast, the words of the Declaration which follows the Promises and Marriage Blessing are obscure, declaring the couple to be 'husband and wife according to the witness of the one holy catholic and apostolic Church.'

The Order for Thanksgiving for Marriage, with the renewal of the marriage vows, is new to the Church of Scotland and its introduction a sign of the times. An opening note explains that the order may be used 'at an anniversary; or after a time of separation; or when a couple has experienced difficulty in their marriage; or when several couples request, or are invited to make, a public reaffirmation of marriage.' Uniquely among these marriage rites this order asks for an affirmation by the congregation that they will offer support.

## VI Funerals

As with marriage, so with funerals the 'national' status of the Church of Scotland is a factor in the composition of the rite, and in the case of funerals an inhibiting factor, at least in terms of eschatology. Ministers in the Church of Scotland will find themselves asked to conduct many 'parish' funerals, i.e., the funerals of persons resident in the parish but not communicant members of the Church, perhaps not baptized, perhaps lapsed from other denominations, or having no religious background at all. The emphasis is therefore on the love of God, his compassion, his goodness, his mercy, his comforting of those who mourn: it is also on the death of Christ 'for all,' with the possibility of universalism and with no hint of demarcation. Judgment belongs to God.

Within this framework of thought simple rites have been constructed. There is a choice of two orders for a funeral service, an Order for use in Distressing Circumstances, another for the Funeral of a Child, and yet another for the Funeral of a Still-born Child. Finally there is an Order for the Interment or Scattering of Ashes. Strangely there is no guidance for memorial services, which are increasingly common. In these rites there is not only simplicity and directness of testimony to the faith, there is also beauty and dignity and tenderness. Additionally there is provided a wealth of scripture passages that may be read and prayers that may be said.

## VII Other Ordinances

Of the remaining ordinances, perhaps only the order for the ordination and admission of elders requires interpretation. The office of the elder is a distinctive feature of Reformed church government, although it evolved in different ways in different national contexts. In all, the concern was for discipline that would safeguard the Church from the abuses that had shamed it in the Middle Ages. In Scotland, confusion long surrounded the eldership. Two rival theories in particular disturbed the peace—the 'lay' theory and the 'presbyter' theory. The latter theory actually associates ministers and elders in one office, the minister being referred to as the 'teaching elder' and the elder as the 'ruling elder,' all of this defended by a reference to scripture.

Happily the eldership has developed in modern times in such a way that, at its best, it is enormously helpful to the Church. Modern thinking finds the model for the eldership in the diaconate of the early church.[18] Elders are usually assigned a 'district' within which they will visit from time to time perhaps ten to fifteen households of members. Elders are appointed for life. On moving to another

---

[18] *Reports to the General Assembly* (1989), 200. That report also recognized that the use of the word 'ordination' in relation to elders was unhelpful.

congregation they may (or may not) be invited to join the Kirk Session. If invited, they are admitted—hence the word 'admission' in the title of the order. The order itself envisages a ceremony during worship and after the sermon. It involves the reading of an excerpt from the preamble prescribed in the 1929 *Basis and Plan of Union* for the ordination and induction of ministers. Reference in this to the Westminster Confession of Faith as the Church of Scotland's 'subordinate standard' is an embarrassment to many, as is a conscience clause covering items of belief which are not of the (undefined) substance of the faith. The General Assembly has to date resisted change to this wording, even to the reasonable suggestion that the Westminster Confession be associated with the ancient creeds and the Scots Confession, and all acknowledged as historic statements of faith.

## VIII Language

Two hundred pages of *CO* are devoted to extra prayers of different kinds. The book then concludes with the Revised Common Lectionary, which runs on a three-year cycle and is used in the majority of English-speaking Churches in the West, and with scripture sentences and collects for every Sunday of the year.

Throughout the book scripture is quoted from the Revised English Bible. In prayer God is addressed in the 'you' form, and the committee 'wherever possible avoided male-dominated language to describe God. Traditional metaphors like Father, Judge, King remain, though they are used sparingly.'[19] Language about people is inclusive. Personal pronouns are italicized where appropriate: *she* sometimes occurs rather than *he*. Likewise *sister* sometimes occurs rather than *brother*.

---

[19] Charles Robertson in *To Glorify God*, 7.

For prayer language in general, Charles Robertson claims that every effort was made to ensure that in *CO* it was 'simple, fresh, and relevant.'[20] The aim was also to make the speaking of prayers rhythmical and to achieve dignity and beauty in prayer. In many ways these are laudable aims and in pursuing them the committee will probably be judged to have had considerable success. It can be argued, however, that in two contexts at least these aims were inadequate, perhaps even wholly inappropriate. In prayers of confession there are surely times when dissonance, not euphony, are required - times when a harsh statistic, say of drug-related deaths in our communities, needs to be brought to mind. Confession of shame in relation to social evils of this kind calls for language that is disturbing, incisive, and arrhythmic. Likewise, in intercession, the prayers will often arise out of remembered pain or distress. In such contexts as these silence may outdo speech in the actual prayer to God and bidding to prayer may be what is required. Newspaper headlines can be quoted in biddings addressed to the congregation with rather less inhibition than if they are addressed to God!

In *CO* biddings are never used in confession and only once in intercession. But these intercessions are bland, not contextualized in a real week in the real world, nor could they be. And yet perhaps that is what they have to be and rubrics could be used to indicate this. Better still, a model could have been reproduced in this expansive book from a particular week with topical references and with a clear indication for the unwary that (of course) it could not be used as printed.

On a more grateful note: the compilers are to be congratulated on references to God in creation within the eucharistic prayer. So often in the past these have seemed perfunctory. In the second order for Holy Communion, which is claimed to reflect the Celtic tradition,

---

[20] Ibid.

there is a welcome hint of Gallican exuberance of expression. For dwellers in the space age there is clearly scope for ever more dramatic and poetic allusion to God's versatility in creation, and if this can be represented as a gauge for God's versatility in salvation, then the exercise is heart-warming.

## IX Conclusion

*CO* has within it enough of catholicity, enough of Reformed doctrine, enough of Scottish tradition, and enough of modernity to make it widely acceptable in the Church of Scotland. As with all liturgical books, the earnest hope is that the material in it and also that modelled on it will do honour to God and prove serviceable to him, for he is the chief actor in worship.

# The Christian Year

## *R Stuart Louden*

In the *Church Service Society Annual (1954)* I wrote that 'the Christian Year is a true handmaiden of the Gospel in helping to keep the Church's worship rooted in the Word of God and close to the Holy Scriptures', while also suggesting that a responsible use of the Church Calendar can help to bring the Church back to the Bible. Careful re-examination of the structure of the Christian Year in relation to the Scriptures and to the sequence and seasons of the natural year, in order to ensure a sound evangelical and theological basis for the Church Calendar, is a continuing task in the Church *semper reformanda*. Ecumenical effort along these lines resulted in the publication by the Joint Liturgical Group in 1967 of *The Calendar and Lectionary, a Reconsideration*, edited by Ronald C D Jasper.

As the Church of Scotland norm for public worship *The Book of Common Order (1979)* has adopted with some minor modifications the Joint Liturgical Group's helpful restatement of the traditional Christian Year with its emphasis on the main festivals of Christmas, Easter and Pentecost. The Calendar and accompanying Lectionary[1] offer a two-year cycle of Scripture Lessons for each Lord's Day throughout the year with the addition of Christmas Day, Ash Wednesday, Good Friday and Ascension Day. The use of this Lectionary in the arrangement of weekly Sunday services has been usefully supplemented by the publication in 1976 of *The Year's Praise* which links the choice of items from *The Church Hymnary: Third Edition* to the two-year Lectionary according to the sequence of this clearly structured Christian Year.

---

[1] Since this paper was written the Church of Scotland has adopted the 3 year Revised Common Lectionary which takes a different approach to some of the matters described below.

Scripture lessons and praise chosen according to the Church's calendar, with its carefully selected themes and subjects, ensure that the Gospel in its wholeness and fullness is the substance of the Church's public worship. In this context Preaching finds its regular themes in the Word of God, ensuring a faithful exposition of the mighty acts of God unto salvation in Jesus Christ. This prevents public worship from drifting into too much merely occasional preaching which so easily degenerates into the word of man. Again, it guards against the weakness in too many sermon themes arising out of the particular preacher's interests, not to say whims.

**The Lord's Day**
The celebration every week of a lesser Easter on the first day of the week, the Lord's Day, is essential in relating the Faith to the sequence in the natural year of four seasons and to the scene temporal in general. From earliest Christian times the Lord's Day has been marked by obedient Christian response to one of the few precise instructions of the Church's Lord to His people: 'Do this in remembrance of Me' (1 Corinthians 11:24). The celebration of a weekly Eucharist, recommended by the General Assembly as eventually to be accepted as Church of Scotland practice, the Lord's Supper on the Lord's Day, is the basic link between redemption and the passing of time in Creation, and undergirds any Christian Year and Church Calendar. Study of the gradual evolution of the Calendar can lead to a theologically sound and a liturgically profitable following of the Christian Year by ministers.

**Christmas, Easter and Pentecost**
The Feast of the Epiphany (January 6), known first in the Eastern Roman Empire from the close of the first century, was among the earliest of Christian festivals, anterior to any Christmas or Nativity

celebration. Epiphany arose as a unitive commemoration of the birth and baptism of Jesus. This Greek name, 'manifestation', in honour of our Lord's baptism in Jordan indicates that from Apostolic times the faithful had an instinct for a yearly remembrance of the dawning of the Light of the World, the Coming of the Saviour, and therefore, subsequently, of His Birth.

The so-called Philocalian Calendar of 354 AD is the earliest mention of December 25 being observed as the date of the Nativity; and this dating is quite arbitrary, possibly chosen to oppose the pagan observance of *Natalis Solis Invicti*. But proper gratitude for the Light of the World, manifest in Jesus at His baptism, encouraged interest in His Nativity, although it was the fourth Christian century until the whole Bethlehem tradition from the Synoptic Gospels was much heeded. The Coming of Jesus is thus the divine event requiring annual celebration, and accordingly Christmas, the Nativity, becomes one of the three controlling feasts in a relevantly restructured Christian Calendar (When the Eastern Church declined to change from the Julian Calendar of 46 AD to the Gregorian Calendar of 1582 AD, January 6, the original Epiphany, has remained Christmas Day for most of the Orthodox Churches).

Since doctrine (Gospel) rather than commemoration was the formative influence in developing a Christian Year, the Cross and the Resurrection of the Lord Jesus Christ, Passiontide and Easter, were the supreme events in time and history particularly to be marked in every natural year, as the mighty acts of God in Redemption. These events had their definite dating in the Jewish Passover, hence the Christian *Pascha*. Jewish festivals had a very close connection with the cycle of the natural year, and the Pascal moon remains the key for dating Easter.

As a Christian Passover, Holy Week emerged in the 4th century: it was the actual record of the events in our Lord's Passion week, as interpreted from the Synoptic and Fourth Gospels, allowing for their variations, which formed the traditional Holy Week. This makes Holy Week and Easter the second essential pivot in the Church Calendar.

In the Jewish Calendar, Pentecost, the Feast of Weeks or Harvest, fell on the fiftieth day after Passover, and according to the Scriptures, it was 'when the day of Pentecost had come' (Acts 2:1), that the Apostolic Church had its unique experience of the Descent of the Holy Spirit, an event which was virtually the birthday of the Christian Church. Pentecost thus continued to be observed by the Christian faithful as a unitive commemoration of our Lord's Ascension and the Gift of the Spirit.

The Lord's Day following Pentecost was marked as the Octave of Whitsun until medieval practice named that Sunday as a separate feast in honour of the Holy Trinity. Pentecost is the third event in the history of Salvation which brings a revised Church Calendar into focus. Modern Roman Catholic as well as Reformed practice is wise in identifying the remaining six months of the natural year as Sundays after Pentecost, rather than Sundays in a prolonged Trinity season.

For the Church's edification and guidance in arranging the content of public worship, it will be noted that the Christian Year is most appropriately laid out round the great Salvation-events of Christmas, Easter and Pentecost, the scheme adopted in the Joint Liturgical Group's *Calendar and Lectionary* (see *The Book of Common Order (1979)*).

## Advent and Lent

That through their liturgical revisions, the churches have improved their Calendar by making the axis of the Christian Year revolve round the main festivals of Christmas, Easter and Pentecost, should not exclude from observance other traditional elements in the Calendar which are required within the sequence of the natural year for the proclamation of the Faith in its fullness. In particular the observance of Advent and Lent ensures that annually the notes of expectancy and penitence are included, notes vital in the Church's kerygmatic and homiletic tasks. Advent and Lent help to keep public worship 'rooted in the Word of God and close to the Holy Scriptures'.

In the 'run-up' to Christmas it is didactically sound to arrange Biblical themes covering a sequence of nine numbered Sundays before Christmas, as a longer preparation for celebrating the Nativity of the Redeemer. This in no way alters the relevance and value of Advent Sunday, the fourth Sunday before Christmas being observed as very particularly the beginning of a new Christian Year and the First Sunday in the season of Advent, the season of expectancy for the coming of Christ.

Since the 6th Christian century, Advent Sunday has been observed in this manner, traditionally not only a time of preparation for Christmas, but also sounding the eschatological note of the Second Coming of Christ and the Last Judgment. This eschatological orientation is basic to the primitive Gospel, which according to Saint Mark commences with 'prepare ye the way of the Lord', while the Saviour's first recorded word is 'the time is fullfilled and the Kingdom of God is at hand' (Mark 1:3 and 15). All Christian faith and worship are celebrated 'until He come'. Watchfulness towards our Lord's Second Advent made this season of the Christian Year a 'fast', though literal fasting has had very little place in Christian practice for many centuries.

Expectancy is the significant theme for the nine pre-Christmas Sundays and in particular for the four Sundays of Advent. This is the rationale of the Christian Year having its annual beginning with Advent and with this emphasis on the eschatological element in the Primitive Gospel.

The Lenten fast of forty days before Easter sounds the note of penitence in preparation for the Church remembering the Death and Resurrection of the Lord Jesus Christ. This once more is faithful to the Primitive Gospel: 'the time is fullfilled, and the kingdom of God is at hand: repent ye, and believe the Gospel' (Mark 11:15).

Revised lectionaries adopting themes for nine Sundays leading up to the Easter celebration, have dropped the traditional names for the three pre-Lenten Lord's Days. In practice, the names, Septuagesima, Sexagesima and Quinquagesima, indicating 64 not 70, 57 not 60, and 50 days before Easter, for these 9th, 8th and 7th Sundays before Easter, are no longer current. Such themes as the Creation and the Fall gave these Sundays their initial pre-Lenten significance.

The actual Lenten Season, beginning with Ash Wednesday forty days before Easter, remains the appropriate preparation for celebrating the Passion and Resurrection of the Saviour of the World, and Lent is traditionally a 'fast'. Lent probably means Spring, and the fast absorbed into its observance the Biblical account of our Lord's Forty Days' Fast and Temptations in the wilderness. In medieval tradition Shrove Tuesday, a day for the confession and absolution of the faithful (shriving) preceded Ash Wednesday, so-called after the 'dust and ashes' image of penitence. Thus were introduced the five Lenten Sundays before Holy Week which is observed from Palm Sunday, also called the Sixth Sunday in Lent, to Easter Day.

The Lenten Lord's Days are all based on very significant Biblical themes related to the mighty acts of God in redemption. Themes included are our Lord's Temptations and the Transfiguration. The fourth Sunday in Lent, third before Easter, is called Mothering Sunday (the reference is to Mother Church); and the fifth Sunday in Lent, second before Easter, is traditionally Passion Sunday with Calvary as its theme.

**Holy Week**
The themes for worship in Holy Week have developed out of a study of the Synoptic and Johannine records of the Passover Week when Jesus Christ was crucified. The observance of the days of Holy Week, followed by a full Easter celebration, has been one of the most effective devotional influences in the Christian fold and a vital contribution to spirituality.

The first Sunday before Easter, Palm Sunday, recalls our Lord's Triumphal Entry into Jerusalem, the city where He was to die. Monday and Tuesday in Holy Week are connected, respectively, with the Cleansing of the Temple, and with our Lord's Parables and Teaching in the Temple precincts during the week of the Crucifixion. Wednesday in Holy Week, often referred to as the Day of Silence, marks the quiet day spent by Jesus in Bethany.

Thursday in Holy Week bears the English name of Maundy Thursday, a reference to the Feet-Washing and the new commandment of love: *mandatum novum* (John 13:34). The institution in the Upper Room of the Sacrament of Christ's Body and Blood gives an especially significant place to this day in the Church Calendar: 'the Lord Jesus the same night in which He was betrayed, took bread' (1 Corinthians 11:23).

To Good Friday belongs its quite unique place not only in Holy Week but in the entire Christian Year: in some Christian practice the Friday of every week is observed throughout the calendar year as a lesser Crucifixion-day, as every Lord's Day is for the Church universal a lesser Easter. From the Scripture records, marking 9 in the morning as the hour of Crucifixion, with the darkness and the Agony on the Cross running from 12 noon until 3 o'clock when Jesus died, has come the devotional practice of making the Three Hours, 12 noon to 3 o'clock, a special time of vigil and Good Friday devotion.

Saturday in Holy Week marking the period when our Lord lay in the tomb, leads into Easter, this eve of Easter theme being Christian baptism: 'buried with Him in baptism, wherein also ye are risen with Him' (Colossians 2:12).

A devotional observance of Holy Week not only illumines the meaning and deepens the joy of the Resurrection Day for believers, but it contributes to a more adequate proclamation of the inexpressible Victory and Triumph in the Easter Message.

**Liturgical Colours**
The use in churches of colours traditionally associated with the revolving seasons of the Christian Year can be a helpful 'visual aid' identifying particular days and seasons in the Calendar and indicating the facet of the Gospel being particularly presented. Eucharistic vestments in the various liturgical colours are not part of the Reformed tradition, but these colours can be used quite usefully for pulpit falls and Bible markers in our churches.

White is the high festival colour appropriate to the twelve days of Christmas and the octave of Easter. For Pentecost red as the colour of flames of fire is traditional. The colour for fast-seasons is purple or violet for use in Advent and Lent. A variant colour for Lent is unbleached linen (compare hodden grey), and in that usage purple or violet can then be restricted to Passiontide (Palm Sunday to Holy Saturday), with the possible use of black on Good Friday. Green, the colour of the earth's verdure and symbolic of the ongoing natural Creation, is the liturgical colour for seasons not otherwise distinctly marked. Green is normally in use for the six months of Sundays after Pentecost, and also between Epiphany and Lent.

The traditional liturgical colours are listed as white (*albus*), red (*rubeus*), green (*viridis*), purple or violet (*violaceus*) and black (*niger*). These colours and others such as blue or yellow can be varied according to local situations and particular events in the natural or Church Calendars, e.g. Saints' days and local celebrations.

Such a use of liturgical colours, dating from early 12th century practice in the Western Church, offers didactic support in keeping the themes of the Christian Year before the eyes of worshippers. In this way even such a 'visual aid' can help to bring the Church back to the Bible as the record of God's mighty acts in Salvation.

# Celebrating the Christian Year

## *William T Hogg*

The rhythm of the seasons has always affected and inspired human beings. Even today, in urban and air-conditioned environments, people are still aware of the changes each season brings; and those who live in rural areas know that each season brings its own tasks and problems. The changing appearance and feel of the created world demonstrate both continuity and change.

It is the same in the life of the Church. Every congregation has a rhythm of life marked out by different events from the Sunday School Picnic to the Sale of Work. Other regular events are then added. Harvest Thanksgiving has its place, as does Remembrance Sunday and the celebration of Holy Communion. Such patterns are important and comforting, representing continuity and security.

The observation of Christmas and Easter takes its place in this pattern. This can be developed, if so inclined, into more comprehensive patterns. Just as the seasons of the calendar year impinge on our lives, so the seasons of the Christian Year take their place in our consciousness. These can play much the same part in our lives by providing a sense of continuity and change, of familiarity and progress.

There are several advantages to observing the Christian Year. It gives a structure to our worship and it has an educational purpose. Even in its simplest form we are kept in touch with the major events of the Christian story in a purposeful way. It is now common for the major celebrations of Christmas and Easter to be accompanied by the appropriate season of preparation, with their opportunities for teaching and focusing worship on challenging themes. For the worship leader it is a great aid to preparation and planning to have a guide which will fill in and inspire in times where there is little leisure or when the spring of ideas has run dry.

Resources, such as the various versions of the Revised Common Lectionary, show how this can be expanded throughout the year. The Church of Scotland's book, *Common Order*, provides a rich source of basic material since it contains appropriate readings, prayers and other worship material for every Sunday of the year. The Church of Scotland website now features additional material for each Sunday. Since the Church of England adopted the Lectionary a great number of other British resources have become available to join that from other denominations throughout the world. One of the attractive aspects of the Lectionary is its international and cross-denominational use in Roman Catholic and Reformed Churches.

It is not just in words that the seasons of the Christian Year can be marked. As we experience the created world, colours are valued and enjoyed. People flock to observe the rich autumn colours before they disappear into the dark and grey tones of winter. That sparse season is ended by the fresh greens and splashes of yellows which characterise spring for so many of us before they merge into the brilliance of summer foliage and flowers. The Church can take its cue from that annual progression and, by the appropriate use of colours and symbols, provide a visual reminder of the rhythm of the Church's Year.

In the Church a pattern of seasonal colours has emerged over the centuries. It has regional and denominational variations and has never been altogether a rigid system. For instance, whereas today Christmas and Easter are assigned the celebratory colours of white or gold, in the medieval period the best and newest vestments and decorations could be used irrespective of colour.

An example of this freedom can be found in the first Season of the Christian Year, which is Advent. This has been regarded as a penitential season of preparation for Christmas on the pattern of Lent, which was developed earlier. Accordingly the colour violet or purple has been used for these four weeks before Christmas Day. When this period is strictly observed - that is without anticipating the joy of Christmas - this is an appropriate colour. However it is one of the challenges of modern life that the world as a whole does anticipate Christmas, and even the Church will present celebratory events such as Carol Services and Nativity Plays in the Advent Season. Opinion will differ on the appropriateness of this and how to achieve a solution which will both respect the Church's traditions and reach out to those who have that sense of celebration which is such a great opportunity for outreach. In the minor field of liturgical colours, this can be illustrated by the choice of blue for the Advent season. Based on the ancient Sarum (Salisbury) usage, blue is presented as the colour of hope, a legitimate Advent theme. As an alternative theme to penitence it can suggest eager anticipation rather than sombre preparation.

Many American Churches have a ceremony at the beginning of Advent called 'Hanging of the Greens' when evergreen branches are used to decorate the building, including a tree, which may be decorated with appropriate Christian symbols (chrismons). The evergreens represent everlasting life and can be put up with appropriate liturgical formality and scriptural readings, such as provided by the United Methodist Church in the United States.

On Christmas Eve the season of Christmas properly begins. The liturgical colour is white or gold for celebration and the predominant theme is light. Whatever has been done in Advent, and to whatever extent the world has anticipated this moment, the Church must mark it out as special. The possibilities are too vast to list here but imagination and joy will suggest how the burst of light at Christmas midnight may be extended through all the seasonal services.

The Christmas season proper extends to 6 January, the Day of the Epiphany, or a Sunday close by on which the Visit of the Magi is celebrated. However the Season of Epiphany which follows can be treated as an extension of the Christmas celebration. The Church of England's book *The Promise of His Glory*[1] suggested that it might run through to the Presentation of Christ in the Temple or Candlemas (2 February or the nearest Sunday). In this case, the colour white could continue in use and the Church's celebration extended for those 40 days.

Otherwise, the season after 6 January is treated as regular or ordinary Sundays and green would be used through to Lent. In any case there are usually a few Sundays in February before Lent begins and these would use green. In the Lectionary, the Sunday before Lent is assigned the Transfiguration readings, as a kind of transition from readings about Christ's life on to the journey to Jerusalem, and once again white is used.

Purple is the colour for Lent, although some traditions use unbleached linen. The tone of worship and the sense of the build up to Holy Week dictate a sombre look. Holy Week itself has some variations. Palm Sunday and the first part of Holy Week is traditionally red. This is a royal colour but also the colour of blood. Red is also used at Pentecost but ideally this should be a different shade, perhaps lighter than the Holy Week colour.

---

[1] *The Promise of His Glory* published 1991 by Church House Publishing and Mowbray for the Church of England. This contained a wealth of seasonal material and ideas which has influenced later liturgical publications such as *Common Prayer*.

Modern practice is for white to be used on Maundy Thursday when the Sacrament of Holy Communion is celebrated. Sometimes this service is followed by the removal of all colours and hangings from the sanctuary, leaving it bare until the Easter services. Red may also be used on Good Friday.

Easter begins at different times for different Churches. It may follow a vigil on the Saturday night or a dawn service and so on. However we do it, the primary importance of the day needs to be marked and the colours of white and, perhaps best of all, gold will do this.

The use of white continues through the seven Sundays of the Easter Season as the Lectionary explores the growth of the early Church and the resurrection appearances of Jesus. At the end of this we have the Day of Pentecost – the traditional colour for which is red. Another approach would be to use the colours of flame. The rich symbolism of Pentecost – wind and fire, the Spirit and the proclamation of the Gospel – can be used in many ways. For instance, it has been suggested that the congregation be invited to come along on that Day wearing the flame colours – red, yellow and orange.

Imagination could well be the key to the use of liturgical colours throughout the Christian Year. Some of us may use them minimally or conventionally but others will find ways to use them dramatically and extensively. This would be particularly useful in the season following Trinity Sunday, which is the Sunday after Pentecost. The colour for the day itself is white and its theme an important doctrine which can be difficult to talk about but can easily be celebrated in signs and symbols.

John Meade Falkner wrote of the Sundays which follow Trinity Sunday:

> We have done with dogma and divinity,
> Easter and Whitsun past,
> The long, long Sundays after Trinity
> Are with us at last;
> The passionless Sundays after Trinity,
> Neither feast-day nor fast.
>
> Christmas comes with plenty,
> Lent spreads out its pall,
> But these are five and twenty,
> The longest Sundays of all;
> The placid Sundays after Trinity,
> Wheat-harvest, fruit-harvest, Fall.[2]

These are the ordinary Sundays of the year – which does not mean they are plain but simply that they have no special celebrations attached. The colour of the season is green, a colour of life and growth. This is helpful because these are the Sundays when the Lectionary explores the life and teaching of Jesus; the letter writers of the New Testament; and the stories of the Old Testament.

Traditionally the liturgical colours are used on pulpit falls, bible ribbons and a cloth or cover on the Communion Table. The minister may also wear a stole of the appropriate colour. Strictly speaking this should be confined to Communion services but, given the relative infrequency of these in our Church, there is no reason not to make standard practice. As has already been said, colours may be used in other ways to decorate the church and help people feel the movement of the Christian Year. Banners and hangings would be good examples of this.

---

[2] 'After Trinity' by John Meade Falkner.

Falkner caught a note of tedium in his poem, but also noted that there are other celebrations in this season. Harvest, All Saints-tide and Remembrance Sunday all come towards the end of it. In each appropriate colours can be used such as white for All Saints or red for Remembrance Sunday.

Throughout the year there will have been special celebrations of Holy Communion or Baptism. Traditionally the colours of the day do not change for these occasions since they are part of the ongoing life of the Church. Nevertheless, when these occasions are rarer than some might desire, it is perhaps appropriate to change to a celebratory colour when they occur. The Scottish tradition of decking out a building in white when Communion is celebrated is very impressive. However, when such events occur within a special season, especially Advent or Lent, retaining the colour of the season should be seriously considered to maintain the theme and the feel of the time.

The use and observance of the Christian Year is a pastoral tool, a witness to the fact that the Church marches to a different drum and a corrective to following a too well worn path. By coupling it with the use of colour and symbol, we can enrich the experience of worship and move nearer to achieving what the Shorter Catechism tells us is our 'chief end':

>  To glorify God and enjoy Him for ever.

# Music for Worship
## *Douglas Galbraith*

**Hymns and songs**

There are three kinds of congregational song. The staple, 'classic' hymn has twin roots. One reaches back to earliest Christian practice (the Epistles contain passages which quote or derive from words that were sung, e.g. Colossians 1:15-20)[1] and to the Latin hymns of the first millennium, such as 'Veni, Creator Spiritus'.[2] The other draws more immediately from the metricised[3] versions of the psalms which followed the Reformation. In the hands of such as Isaac Watts and Charles Wesley, and of those who have continued this tradition to the present day, these hymns have become the shapers of Christian witness. Solidly founded in Scripture,[4] they wrestle with the meaning of the faith against the backcloth of the life of their time. In their repeated use, congregations sing their way into knowledge and understanding, into spiritual experience, into the conduct required of a disciple of Christ.

A second kind of song is equally ancient, settings of key moments in an unfolding act of worship which allow the congregation to participate more fully. These may be texts of long standing, such as 'Lord, have mercy' or 'Holy, holy, holy', or songs and chants which accompany gathering or dismissal, listening for the Word of God or punctuating

---

[1] A version for singing today can be found in *Church Hymnary: Fourth Edition (CH4)*, 2005, at no. 453.
[2] See *CH4* no. 586.
[3] 'Measured' in that there was a regular number of syllables in each line, each verse identically fitting a given tune and facilitating congregational singing. See *With Heart and Hands and Voices*, a church music pamphlet from the Office for Worship and Doctrine, Church of Scotland, for further explanation: wordoc@cofscotland.org.uk, 0131 225 5722, ext.359.
[4] The extensive biblical indices in *CH4* bear witness to this.

spoken prayer, alleluias or doxologies (utterances of praise). The use of such 'short songs' is becoming increasingly popular in today's more openly participative style of worship and explains why the new *Church Hymnary (CH4)* provides no less than 75 examples.[5] Some of these are 'world church songs', bringing with them not only a more spontaneous singing style but an opportunity for sharing in the prayer and praise of Christian communities for whom living the faith may be difficult and even dangerous.[6]

A third genre is the praise and worship song, a result of (but not the sole example of) the search for ways of expressing worship through contemporary cultural forms. Stylistically they derive from a range of more popular music styles, current and recent, and typically would be accompanied by groups of instruments including percussion. The stronger rhythmic element and the accessible nature of their melodies make for instant appeal, and this is seen as advantageous for the drawing in of people not familiar with the traditional vocabulary of Christian life and worship. Another feature is that they are not tied to the musical score and require to be 'realized' in performance, thus calling on the improvisatory skills of the musician. Given their origins in performance-oriented music, they are not always easy for a congregation to sing and rely on a strong lead from a 'praise band'. Often criticised for their lack of musical quality, it is a fact of life that each new age produces far more ephemeral songs and texts than those of lasting value,[7] and discrimination is required to gauge what will be strong enough to support a witness and worship sufficiently robust for our day. Some texts are overtly biblical, but often without the 'tapestry of texts' and the working through of themes typical of classic hymns. Texts with an individualist bias need to be balanced with others which

---

[5] Nos 750-805.

[6] The Office for Worship and Doctrine pamphlet *Assist our Song* contains an extended section on the use of short songs.

[7] For example, only a smallish proportion of Victorian hymn tunes have survived to this day.

recognise the corporate nature of the worshipping community.

## Psalms

Although psalms are not distinct from the above categories - and all three of the above styles have set psalm texts - they deserve separate mention because of their particular history and use. For centuries the staple of Scottish worship, they were joined by hymns (officially, at any rate) only in the last quarter of the 19th century. Now the psalm 'survives' often only as the first singing in a service, a custom which can go against the content of a particular psalm. With the now widespread use of the lectionary, a psalm is provided for each week, its intention being to 'comment' on the Old Testament reading. It is not a fourth reading but a communal utterance, usually sung, and finding its appropriate place after the first reading. *CH4* has placed the psalms at the front of the book as a separate section[8] and has provided a wider range of settings and translations, sometimes more than one to a psalm. Ministers and organists will be interested in the opportunities not only afforded by the new metrical versions for bringing home the meaning of the psalm but by the variety of musical setting which sometimes enables the psalm to be used in the pre-metricated form of the original poetry. Chanting the psalms is not new in our tradition; there was a time (prior to 1900) when all three major pre-union Presbyterian denominations published versions of the psalter entirely set in chant form.

## Expanding the repertoire

Today, much enrichment is being offered by writers, composers and hymn book editors through music in different styles, which encourage greater participation, enjoyment and meaning for the singing congregation, as well as new texts which seek to embed the

---

[8] In *CH3*, they were placed throughout the book according to content, a feasible arrangement which reminds us that a psalm may find its place at any point in worship.

Gospel in the quite new situations which face us today. There is an obligation upon those who select hymns for worship to explore what is on offer, but there can be limits set by local attitudes or experience. The publication of *CH4* has been accompanied by the establishment of a network of precentors ready to visit congregations and introduce some of the new material, a scheme operated through the Church's Office for Worship and Doctrine.[9] The experience has been that, where an unfamiliar hymn might be greeted with reserve in the context of Sunday worship, an evening of new songs brought by an outside visitor has seldom been met with anything less than enthusiasm.

Increasing the repertoire is more than simply having more songs to sing but can have an effect on the congregation in terms of the health of its own life and witness; new ideas and directions may be opened up in the words sung while new (and some older, recovered) melodies and styles of music may lead to a deeper feeling of engagement in worship. The song of the Church has developed since the late 19th century through a succession of 'official' books, usually prepared with other Churches in the same 'family', or, in the case of *Common Ground*,[10] with the other Churches in Scotland. It was felt important to continue production of a denominational collection since the many independent publications now available tend to be market-led, lack an awareness of the Scottish context, and contain little Scottish writing.[11]

---

[9] See footnote 3 for contact details.

[10] Saint Andrew Press, 1998. This was also seen as a 'supplement' to the edition of the *Church Hymnary* then in use, and, in this role, succeeded *Songs of God's People*, still in use in many congregations.

[11] *CH4* contains the work of some 50 Scottish writers and composers, together with texts and tunes from both the Gaelic and Lowland traditions, as well as the psalms and paraphrases. The latter are a group of 67 metrical versions of passages of Scripture other than the psalms, the response of the General Assembly (finally in 1781) to the call for a wider repertoire and one which included New Testament themes.

## Choosing hymns

The choice of hymns for worship is a delicate and creative process that takes into account the place in the unfolding drama of the service, the themes which emerge from the readings, the point reached in the Christian Year, issues or events in the surrounding local or world community, and what the congregation is familiar with or might be encouraged to try. This is a skill which requires some honing on the part of the minister. In the first place, familiarity with the contents of the books or sources used is necessary, not least because what might make a hymn exactly right is not the familiar first line but, say, the second half of a later verse. This is no hardship, since in our tradition we have looked on the hymn book not merely as a tool for Sunday worship but a devotional book for people's own use, offering as it does insights into Scripture and into Christian life and prayer.

In partnership with the Church's musician(s), the minister will also be aware of the tunes, since a hymn consists of both text *and* melody, together creating a new form of expression. It is for this reason that the congregational edition contains the melodies. Reading music in what is called 'staff' is no more difficult than reading it in sol-fa, with which both choirs and congregations used to be familiar.[12] Resources such as *HymnQuest* are able to play melodies to assist those making choices.[13]

Those choosing hymns now have more assistance than ever before. Biblical indices are now becoming standard in hymn books, with *CH4* the most comprehensive so far. Reference to the passages used in the service often throws up many possibilities. Thematic indices

---

[12] An increasing number of school students are becoming familiar with staff notation today.

[13] Earlier issues of the Scottish church music quarterly *Different Voices* contain 'lessons' in reading music for those who do not yet have this skill. Back numbers are available from the Office for Worship and Doctrine (see footnote 3).

also help. Congregational or individual members of the Royal School of Church music receive the quarterly publication *Sunday by Sunday*, which not only lists suitable hymns but choral music and organ voluntaries as well. The Church of Scotland's own 'Starters for Sunday' feature on its website also makes suggestions for hymns to go with its commentaries and sermon ideas.

Reference has been made to the location of hymns in a service. Erik Routley commented that the right hymn at any point was the one which the congregation was on the edge of its seat waiting to sing. Such precision - a tall order, perhaps - depends not only on thematic relevance but what part of the service has been reached. Broadly, in most traditions, including our own, an act of worship will have four (or five) 'movements': the *gathering* of the people of God, the *listening* for the Word of God including preaching and reflection, the *response* to the Word - which will include self-offering and prayer for the world, and the *sending* of the people in mission, a brief but very significant part of worship. The Sacraments of Holy Communion or Baptism may also be part of the service. Hymns, psalms and songs help to shape and clothe this skeleton.

The *first hymn* is sung as on a threshold and helps to bring the worshippers into the presence of God. Most commonly it focuses on God in adoration and praise, 'big' in its statements and its tune. Or it may express delight in being in God's house and more quietly prepare the mind to recognise the presence of the One who promised to be where two or three have gathered together, helping create a feeling of unity among them. On special Sundays, it can strike the appropriate note for the day or season. At a time of sorrow or threat, it may express contrition, searching or longing - a time when an opening psalm may be particularly appropriate. In some congregations, a group of choruses, chants and canons fulfil the function of gathering and preparing the people for worship.

Following the first prayer, many Churches will have a first or children's address, which usually ends with a *children's hymn*. This may be one written specifically with children in mind or it may be one of the vivid hymns of the Church, with clear images and a telling tune, which children can appreciate and respond to as well as adults. There are also styles of music (participatory, using percussion, rhythmic - often from other cultures) which particularly engage children. In the new *Church Hymnary (CH4)*, a criterion was that such hymns should be capable of being sung by adults and children together.[14]

In conjunction with the *readings*, reference has already been made to the suitability of singing/speaking the psalm at this point, but there may also be a place for a hymn that celebrates Scripture (either directly or by retelling and reflecting on an incident from the Gospels) or seeks the guidance of the Holy Spirit before the sermon. In this section may also come the anthem, which is usually a setting of words from Scripture, or an alleluia or other 'short song' that expresses a waiting with expectation on the Word.

After *the sermon*, a hymn may enable an outburst of affirmation, of praise, take a credal form, or point forward to the worshippers' renewed concern for the reconciliation of all creation to God which will be expressed in the prayers of intercession. A *closing hymn* may express praise, dedication and commitment, encouragement, discipleship and service.

Many, citing the earliest Reformers' hopes, would wish that the 'four movement' shape outlined above might be five, with Holy Communion being a more frequent part. In terms of hymns and music, some of our traditions are not so venerable as often thought. Before 'Ye gates,

---

[14] The Office for Worship and Doctrine pamphlet *Assist our Song*, as well as discussing the shape of worship more fully, contains a section on children's hymns.

lift up your heads on high' sung to St George's, Edinburgh (Psalm 24:7-10), it was more common to sing Paraphrase 35 ('"Twas on that night') as the elements were brought in - although earlier still, before the tune named was written, Psalm 24 was apparently a frequent choice. This setting is a demanding one, depends on reasonable forces to fulfil its intention, and perhaps might be said to contribute to an invariably formal style of celebration. There are many other possibilities for surrounding the celebration with music (the current and previous Church Hymnaries greatly expanded the relevant sections), which allow for Communion to be celebrated in different ways and with different 'accents', depending on the setting and the participants. *CH4* also offers short songs and settings that potentially enhance the celebration. While it has been most common to have silence during the distribution of the elements, some congregations have experimented with tasteful organ music or with choral items (which could be hymns) at that point.

**The use of screens**
Those who advocate the projection of the words of hymns and songs legitimately argue that the attendant holding up of the heads greatly enhances the enthusiasm and the corporateness of the singing. Perhaps, however, the distinctions made at the outset between classic hymn and worship song need to be recalled. There it was suggested that the structure of these genres was different. The hymn is a continuous 'document' where there is a progression towards a climax, an 'argument' or spiritual reflection which has an outcome. It can help greatly to 'see where we are going' in such a structure, to be able to make connections between verses as we sing. 'Dependency on books' is not necessarily a bad thing when such books have a devotional purpose and are not just 'tools for worship'. On the other hand, the worship song is one that very often depends more on the immediacy of an inspired alliance between words and melody and is usually more 'episodic' in character. To project the words can thus be freeing.

### Announcing hymns

Those who print the words of hymns and songs on a service sheet (or project onto a screen) may be able to proceed without announcement. Thus a hymn is allowed to 'speak for itself' and the attention is immediately focused on what is to be sung. Where announcement is necessary, it is desirable to keep this to a minimum. The stereotypical 'let us sing to God's praise and glory in ...' and other predictable introductions can, with repetition, induce monotony and reduce expectation. Giving a number may be sufficient, but if a first line is necessary it should only be a first line and not a first verse. A hymn is a musical utterance and there is little point in reciting the words without the tune. On the other hand, on occasion, the point and relevance of a hymn can be assisted by a brief but well prepared introduction which underlines the significance of the words or the reason that this hymn has been chosen. For a psalm, the fact that it is a psalm, coming from a distinctive corpus of material, should be acknowledged in announcement or on service sheet, even if it is necessary also to give a hymn number.

### The place of other music

While we are increasingly becoming conscious of the congregation's musicianly role, there is at the same time no undervaluing of the special contribution of musicians who work at their gift and are able to offer more to worship. A choir may be able to sing an anthem or other music (for example as an introit at the beginning). This should not be seen as an 'item' and certainly not as a performance item, but music in which the congregation participates by listening and reflecting.[15] This is greatly helped if they can be told (e.g. in a service sheet) what the words set are. There may be other musical groupings which can enhance people's worship, ad hoc singing groups that explore

---

[15] The writer has heard of a congregation which, in living memory, used to stand while the anthem was sung.

and share new material, groups of instrumentalists or praise bands, and solo players whose contribution can focus one of the 'events' within worship.[16] The understanding of the choir as contributing to and enhancing worship is underlined by the number of settings in *CH4* which allow a choral group or 'cantor' and a congregation to combine in the same piece of music. The placing of the choir can also give the right or wrong signals (the latter, for example, when placed on a platform in a solid phalanx facing the congregation).

## Musicians

A lack of common vocabulary has often made it difficult for ministers and organists to communicate effectively. However, both share in the intention that worship will be full and inspiring and each holds a part of the jigsaw. Assumptions are often made about organists' attitudes to new material, when a more productive approach would be to ask their help in assessing the suitability of an item and consulting as to how it might be introduced or performed. Conversely, organists may assume that a minister will know nothing about music, when that minister, like other members of the human race, is naturally musical. Ways of collaboration will be different in each case but the result will strengthen the role of both in the choice of music for worship. Certain courtesies should be maintained, such as that of consultation and of ensuring that the organist or musicians know far enough in advance what the minister proposes or has chosen. The commonest complaint from 'beginner' organists is that they do not receive the hymns in time to practise and embarrass themselves and the congregation with their unpreparedness. For a minister to say that 'they are quite straightforward' may not meet the need to insert a functional pedal line.

---

[16] The Office for Worship and Doctrine pamphlet *Assist our Song* contains a discussion of the place of choral music.

Ministers may wish to encourage their musicians to consider taking part in one of the many opportunities for musicians to improve their skills, through the Scottish Churches Organist Training Scheme (SCOTS),[17] through the Royal School of Church Music (RSCM),[18] through the Royal College of Organists (RCO),[19] and through the quarterly magazine *Different Voices*.[20] Sometimes the problem is not so much relating to musicians as having any at all. Where there is no organist, it is often assumed that the nearest electronic equivalent is the answer, for example in the purchase of a digital hymn book or discs that reproduce accompaniments through a midi system, and in some situations this may be the best way forward.[21] Our traditions, however, are more varied than organ accompaniment and it may be that before making such expensive purchases we should look at the power of unaccompanied singing and the use of natural musicians in the parish, whether of voice or instrument. Further, reproducing the forces of a large parish church in a small country setting can sound incongruous.

**Copyright**

Today the copyright laws are being applied in a stricter way than before in the hope of protecting those whose ministry is the writing of material for Churches and those who publish them. It is often wrongly thought that copyright applies to a whole book but in fact copyright is held by each writer and composer. It is true that the publishers of some collections appear in lists covered by a licensing conglomerate (see below) but this applies to the 'imprint' of the book, the way the hymn

---

[17] Information through the Office for Worship and Doctrine (see footnote 3).
[18] In Scotland events and workshops are run (see www.rscmscotland.org). Nationally, there are distance learning courses in Sacred Music Studies through the University of Wales Bangor: mus006@bangor.ac.uk
[19] www.rco.org.uk
[20] See www.churchofscotland.org.uk
[21] Outlets like the Edinburgh Organ Studios can give information.

appears in that publication, and is relevant only when someone wishes to photocopy the page layout - permission for the words and/or tune having separately been sought. Some writers may be administered through a company (e.g. CopyCare), and it is to this that application is made. The necessary information is nowadays usually included on the relevant page of the hymn book.[22] Some congregations have found it is relatively easy to satisfy these requirements by taking out an inclusive Christian Copyright Licence which means that they can reproduce work by those composers and writers who have opted to place their work under that licence. This licence also covers the recording of copyright material, e.g. in making services available for the housebound.[23]

**What kind of Church?**
Questions about Church music are not simply about repertoire. What a congregation needs to sing is related to its understanding of itself and the pattern its discipleship is to take. Decisions made about its music are paralleled by decisions about the quality of its life and structures. 'Inclusive' music, for example, without the effort to include newcomers in other ways in the worship and life of the church, will not achieve much. How it treats its musicians is concomitant with how it looks upon and nurtures the giftedness of its members in all its variety. The music of the Church is not a decoration but an integral part of its life. Its health and the health of the congregation go hand in hand.

---

[22] In earlier editions of *CH4*, this was printed on the inside of the page vertically up the spine, and could often be missed.
[23] www.ccli.co.uk

# Our View of the Ministry Today[1]

## *A Stewart Todd*

The Council of this Society in assigning this task to me and suggesting this title had in mind that I should speak about the holy ministry of word and sacrament, that I should differentiate between this ministry and other ministries and that I should also refer to the controversial candidacies for the ministry which have been before the General Assembly this week.[2]

The **popular** view of the ministry is undoubtedly coloured by observations of a sociological nature and at the moment these observations are so sombre as quite to overshadow the theological and eschatological winsomeness of the minister's role. The sociologist looks at the minister of the Church of Scotland and he asks the question, 'Are the arrangements pertaining to this man's role in society functional or dysfunctional?' and at the moment the answer would seem to be that they are in many respects dysfunctional. There is first of all the marginality of the role. While ministers still retain some respect in society they no longer occupy a position of prominence or centrality in the social, cultural, intellectual, political or any other aspect of national life. Only in the area of ritual do the clergy retain a residual centrality for they are still required to solemnise and sanctify events in the national, civic, local and family life of the nation. For the rest the sociologist speaks of marginality and therefore dysfunction. This particular dysfunction is likely to be aggravated by the policy of our Church, which creates ever bigger parishes and makes a minister responsible for perhaps two, three

---

[1] This paper was read at the Annual Meeting of the Scottish Church Society, 25 May 1984 and published as an occasional paper.
[2] Both had been imprisoned for serious crimes.

or four congregations within a parish. The demands made upon the minister in regard to ordinary pastoral work and administration are then so great as to cocoon him in an ecclesial world cut off from the mainstream life of the community.

The sociologist will also make much of the fact that still today so many ministers share the middle-class culture of most of their members. This is supposed to be a terrible handicap and contributes to dysfunction.

Dysfunction is also said to be attributable to our traditional leadership role - clerical monopoly and so forth. The Church being in the sociologist's terms 'a voluntary associational organisation' professional leadership is increasingly questionable: leadership ought to emerge from the local membership. The minister's very professionalism is a disincentive to the growth of a congregation it is claimed: his mode of leadership is also inherently inflexible and impervious to social change and new conditions.

I do not think I am guilty of caricaturing the sociologist's view, which colours the popular view. And if any of the observations do seem too sophisticated for the average layman at least the widespread acceptance today of the fact that the minister's role is marginal will not be disputed. The amount of money which a role can command may be regarded as some indication of the significance society affords it. None of us is in any doubt that stipends have fallen far behind the salaries of other professions and seem unlikely to catch up for a very long tine.

In the popular view of the ministry today the minister probably does still however have a certain moral standing. People recognise that by and large (there are scandalous exceptions!) - by and large clergy do conform to the standards set out in 1 Timothy chapter 3. You remember how the passage goes, substituting 'minister' for 'bishop', 'Now a minister must be above reproach, married only once, temperate, sensible, dignified, hospitable, an apt teacher, no drunkard, not violent but gentle, not quarrelsome, and no lover of money. He must manage his own household well', and so on. The popular view, vaguely informed by that passage of Scripture, may well be therefore that a person with a criminal record cannot possibly become a minister and the Church must be crazy to risk making more disreputable the already battered image of the clergy by admitting not just one but two ex-criminals to the holy ministry. The information that six others with significant criminal records have sought to be accepted as candidates must serve only to increase the dismay and disillusionment. A gloomy picture of the ministry and I don't think it is a caricature!

The sociologist's view of the ministry which I have sketched does not only represent the popular view it also influences the view of many Church people and infuses much of the pragmatism that passes for Christian planning these days. One recognises details of the sociologist's picture in the contributions of many churchmen today to the discussion of ordination - the error of ministerial monopoly and the inappropriateness of professionalism in the voluntary associational organisation, as a congregation is described, are frequently dressed in theological attire and offered as logical deductions from the doctrine of the priesthood of all believers. Before you or I know where we are, we are quietly made more or less redundant, labelled enablers, the primary objective of which enabling seems to be to enable Tom and Dick to preach in your stead and Harry to celebrate Holy Communion as well. For thirty thousand pounds extra they will provide statistical evidence that by the end of the century this is how it is going to be in any case.

I turn then to speak of the **priesthood of all believers** or the ministry of the whole Church. There is one, unique priesthood, the priesthood of Jesus Christ. He is the true priest, he is the true minister. 'The son of man came not to be ministered unto but to minister'. ***Diakonethenai - diakonesai.*** The word or its Aramaic equivalent was in our Lord's vocabulary, it would appear, and as he used it, it was not the description of any circumscribed office but rather covered that far-ranging service, that unstinted dedication, that zealous commitment to the working out of God's plan of salvation which carried him from his baptism in the waters of Jordan through his life on earth and through a bitter baptism in blood to the bliss of resurrection and exaltation to the heavenly places. By baptism all Christians are incorporated into Christ and thereby involved in the royal priesthood of the whole Body of which he is the head. The priesthood of the whole body is not identical with the priesthood of Christ and is yet not to be separated from it: it is humble participation in the continuing ministry of the man in heaven, in his continuing ministry of love and intercession; the ministry of the whole people is also a prophetic, priestly, kingly ministry appropriate to the age of the Church. It is to perform this wide-ranging ministry to the Church and to the world that the whole body is enabled and empowered by the Spirit, through the means of grace. This is the priesthood of all believers in which we all share.

Within this far-ranging ministry there are charismata, gifts, and even if, in a moment, we find ourselves speaking of an ordering of these gifts and an ordaining of some 'gifted' to dispense the word and sacraments I would argue that all talk of ministerial monopoly and congregational passivity is wholly inappropriate and reveals a complete lack of understanding of the mystery of Christian worship. Minister and people assembled for worship are an ordered whole and the ordering is done in terms of that best of all Christian charismata, love. Such mutual ordering in love means that not all will be prophets, nor all teachers as Paul indicates in 1 Corinthians 12. Suppose we decide and tradition persuaded us that by and large and normally we have one preacher: if that preacher speaks the Word of God that is of God. But that word which requires to be preached because it is good news for a fallen world and which requires to be given rich content and imbued with all wisdom-that word also needs to be heard and if it is heard that also is of God and if by the grace of God those who have been hearers of the word also become doers of it, is this not cause for gratification rather than girning about monopolistic ministry? No doubt leadership monopolies are inappropriate in voluntary associational organisations but if the sociologist has got quite the wrong model for the Church, as indeed he has, if he is moreover unable to describe the nature of the Church in his own terms then the monopoly complaint is irrelevant.

Similarly in the Lord's Supper if the minister has a distinctive part to play in giving thanks to God, if in grateful, confessional anamnesis he is to be lyrical in prayer to the utmost of his ability, the people also have their part in Dialogue, in Sanctus, Benedictus, Hosannas, Lord's Prayer, Amen sufficient in spiritual eloquence surely, rich in eschatological overtones and if in the dispensing of elements one man gives in faith the whole action cries out for others to receive in faith. There is much more to the people's part in worship as we all know–but I digress.

If there are special charismata within the whole of the Church they are the gifts of Christ's love for his Church (Ephesians 4:10-16) and they are for the Church's sake and for the glory of God and they are exercised in and with and through Christ and with the people and with the saints, and if you and I honour these special charismata and guard them jealously from confusion it is in love for Christ and for his Church and in humble gratitude not in clerical arrogance. Also these charismata are not less significant just because sociologists find the ministry in this part of the world and in this particular age marginal.

It will be noted that in the important Pauline passages to which I have referred the ministry of the word is spoken of **not in terms of an office but in terms of a charisma** - a gift. That is, it seems to me, of the utmost importance. Whatever nature or personality the Church has, she has from Christ. The Church is the body of Christ, 'the fulness of him that filleth all in all'. The building up of the body by means of any of the ministries in the Church and not least by the ministry of word and sacrament is a dynamic process. Of course the ministry and other ministries within the Church take on an institutional character. Quoting Professor Schmaus in his *Katholische Dogmatik* Professor Tom Torrance describes orders in the Church as forming a 'scaffolding in space and time for the building up of the body of Christ as an habitation of God', and 'luminous signs'. But no more than a scaffolding! Hans Urs von Balthasar will not even allow the scaffolding metaphor. Such a conception of the Church, he writes:

> would in no way be transparent to Christ: this would, indeed, be the last kind of thing one could expect of Christ, who abolished the old ritualism and formalism (Epistle to the Hebrews, Epistle to the Romans). The institutional element in the Church is not absolute... it is relative to love, and the love of the Church, in turn, is not absolute, as if it ever reached perfection: rather, it consists of a steady progress towards an eschatological form which at present is in the process of becoming.[3]

He would have us think of the Church and of the ministry as a medium, as a system of relations. The servant of Christ cannot be identified with the powers conferred on him: he performs only a service and yet on the basis of this service, this office, this function, this charism another Christian or Christians can love the Lord purely and effectively.

---

[3] Von Balthasar, *The Glory of the Lord*, 559.

In this scenario it is, I believe, possible to place the ministry in its institutional character without apology and awkward candidacies for the ministry without embarrassment. The 'ethical lists' as they are called in Timothy, taken over from the secular sphere, are useful as guidelines and as a spelling out certain patterns of behaviour that are normally appropriate and certain that are normally inappropriate to a person who is going to be a minister but when you look at them they are arbitrary and unreliable. We clergy are sinners all: not many of us are fit for the cloth if you examine us too closely and how God called **us** is still for some of us, I am sure, a mystery of grace. No, the awkward 'candidacies for office' of Peter and Paul point me more authentically to Christ than do the ethical lists of the Pastoral Epistles.

In the case of Peter there is no question of ethical achievement, only an incomprehensible grace from the Lord. The conferral of office follows immediately after the anamnesis of Peter's guilt. With Christ there is not only no incompatibility between humiliation and elevation to office: there is even simultaneity. Or we look at Paul who was 'consenting unto' Stephen's murder, who is never quite taken seriously, who is feared, who is persecuted, criticised. Von Balthasar writes:

> Paul is the precise anatomy, we may even say the precise vivisection, not only of the Christian in general but of the hierarchical Christian who holds office in the Church, and this Pauline existence makes the form of the office-holder credible.[4]

Later in the same paragraph he writes magnificently:

> Here [meaning this model] the institution is what it should be - a means for the preservation and the intensification of the relationship between the Head and

---

[4] Ibid, 568.

the members, a channel (corresponding to God's Incarnation) through which the Head may work in the members in a living manner, that is to say, in a mode that is mediated through living persons and which yet remains pure, unmuddied and unobstructed by sinners.

Still with our disputed candidacies in mind it is constructive to note the form of the post-resurrection commissions to the disciples as they are given in the gospels. While in Matthew and Mark there is a more or less general commission to preach the Gospel, in Luke's gospel Jesus is represented as having first clarified their understanding of the Cross and Resurrection and then indicated that what they should preach in his name among all nations is repentance and remission of sins. John's gospel in the corresponding passage has unmistakeable echoes of Luke's emphasis. '[Jesus] saith unto them, *Receive ye the Holy Ghost, whosoever sins ye remit, they are remitted unto them: and whosoever sins ye retain they are retained*'. It would seem that Our Lord himself, or Luke, or the school of thought Luke represents is going so far as to say: here is the final reduction of the Gospel, this is what it is all about – Cross and Resurrection and repentance and forgiveness of sins – preach that to the world.

I say nothing of the particular circumstances of the cases that have been before the Assembly or of the particular means available for testing the sincerity of their repentance and of their call, but in the light of what I have said it seems to me that given repentance and forgiveness and a call there is no sin that can be an impediment to the grace of God and therefore to the conferring of charismata appropriate to the ministry.

I said a moment ago that in this context of grace there was no incompatibility between humiliation and elevation to office. I think it is proper to speak of elevation for all of us. My view of the ministry is that it is ennobling: it does render the servant distinctive; it accords the servant despite his imperfections enormous privilege; it does impart to the servant even a kind of beauty. In the Pauline lists of the charismata the Apostles come first: their position is unique. Thereafter within the Church however the ministry of the word, through evangelists, prophets and teachers, occupies the primary place: it is the ministry of the word that continues to beget and maintain the Church. That is still true today. Marginality doesn't make it less true only more challenging. This primacy and distinction does not accord us clergy a monopoly of right answers on all matters of national and international politics, defence policy, ecology and all the rest, it does accord us, (the essence of the word being good news, and having an eschatological dimension and there being so little good news around these days) – it does almost accord us a monopoly of optimism that with Christ in their lives politicians, nuclear scientists, ecologists and others will be able to find right answers or at least better answers. The optimism of the message is these days just about unique. No wonder I dare to speak of the beauty of our role! I merely mention in addition the great tradition of preaching down the Christian ages of which we are heirs; and a rich experience in our own land, the very memory of which is ennobling and immensely inspiring.

And then the Word proclaimed is fulfilled as Word in the sacramental ordinances given to the Church by Christ and we are to be accounted stewards of the mysteries of God. In the eucharist is the order par excellence for which we are ordained. In the eucharistic fellowship the whole interrelation of the members of the Body with the Head and with one another becomes clear. There is no higher ministry in the Church than the ministry of Word and Sacrament for that would mean that there was a higher authority than that of the Word and a more excellent means of grace than the sacraments. The celebrant at the Lord's Supper is therefore inestimably privileged. All the facets and overtones of the eucharist ask for the privilege to be safeguarded and honoured in love. And again one thinks of the experience of the Christian ages. The Lord said, 'do this in remembrance of me'; no command in the world has been obeyed as this one has been obeyed – every Sunday for nineteen hundred years.

I conclude therefore as Bill Cant concluded his fine paper to the Church Service Society last night. Article XVIII of the *Scots Confession* is entitled 'Of the notis, be the quhilk the trewe kirk is decernit fra the false' of which notes two, and these the first two, are preaching the Word and the right administration of the Sacraments of Christ Jesus. 'Wheresoever...thir former notes are seene', says the Confession, 'there, without all doubt, is the trew Kirk of Christ'.

# Order, Ordination and the Ministry of Word and Sacrament: The Tradition of The Church of Scotland[1]

## *John L McPake*

### Order in the Church of Scotland: The Tradition Expressed

The traditional understanding of Order in the Church of Scotland is given quintessential expression in *A Manual of Church Doctrine*.[2] As we shall see, the primary basis upon which this understanding is established is the view that the Church of Jesus Christ is brought into being 'from above'. Thus, it states:

> The Church of Jesus Christ is ordered from beyond its empirical being and existence by the power of the Word of God. By that word it is called and formed to be the community in the midst of the world which is given to share already in the new creation and its new order through the Communion of the Spirit.

Therefore, we note that the life and being of the Church - and its ordering – derives, not from historical accident, but, from the providence and will of God. Further, it may be suggested that our understanding of the nature of the Church's order flows from a prior comprehension of the fact that: 'There is one body and one Spirit... one Lord, one faith, one baptism, one God and Father of us all'. (Ephesians 4:5-6; 4:1*ff*.)

---

[1] This paper was read to the Scottish Church Society 2 November 1998 and published in the *Report*, 1998-1999.
[2] H J Wotherspoon and J M Kirkpatrick, *A Manual of Church Doctrine* (1920), revised 1960 and 1965 by T F Torrance and Ronald Selby Wright.

Thereafter, the *Manual* states that

> But this Church is sent by Christ to live its life and fulfil its mission in the midst of a divided and disordered world, both by proclaiming the Gospel of reconciliation and by living it out in a reconciled life. It belongs to the very nature of this Church to manifest the unity of the Triune God in the inner unity of its faith and life in the Spirit, but also to translate that unity into its outward behaviour within temporal and physical existence. It is in and through this reconciliation of its outward life in the world with its inner life in Christ that the Church fulfils its holy ministry in the Gospel.

Thus, we note that the nature of the Church is grounded in 'the unity of the Triune God' and is expressed through the translation of that reality into faith and practice in the midst of the world in which Christ calls the Church to fulfil its vocation. The *Manual* continues:

> Order is therefore the form that the life of the Church takes in its conformity to Christ through His Word and Spirit, and in obedient fulfilment of its mission of reconciliation. True order in the Church of Christ is order that points above and beyond its historical forms to the new divine order in Christ, and points beyond its present forms to the future manifestation of its order in the new creation. Actual order in the Church throughout its historical pilgrimage is thus ambivalent and provisional. It is order that derives from beyond itself and order that exercises a provisional service in history until Christ comes again. That is the doctrine that lay behind the reforming and reordering of the Church of Scotland at the Reformation.

Therefore, the Church is faced with the reality of having to translate its calling to a ministry of reconciliation into concrete and earthly forms. In so doing, the particular form in which that ministry is exercised at any particular moment in time will reflect the permanent, dialectical tension which the Church is called to live through. As such, the calling of the Church in this time of creative tension is an immense privilege and a humbling responsibility. It is also, by its very nature, a calling that is provisional. Thus, we are delivered from imagining that our particular historical forms are necessarily a template of the 'divine order in Christ'. Equally, we are given a freedom to reform our present ordering, to the extent that we believe it will more fully function as a sign of the 'divine order' that is to come.

Thus, the *Manual* may sum up and contend that:

> Church Order has therefore a permanent and stable element that derives directly from the Word and its ordering of the life of the Church through the ministry, but because this ordering of the life of the Church has to be carried out within the conditions of our erring and sinful world it cannot but partake of sin and error, it also has a variable element liable to error. Therefore it must ever be renewed and reformed by reference back to the creative Word of God.

The 'reference back to the creative Word' is the principle by which the Church of Scotland seeks to live, and the traditional understanding of church order and ministry within the Church seeks to reflect and embody this principle, which is typically expressed in the form: *ecclesia reformata et semper reformanda*. Equally, with respect to the practice of Ordination, the Church of Scotland affirms, in the words of the 'Preamble' to the service of Ordination, that:

> In this act of ordination the Church of Scotland, as part of the Holy Catholic or Universal Church worshipping One God, Father, Son, and Holy Spirit, affirms anew its belief in the Gospel of the sovereign grace and love of God.

Thus, Ordination, understood as an expression of one element within the Order of the Church's life, is fundamentally a 'catholic' action that affirms our participation in the Church Universal that lives only in and through the sovereign grace and love of God.

Therefore, we affirm that the theological basis upon which the Church of Scotland is understood as being established is the view that the Church of Jesus Christ is, by its very nature, brought into being 'from above'. Further, we note that the Church is conscious of the need to translate its calling into concrete and earthly forms. With the latter concern in mind, let us now turn to a review of the principal sources upon which the Church of Scotland has sought to establish its understanding of Ordination and the ministry of Word and Sacrament. Thus, let us review the principal historical documents which establish and embody that understanding: the *Forme of Prayers* (1556), *The First Book of Discipline* (1560), *The Second Book of Discipline* (1578) and *The Form of Presbyterial Church-Government* (1645). Thereafter, we shall seek to set that tradition within its contemporary context.

## The *Forme of Prayers* (1556) and *The First Book of Discipline* (1560)

*The First Book of Discipline* reflects the position of the early Scottish Reformers, and the influence of John Knox is undoubtedly present in the conception of ministry that is exhibited here. In formulating their understanding of what constituted the 'Lawfull Election' of a minister the early Scottish Reformers rejected the doctrine of Ordination as understood and practised within the Roman Catholic Church, and the *Book* eschews any reference to 'Ordination', such that the word is not used with respect to the admission of a 'candidate' to a charge. The purpose of the *Book*'s rejection of the word and doctrine was to exclude any notion of Ordination as a sacrament, and to nullify the attendant superstitions that were judged to have attached themselves to the previous practice. Thus, while the *Book* explicitly acknowledges that 'the Apostles used imposition of hands' (that is, the outward form of the act of Ordination), it judges that this particular ceremony was not necessary in character. In so doing, the *Book* is consonant with the *Forme of Prayers* used by Knox at Geneva from 1556-1559 and subsequently in the reformed Church of Scotland, and in this Knox is following Calvin's Genevan usage of 1541.

It has been contended by T F Torrance that Knox actually intended to retain the substance of the doctrine of Ordination, while not reproducing the outward form as established within the Roman Catholic Church. The Panel on Doctrine of the Church of Scotland, in their report of 1963, (and then reaffirmed in 1965) has offered support for Torrance's interpretation and stated that: 'Though the First Book of Discipline omitted reference to the laying on of hands there is no reason for supposing that the practice was departed from.' However, in their report of 2000, the Panel rejected this interpretation, and acknowledged that, in truth, there had been a breach in the practice of Ordination at the time of the Reformation in Scotland. The latter position seems to offer the best reading of an admittedly confusing situation, and it is better to interpret Knox and the early Scottish Reformers on their own terms rather than offering a reinterpretation of their intention for the sake of imposing uniformity and continuity. Therefore, it may be said that:

> The Scottish Reformers saw themselves as making a clean break with medieval understandings of ministry and ordination.

In stating the above, we should not thereby think that *The First Book of Discipline* embodies a relative lack of concern, with respect to the ordering of the ministry of the Church. On the contrary, the *Book* stresses that:

> In a Church reformed, or tending to reformation, none ought to presume either to preach, either yet to minister the sacraments till that orderly they be called to the same. Ordinarie Vocation consisteth in Election, Examination and Admission.

Thus, in the absence of any stress upon this element of 'Lawfull Election' within the Roman Catholic tradition, the *Book* emphasises that: 'It appertaineth to the people and to every severall Congregation to elect their Minister'. Thereafter, the 'man' is to 'be examined as well in life and manners, as in doctrine and knowledge'. In the course of the examination, the prospective minister 'must give declaration of their gifts, utterance and knowledge by interpreting some place of Scripture to be appointed', and give an acceptable confession of their faith.

In turning to the 'Admission of Ministers', the *Book* affirms again that this 'must consist in consent of the people, and Church whereto they shall be appointed, and approbation of the learned Ministers appointed for their examination'. As to the particular ceremonies that may be thought of as integral to the act of admission, the *Book* makes clear that:

> Other ceremonie than the publick approbation of the people, and declaration of the chief minister, that the person there presented is appointed to serve the Church, we cannot approve, for albeit the Apostles used imposition of hands, yet seeing the miracle is ceased, the using of the ceremonie we judge not necessarie.

In suggesting that the Apostles' practice of 'imposition of hands' was a temporary and expedient measure, the *Book* indicates its belief that the 'imposition of hands' was linked to a particular and distinct dispensation of grace, and, given that this dispensation is complete, the practice is unnecessary. In so suggesting, the *Book* is consonant with Calvin, when he writes:

> If this ministry which the apostles then carried out still remained in the church, the laying on of hands would also have to be kept. But since that grace has ceased to be given, what purpose does the laying on of hands serve?... [T]hose miraculous powers and manifest workings, which were dispensed by the laying on of hands, have ceased; and they have rightly lasted only for a time.

Thus, *The First Book of Discipline* takes our understanding of Ordination in a direction that is radically different from that which it has followed in its subsequent development within the Church of Scotland. This impression is confirmed by J K Cameron's commentary on the *Book* when he writes, with respect to the admission of a minister, that:

> Two points are regarded as essential in this service of admission, namely, the public approbation of the people and the declaration of the 'chief minister' (by which, in all probability, was understood the minister who was presiding at the service) that the minister presented is appointed to that charge. The laying on of hands is stated to be unnecessary.

Therefore, we note the essential elements in our tradition, embodied in the *Forme of Prayers* and *The First Book of Discipline*, which have been retained throughout the subsequent development of that tradition and we ought not to lose sight of the significance of this. Equally, we note the element of our tradition, as it has subsequently developed, that is here declared to be unnecessary.

## *The Second Book of Discipline* (1578)

In turning to *The Second Book of Discipline*, we see a development in the Church's doctrine and practice that reflects a certain continuity, and a certain discontinuity, with that of *The First Book of Discipline* of 1560. The continuity may be found in the fact that it affirms that the first element of the 'ordinarie and outward calling' to any office of the Kirk is 'electioun'. The discontinuity is found in the affirmation that the second part is 'ordinatioun' (The particular and specific sense in which *The Second Book of Discipline* understands this term will be clarified hereafter). Indeed, it may be said that *The Second Book of Discipline* establishes the basis of the subsequent development of the doctrine and practice of Ordination within the Church of Scotland. In saying this, it should be noted that the General Assembly of 1566 had ratified the *Second Helvetic Confession*, containing as it did an explicit affirmation of the legitimacy of the practice of Ordination (18:4, 8), and had offered no reservations on the *Confession* in respect of this matter. The significance of the ratification of the *Confession* is debatable and whilst it is true to say that, nominally speaking, a particular doctrinal position was approved, it is clearly not the case that the *Forme of Prayers* and *The First Book of Discipline* were overturned by this ratification. Alongside this, we do note that there is some evidence to suggest that the practice of the 'imposition of hands' continued within the reformed Church of Scotland after 1560, notwithstanding the strictures of *The First Book of Discipline*.

In stating the above, and setting out the teaching of *The Second Book of Discipline*, we ought to be clear that the practical impact of this *Book* was in no sense immediate. The *Book* failed to secure the approval of the Scottish Parliament in 1578 and was subsequently 'engrossed into the proceedings of the General Assembly in April 1581' before being affirmed by an Act of Assembly in 1590. This was re-affirmed in 1591 before 'parliamentary approval' was obtained in 1592. The establishing of episcopal government thereafter within the Church of Scotland nullified the impact of the *Book*, whose 'real influence' upon the practice of the Church was found only after the cessation of episcopacy in 1638. Equally, we may infer from this that *The First Book of Discipline* continued to influence the practice of the Church for a considerable time after 1578. In all of this, we may further infer that there was a certain fluidity in the practice of the Church of Scotland.

What did *The Second Book of Discipline* intend by the use of the term 'Ordinatioun'? J Kirk suggests that:

> In defining procedures for admitting candidates to ecclesiastical office, the third chapter of the book strongly emphasized the concept of vocation or divine

calling, an idea deeply rooted in renaissance and reformation thought and not confined to a calling to the ministry. Each individual as a member of society had a variety of functions to perform to which he had been called by God and through which he could serve both his creator and his community.

That is, the use of 'ordination' by *The Second Book of Discipline* must be understood within a context in which every person is seen as called to fulfil a vocation within an ordered and orderly society. Thus,' Vocatioun or calling is commoun to all that sould bear office within the kirk'. The *Book* distinguishes between two callings. On the one hand, there is the extraordinary calling such as came to prophets and apostles, which 'in kirkis establishid and weill reformit hes na place'. On the other hand:

> The uther calling is ordinar quhilk, besyd the calling of God and inward testimony of guid conscience, hes the lauchfull approbatioun and outward jugement of men according to Goddis word and ordour establischid in his kirk.

Both of these callings, though distinct, are outward callings, but as noted there is also 'the inward testimony of guid conscience', and the *Book* affirms that:

> Nane aucht to presume to entir in ony office ecclesiasticall without he have this good testimony of conscience befoir God wha onlie knawis the hartis of men.

This distinction between the outward calling and 'the inward testimony' echoes Calvin's distinction when he writes:

> I am speaking of the outward and solemn call which has to do with the public order of the church. I pass over that secret call, of which each minister is conscious before God, and which does not have the church as witness. But there is the good witness of our heart that we receive the proffered office not with ambition or avarice, not with any other selfish desire, but with a sincere fear of God and a desire to build up the Church. That is indeed necessary for each one of us (as I have said) if we would have our ministry approved by God.

As stated above, *The Second Book of Discipline* stands, in essence, in continuity with *The First Book of Discipline*, in respect of Election. Equally, it is in respect of Ordination that an essential discontinuity is to be found Thus, *The Second Book of Discipline* states that:

> Ordinatioun is the separatioun and sanctifeing of the persone appointit of God and his kirk eftir he be weill tryit and fund qualifeit... The ceremonyis of ordinatioun ar fasting and earnest prayer, and the imposition of hands of the elderschippe.

Thus, we note that there are three elements integral to the act of Ordination: 1) Fasting, 2) Prayer, and 3) The imposition of hands. In respect of 3), we note that the power to ordain is ascribed to the 'elderschippe', which J Kirk takes to be a reference to the 'presbytery' as a whole. Further, he amplifies his understanding of what is intended, when he suggests that: 'By 'eldership' is understood the assembly of ministers, doctors and elders from several contiguous congregations'. This is consonant with the *Book*'s affirmation that the power to elect lies with 'this kind of assemblie' constituted as it is by the pastors and elders.

What then is the theology that informs the practice of Ordination in *The Second Book of Discipline*? The *First Book of Discipline* rejected the term 'Ordination' and the 'imposition of hands', and did so to avoid any suggestion of a sacramental understanding. However, in its approbation of the term 'Ordination' and 'the imposition of hands', it should not be thought that *The Second Book of Discipline* sought to reinstate such an understanding. We may interpret 'the imposition of hands not as an act but as a sign of ordination'. The 'imposition' is thus an element integral to the 'act', with the 'act' referring to the whole action whereby a vocation, or calling, is brought to fruition, and as the complement to the process of 'Election'. Further, we might amplify this interpretation and suggest that 'the imposition of hands' is the 'sign' that confirms the 'spiritual grace' given to the candidate for the ministry. That is, the 'sign' confirms that which God has given, rather than the means whereby the 'spiritual grace' is conferred. Thus, Ordination is an action of the Church in response to the grace of God that is given.

## *The Form of Presbyterial Church-Government* (1645)

*The Form of Presbyterial Church-Government* gives expression to the ecclesiology of the Westminster Assembly and states the doctrine of Ordination in what is essentially a thesis form, with only a limited interlinking commentary, in a brief and summary manner. Thus, Ordination is defined as 'the solemn setting apart of a person to some publick church office' following a 'lawful calling', and is to be regarded as a perpetual feature of the life of the Church. The sign by which Ordination is enacted is as follows:

> Every minister of the word is to be ordained by imposition of hands, and prayer, with fasting, by those preaching presbyters to whom it doth belong.

Thus, we note that the *Form*, in large measure, reproduces the teaching of *The First Book of Discipline* and *The Second Book of Discipline*, with respect to 'lawful calling'. Equally, we note that it reproduces the teaching of *The Second Book of Discipline* regarding the latter's contention that: 'The ceremonyis of ordinatioun ar tasting and earnest prayer, and the imposition of hands of the elderschippe.'

Further, the *Form* states that 'such as are to be ordained ministers, be designed to some particular church, or other ministerial charge'. Thus, the purpose of the act of Ordination is to enable the exercise of ministry in a particular sphere.

'Ordination is the act of a presbytery', such that: 'The power of ordering the whole work of ordination is in the whole presbytery', and no single congregation can 'assume to itself... sole power in ordination'.

Therefore, with respect to the agents of Ordination, the *Form* specifies that they are 'those preaching presbyters to whom it doth belong', with Ordination being understood as 'the act of a presbytery'. In so specifying, the *Form* may be said to enunciate a particular 'doctrine of succession', which is further affirmed by an Act of the General Assembly of 1698 that states:

> The Church of Scotland allows no power in the people, but only in the Pastors of the Church, to appoint or ordain Church officers.

The theology and ecclesiology of the *Form* are expressed with clarity and succinctness in the following:

> The Church of Scotland holds that the authority of its preaching presbyters (ministers) is drawn from the blessing of Jesus Christ, not from an election by the people. Thus, ordination is to the holy ministry, and involves both a spiritual part (consecration) and a legal part (of commissioning and answerability to authority). Ultimately this is understood as a biblical doctrine. Ordination is the act of a presbytery. A presbytery includes representative elders, and these act with the minister in the legal process. In the ordination itself, the elders do not act Ordination is conferred by the presbyters of the court, acting on a resolution of the court as a whole. Thus the 'magisterial power to ordain' is given to the presbytery, and the 'ministerial (or executive) power' is given to regularly associated preaching presbyters. Such presbyters must be 'orderly associated' as the ministerial part of a regular court (a presbytery). Individual presbyters cannot ordain, nor may they voluntarily associate themselves to ordain. Behind them there must be the authority of the Church as a whole.

The right of ministers to act as the agents of Ordination has been zealously guarded since the inception of the Reformation in Scotland, although J L Ainslie notes the suggestion that George Gillespie, one of the Scottish Commissioners at the Westminster Assembly, 'had favoured elders having their part'. In truth, it cannot be said that the expression 'those preaching presbyters to whom it doth belong' is a particularly happy one. It tends to suggest that that which is conferred is in the possession of the 'preaching presbyters', in virtue of the fact that they *are* 'preaching presbyters'. An expression emphasising that that which is conferred is the gift of Christ and that it is His possession, entrusted to the ministry as stewards who are always dependent upon the grace of Christ, would surely have been better. Equally, a form of expression emphasising the act of Christ in Ordination would have complemented this.

## The Tradition of the Church of Scotland in its Contemporary Context: 'Criteria for Ordained Ministries'

From 1960-2005 the Panel on Doctrine served the General Assembly of the Church of Scotland as the principal body within which doctrinal reflection took place. From its very inception, and throughout its history, the doctrine of Ordination was a matter of perennial concern to the Panel, as evidenced in the Reports to the General Assembly of 1960, 1961, 1963, 1964, 1965, 1967, 1976, 1977, 1985, 1988, 1989, 2000 and 2001, amongst others. Indeed, it might be said that no issue exercised the attentions of the Panel more fully than that of Ordination. In large measure, the Reports of the Panel maintained the tradition of the Church as stated above. However, the recurrent calls to return to the doctrine of Ordination were undoubtedly indicative of a growing challenge to that tradition and that is most fully evidenced in the most recent Panel on Doctrine Reports.

Thus, the Report of 2000 observes:

> It should perhaps be no great surprise then that these issues are back on the Panel's agenda. This suggests strongly that ministry and its inauguration have been important and problematic issues for the Church for some time. It is hard to resist the suspicion that established views of the Church and its ministry are increasingly being found wanting... There is a popular perception that the Church's present structures of ministry are inflexible, idiosyncratic, and in some respects out of date.

In the face of this 'popular perception', the Panel sought to establish particular criteria for identifying ordained ministries, and suggested that:

> 1. Ordained ministries should be those which are concerned not just for one part of the Church's life and activity, but for the Church as such, for its character as the Church. They are ministries whose concern is to keep the Church faithful to its nature and calling.

In so doing, we note that the Panel is speaking of the variety of 'ordained ministries' and not exclusively of the ministry of Word and Sacrament. Thus, the Panel sought to identify the significance of the 'ordained ministries' within the context of the Church, in terms of their contributing to the maintenance of the very integrity of the Church. This is further developed when the Panel states that:

> 2. The fact that such ministries are concerned with the Church's fidelity to its nature and calling means that they are answerable to the Church - the whole Church. They are therefore understood to be ministries of Christ's Church, the Church Catholic, not simply the local Church... this does not mean that when the Church of Scotland ordains it presumes that the ordained person is authorised to conduct his/her ministry outside its discipline; nor does it imply unlimited authorisation to exercise a ministry within the Church of Scotland. It is still for the Church to determine the sphere in which the ministry operates, with a concern for order.

At this point, the Panel offers a helpful corrective against any tendency to view the ministry of the Church exclusively in terms of the 'local'. Of course, there can be no 'Church Catholic' apart from the local. Indeed, the 'Church Catholic' is to be understood as embodied in particular, worshipping communities. Nevertheless, the Panel's perspective reminds us that the 'ordained ministries' are the ministries of 'the whole Church', and not simply the functionary activities of parochial gatherings whose relatedness to one another is not perceived as fundamental to the well-being of the One Body. Thus, the Panel affirms that:

> 3. Such ministries, being answerable to the wider Church, are recognised and authorised by the wider Church. Ordination is therefore consequent upon the testing of vocation by the wider Church.

Finally, the Panel contends for the 'enduring' nature of the 'ordained ministries', and reminds us that the Church throughout its history has been nurtured by the exercise of those ministries. This is not to be understood as merely accidental. Rather, it is providential and, once more, concerned 'to keep the Church faithful to its nature and calling'.

> 4. Since the Church is one throughout history, and not simply throughout the world, this also implies that ordained ministries are enduring, and not temporary expedients. This does not mean that a particular ministry must be exercised in exactly the same manner eternally, nor that ordained ministries do not adapt to changing circumstances. They can and must be flexible in their methods and forms, since the Church lives in history. But an ordained ministry will be concerned with the Church's fidelity to its nature and calling, and these do not change. Equally it recognises that *persons* are called to ministry, and a person's character and personal integrity are presumed to endure through time.

The ministry of Word and Sacrament, though not to the exclusion of other ministries, is most surely concerned with securing 'the Church's fidelity to its nature and calling', and any undermining of the significance of that ministry tends towards the undermining of that very 'fidelity' which is the concern of the whole Church. That is not to say that the tradition of the Church of Scotland has bequeathed to the contemporary Church an inflexible and unvarying pattern for the ministry of Word and Sacrament which must be unthinkingly replicated irrespective of context Rather, the tradition seeks to embody and transmit to successive generations that which is perceived to be integral to maintaining our fidelity to the calling of Jesus Christ

## The Tradition of the Church of Scotland in its Contemporary Context: The Royal Priesthood

A charge made against the Church from time to time is that it is clerically dominated, and that there is an undue emphasis placed on the ordained, to the neglect of those who are not ordained. Indeed, our focus so far might seem to lend credence to that charge. However, while our focus is, by choice, a narrow one, that should not lead to the conclusion that it is an exclusive one. Thus, we must consciously place our reflections on Ordination and the ministry of Word and Sacrament within the wider context of the Order of the whole Church of Jesus Christ. What then is the appropriate response to the charge?

Let me suggest that we find an appropriate context within the doctrine of the Royal Priesthood. I consciously choose this form of expression, as against that of the doctrine of the priesthood of all believers', because, in truth, the latter receives little formal endorsement within classical Reformed theology. Thus, G D Badcock notes 'that in the whole of Calvin's constructive treatment of the theology of ministry, there is no substantive discussion of the priesthood of all believers'. Indeed, he goes further and suggests 'that the doctrine of the common priesthood is actually foreign to Calvin's approach'. How then do we understand the doctrine of the Royal Priesthood? Calvin writes:

> [Christ] once for all offered a sacrifice of eternal expiation and reconciliation; now, having also entered the sanctuary of heaven, he intercedes for us. In him we are all priests, but to offer praises and thanksgiving, in short, to offer ourselves and ours to God... From this office of sacrificing, [that is, 'offering a sacrifice

> of praise'] all Christians are called a royal priesthood, because through Christ we offer that sacrifice of praise to God of which the apostle speaks: 'the fruit of lips confessing his name'. And we do not appear with our gifts before God without an intercessor. The Mediator interceding for us is Christ, by whom we offer ourselves and what is ours to the Father. He... has entered the heavenly sanctuary and opens a way for us to enter. He is the altar upon which we lay our gifts, that whatever we venture to do, we may undertake in him. He it is, I say, that has made us a kingdom and priests unto the Father.

Thus, we see Calvin locating the foundation of the doctrine of the Royal Priesthood in the act of worship offered up by Christ Himself. This is the primary act that constitutes the Royal Priesthood, and is the source from which there is derived the understanding of ourselves as members of the corporate reality which is the Royal Priesthood. This primary act comes prior to the secondary and derivative 'priesthood' that is the common inheritance of all Christians, and this doctrine finds endorsement in Scripture; for example, in Exodus 19:6, Deuteronomy 7:6, Isaiah 61:6, 1 Peter 2:4ff, Revelation 1:5, 5:10, 20:6.

What then of the distinction between the 'clergy' and the 'laity'? Calvin stresses that; 'Peter calls the whole church "the clergy," that is, the inheritance of the Lord [1 Peter 5:3].', and in so doing he signifies that all Christians are called to share in the inheritance of the Christ. Further, he regrets that the term 'clergy' has been applied to a particular order of ministry within the Church rather than the ministry of the whole Church. Thereafter, he suggests that the distinction between the 'clergy' and the 'laity' has arisen 'from error or at least from a wrong attitude'. Thus, we may suggest that the 'clergy' is, in fact, constituted by all who share in 'the inheritance' that Christ prepares and offers, and that it is not a term of exclusion or division. Equally, we may contend that all Christians are called to their share (*clerus*) of the inheritance not as individuals, but as a community whose Head is Christ.

At this point the *Second Helvetic Confession* offers a treatment of the issue that, I would suggest, complements Calvin's approach. The *Confession* states:

> The apostles of Christ do term all those who believe in Christ 'priests'; not in regard to their ministry, but because that all the faithful, being made kings and priests, may, through Christ, offer spiritual sacrifices unto God-..The ministry, then, and the priesthood are things far different one from the other. For the priesthood, as we said even now, is common to all Christians; not so the ministry... for this purpose are the ministers called - namely, to preach the gospel of Christ unto the faithful, and to administer the sacraments.

Thus, the doctrine of the Royal Priesthood, and the sense in which each Christian may be termed a 'priest', does not result in a tension between 'clergy' and 'laity'. Rather, it offers the possibility of seeing each gift of Christ to the Church in mutually complementary terms, with one of those gifts being the ministry of Word and Sacrament.

A feature of discussion within the Church is the interpretation frequently attached to the doctrine of 'the priesthood of all believers', where it is understood as expressing the view that, in principle, *every* Christian is capable of fulfilling any role or ministry within the Church. Thus, the ordained minister of Word and Sacrament does not do anything that, in principle, could not be done by some other member of the Church. I would suggest that the result of this is that the ministry of Word and Sacrament is undermined, and that the said ministers are denied 'their particular identity and 'share' in the priestly work of Christ which, by the grace of God, is their distinctive calling, and to which they are ordained'. Equally, the emphasis in discussion on the 'laity', as against the 'clergy', tends towards the diminishing of the richness of Christ's gifting, as if the promotion of one over the other would somehow elevate the people of God as a whole. This is an unhelpful approach that is to be resisted.

Therefore, as against the tendency of some discussions, I would contend that the doctrine of the Royal Priesthood points to 'the rich variety of complementary gifts' that Christ offers to the Church, and affirm that among this 'rich variety' there 'is to be found the ministry of Word and Sacrament'. This gift is not offered and received to the exclusion of any other gift, nor to the diminishing of any gift whose sign is not Ordination. Rather, in its place and as one gift among others, it may contribute to the mutual enriching of all. When we consciously place our reflections on Ordination and the ministry of Word and Sacrament within this context, there is no diminishing of the Order of the whole Church of Jesus Christ. Instead, there is the renewed affirmation of the place of Christ and the response of praise from those whose shared privilege it is to be numbered as members of the Royal Priesthood.

# The Ministry of the Eldership

*from the Panel on Doctrine Report to the General Assembly, 1989*[1]

*As each has received a gift, employ it for one another, as good stewards of God's varied grace*. 1 Peter 4:10

The difficulties we have already noted in relating New Testament patterns to any specific picture of the ministry of word and sacrament are even greater when we turn to the office of the elder - a distinctive feature of Reformed Church government. It was an office that evolved in different ways in different national contexts. Calvin's elders were different from both those of Oecolampadius and of Bucer, and Knox's were to develop a different role from Calvin's. Common to all the Reformers though was a deep concern for discipline that would safeguard the Church from the abuses of the Middle Ages, and a feeling that something precious had been lost from the life of the Church when authority had been placed more and more in the hands of the clergy. In Scotland today the eldership is often assumed to have developed from the 'presbyters' or 'elders' mentioned in New Testament Epistles – 1 Timothy 4:14, 5:17, Titus 1:5, James 5:14 etc—but this is almost certainly an over-simplification.

During the Reformation there had been extensive research into the history and life of the early Church, and evidence had been found for the existence in some North African churches of *seniores plebis* - lay councillors. Originally civil functionaries responsible for public and moral order, with the spread of Christianity these *seniores* had become associated with bishops, presbyters and deacons in superintending the

---

[1] This report was written while the late Douglas M Murray was convener Dr A Stewart Todd vice-convener, and David M Beckett Secretary.

mores of the people. There is no record of these *seniores* or elders ever being called 'presbyters', but the Reformers found biblical evidence for the office in the 'rulers' of Romans 12:8 and the 'governments' of 1 Corinthians 12:28. Some claimed to find it also in 1 Timothy 5:17, a verse which came later to have a central place in most discussion of the eldership in Scotland: *Let the elders who rule well be considered worthy of double honour, especially those who labour in preaching and teaching* (NEB *Elders who do well as leaders should be reckoned worthy of a double stipend*). Calvin saw elders as an important way by which the Church might exercise its spiritual jurisdiction. His view was that discipline rested with the clergy and the elders, 'provided the elders do not do it by themselves alone, but with the knowledge and approval of the Church; in this way the multitude of the people does not decide the action but observes as witness and guardian so that nothing may be done according to the whim of a few'. (*Institutes* IV, xii, 7). Wishart in Scotland had not proposed any such office, but there is evidence that some elders and deacons were appointed in the 'privy kirks' which developed before the Reformation in several towns.

*The First Book of Discipline* (1560), drawn up in some haste to meet the immediate needs of the Reformed Kirk, conceived of elders as short-term office-bearers providing corporate control of the Church - a concept referred to for convenience by many historians as the 'lay theory' of eldership. Knox's plan was that elders were to be elected annually by congregations and charged particularly with the maintenance of discipline, their function being to admonish and correct the members, without respect of persons, including the minister. Early General Assemblies, however, made no provision for the attendance of elders as such: lay representation was provided by the commissioners of the burghs, shires and universities. *The Second Book of Discipline* (1581) brought a substantial change, defining the eldership as a scriptural order of ministry, along with doctor, pastor and deacon. Elders are to be appointed for life, and ordained, although there is specific provision for them to relinquish their Church duties 'for a time'. They are envisaged as 'ecclesiastical persons' entitled to financial recompense for their services, providing a large part of the pastoral care in the parish and leading the people in response to the Word - 'As the pastors and doctors should be diligent in teaching and sowing the seed of the Word, so the elders should be careful in seeking the fruit of the same in the people.' In fact the Church was not able to afford payments to elders. Not every parish might produce sufficient men of the necessary calibre, and in country districts three or four congregations would share a common eldership. Elders were now regarded as being the 'presbyters' of the New Testament. In practice annual elections to the Kirk Session continued in many places and the ordination of elders remained the exception rather than the rule until the late 17th century.

Both Books of Discipline allowed for the office of deacon, whose main function was to organise poor relief within the parish. It was not, however, confined to that, and there was much confusion over the respective duties of elders and deacons. Deacons were sometimes looked on as assistant elders and they shared in the general work of Kirk Sessions, including the maintenance of discipline, although practice varied from place to place as to whether they were entitled to a vote. Visiting was regarded as a significant part of the deacon's duties, and in many parishes there was a deacon assigned to each elder's district. In some areas elders were specifically set apart to undertake the role of deacon too.

The 'presbyter' theory gained ground over Knox's 'lay' functionaries in the first half of the 17th century. Interference by the civil government in the affairs of the Kirk made it increasingly desirable that Church officials should be seen to have authority in matters spiritual. At the Westminster Assembly (1643-47) the Scots argued that the nature of the eldership was clearly set out in the scriptures, but their arguments were not accepted in entirety by English Independents. The Westminster divines arrived at a compromise: elders were 'warranted' but not 'prescribed' by scripture. 1 Timothy 5:17 was omitted from their proof-texts.

Following the Westminster Assembly, confusion continued to surround the eldership, the 'lay' theory and the 'presbyter' theory each being held by different sections of the Reformed Church. During the 18th and 19th centuries views of the eldership were influenced both by the growth of the secular state and by divisions within the Church. The decline of the Kirk Session's disciplinary activity, and the increasing involvement of the civil government in welfare and education - which had long been regarded as within the Church's province - led to a rather diminished role for elders within the Established Church. Secession ecclesiology, however, gave rise to an increasing association of ministers and elders in one office, the minister being referred to as the 'teaching elder' and the elder as the 'ruling elder'. A number of erudite studies were written in the 19th century, attempting to deal with the confusion. Scholarly United Presbyterians such as David King of Glasgow argued for the presbyter theory, while in the Church of Scotland the lay theory generally (but not uniformly) prevailed. A study by Peter Colin Campbell of Aberdeen, *The Theory of Ruling Eldership*, roundly challenged the presbyter theory and the 'specious' (Campbell's word) use of 1 Timothy 5:17. Campbell asserted that there was only one type of presbyter/elder in the New Testament (analogous to the minister of today's Church) and that the ruling elders were not 'elders' in the New Testament sense but rather the *seniores plebis* of the patristic period.

Most scholars would now agree that there is no indisputable evidence in the New Testament for the Reformed use of the title 'elder' - and none at all for the notion that the minister of word and sacrament is a ruling elder with an added-on teaching qualification. This does not mean, however, that there is no scriptural warrant for the kind of office that our elders have come to hold - though, it is an office probably most similar to that of the diaconate in the early Church. Deacons acted as assistants to presbyters and/or bishops in a variety of roles. They had an important place in the Church's liturgy: reading the scriptures, prompting the people's responses, leading their praise. They assisted the presiding presbyter or bishop in serving communicants at the Lord's Supper and in taking Communion from the central celebration to house-churches in the *parochia,* or parish. They also exercised stewardship over the people's gifts, distributing gifts and alms to the poor. In brief, they were seen as participating in the ministry of the divine mercy, seeking the fruit of it in the life and mission of the Church. These early deacons held together aspects of ministry which were severed in the Church of Scotland when some functions were transferred to elders, and deacons were restricted in their office to the ministry of alms and social care. It is the belief of the Panel that the 'elder-deacon' of the patristic Church provides the most helpful model for the office of the eldership in tomorrow's Church.

All ministry within the Church has as its foundation the ministry of God, Father, Son and Holy Spirit. Jesus was sent into the world by the Father to do the Father's will, and he calls all the members of his Church to follow him in humble service and encourage others to respond. To guide and assist the congregation in making this response is the special calling of the eldership. Theirs is the diaconal ministry of leading the people in their worship, prompting their response to the Gospel, and seeking the fruit of it in the life and mission of the whole Church. This leads to the conclusion that there is much common ground between the diaconate and eldership within the Church of Scotland - the two carrying out the same enabling task in different ways. The eldership, and by the same token the diaconate, should be a visible expression and active demonstration of togetherness and fellowship, that partnership which is so central to New Testament thinking about the Church's mission and ministry. There would be great profit in thorough study of Paul's frequent use of the preposition συν (together) in his references to those who shared with him the work of the Gospel - those who were 'servants-together', 'workers-together' with him - *e.g.* Colossians 1:7 and 4:7 where Epaphras and Tychicus, who are both referred to as deacons, are spoken of by Paul as 'servants/slaves-together' with him in the Lord. This gives a central and crucial role to the eldership in the ministry of the Church, and sets the elder's ruling function - historically so central - in a true perspective. It is only as a servant of the Lord who himself came among us as a servant that anyone can exercise authority within his Church.

The different ways the elders' role has evolved within the various strands of Scotland's Reformed heritage show that there is no single model on which to base the patterns of the future. In the past, changes tended to be initiated for pragmatic or political reasons and justified later by dubious proof texts. But the lack of a given prescription, or of any uniform tradition, allows the Church freedom to develop the corporate leadership and ministry already existing in every parish, in ways that seem best fitted to the Church's needs and insights in the contemporary situation.

It is difficult to exaggerate the importance of Kirk Sessions in shaping the life and character of our people during the centuries following the Reformation; and their influence has never been only in the realm of discipline. The pastoral care which we have come to associate with the eldership always did co-exist with the sternness which seems alien to our minds and which lends itself too easily to caricature. There are today countless members of the Kirk deeply indebted to their district elder for support, encouragement and inspiration; and when a Kirk Session is united in enthusiastic service it can provide the type of corporate leadership and ministry which the Church badly needs. Recent years have seen a welcome emphasis on education and support for elders. The Department of Education is to be congratulated on the efforts now being made to provide training for elders both before and after ordination.

It would be dishonest, though, to pretend that all is well because so much is being attempted. Alongside the tremendous service being rendered by the dedicated, we have to acknowledge the negative witness of some among the elders who have long since lost the vision which inspired them to be ordained in the first place, and who would never dream of attending a training course even though they perhaps need it most of all. There are too many Kirk Sessions embarrassed by elders who seldom attend meetings and who carry out their duties only in a desultory way; too many Church members who feel more of a bond with the magazine distributor than with the elder whom they seldom see; too many elders who are no longer finding fulfilment in the job they were ordained to do twenty-five years ago, and whose sense of guilt inhibits them from appearing at Church at all. There exists, it is true, legislation to dismiss elders who absent themselves over a period of time; but it hardly reflects the spirit in which most Kirk Sessions now operate and (as with the former standard of one Communion every three years for Church membership) it takes no account of those who have chalked up the minimum legal requirement and no more.

For how long should elders be expected to serve? Knox's reason for advocating annual election was to 'suffer none to usurpe a perpetuall domination over the kirk'. *The Second Book of Discipline* allowed for elders being relieved of duties for a while, although appointment was for life. Today there is no reason why an elder who has grown weary after long service or whose other commitments are making the fulfilment of Session duties difficult should not ask for a sabbatical period such as some Presbyteries are now introducing for ministers. In practice, very few elders seem to avail themselves of this opportunity of refreshment, and those who do are sometimes reluctant to resume their duties after it. Perhaps they have not always been encouraged to think positively about the value of a sabbatical break because of the difficulty Sessions might have in recruiting replacements. The question, though, goes deeper than that. As their name implies, elders were first envisaged as being drawn from the senior ranks of their congregation, on the grounds that the elderly had most wisdom to offer. The emphasis in recent years has been more on the importance of youthful voices being heard in the courts and committees of the Church – which raises the issue of whether it is fair to ask young men and women to commit themselves to any form of voluntary service from which death offers the only release.

There is no way of ascertaining what proportion of the Church of Scotland's 47,000 elders are diligently pursuing the duties of their office. Undoubtedly, huge numbers are. Every parish is enormously indebted to the serving elders who by witness and example and by pastoral care often establish closer bonds with the membership than the minister is able to do. But the service they give would still be possible throughout a large proportion of their adult life if a more flexible system of appointment for a term of office were adopted. We believe that the principle now mandatory in nomination to Assembly committees could usefully be adapted to the eldership: that election for a specific period would encourage more men and women to offer their gifts in the Church's service, and that if re-elected all elders at the end of their second term should demit office for one year. Some such practice has long been followed by many of the Reformed Churches. Since the number of available leaders varies hugely from one parish to another, it would be unwise to legislate for one uniform period throughout the Kirk. The appropriate term of office should be decided locally by each individual Kirk Session – with perhaps a lower limit of five years, an upper one of ten.

Such a system would safeguard the Church against Session members caught in a guilt trap after being ordained several decades ago. It would in time widen the potential membership of the higher courts of the Church. With a membership of more than three-quarters of a million, the Church of Scotland must have more than 47,000 whose voice could usefully be heard in its courts. It would also mean that after some years every congregation would benefit from having some former elders *not* on the Kirk Session, who would be able to sympathise with the decisions and priorities being tackled by the elders at any given time, having themselves previously grappled with similar decisions. The closed Session meeting,[2] with power resting permanently in the hands of a few, almost inevitably gives rise to a feeling of 'them and us' in the minds of more than 800,000 who are not ordained, to the detriment of that ministry and sense of corporate responsibility to which we believe the whole Church is called.

This raises the question of how elders should be chosen. Historically there have been many methods used. It was envisaged after the Reformation that Kirk Sessions should nominate twice the number of required candidates and invite the congregation to choose half of them. In the 17th century, Sessions were frequently appointed in the burghs by civil councils and magistrates. Today there are two systems existing alongside each other in the Kirk. One, normally found in congregations of the United Free tradition, is nomination and election by the congregation; the other, more usual, method is selection by the existing elders - which is more or less the system of *The Second Book of Discipline*, in which it was the job of the Session to nominate elders and the job of the people to 'approve'.

---

[2] As of 2001 Kirk Session meetings are no longer to be presumed to be held in private, but shall normally be held in public unless the Session decide otherwise on any specific matter.

Although Presbyterianism and democracy are by no means synonymous, the eldership is often cited as evidence of the democracy of Presbyterianism. In the 16th century context it was a notable advance to give the Church's membership the power to elect its office-bearers. In the 20th century context it seems unreasonable that government should rest permanently in the hands of officials who are generally not elected, who are never subject to a process of re-selection, and who are only in the last resort or in a crisis accountable in any way to the people whom they govern. The Panel believes that such a system, guaranteeing lifelong powers of decision-making to a few (whose meetings are private and firmly closed to the ranks of the governed) should not be accepted without question in the Kirk.

It is understandable why there should be reluctance to adopt more widely the principle of congregational election. Service to the Church is not a field in which any kind of canvassing or lobbying seems appropriate. Nonetheless, the Panel believes congregations should be trusted to be open to the guiding of the Spirit. The Church will give the impression of a two-tier structure, calling for two-tier commitment, so long as its authority is vested in a self-perpetuating group while more than ninety per cent of the members are disenfranchised. The Panel believes it would be to the Church's benefit if elders were elected for a specific term of office. It would be helpful also if the size of Kirk Sessions were not determined only by the number of districts needing to be visited. The body that makes the decisions should be as far as possible representative of those on whose behalf the decisions are made: many congregations have found the benefit of 'specialist' elders with specific insight into education, youth work, social work, etc., who can contribute greatly to the Session's work even if they are not able to do regular district visiting.

How should elders be initiated? When the views of Presbyteries were sought after the Panel's Interim Report in 1986, a large majority of those who replied were in favour of retaining 'ordination' as the term best suited to the elder's office. From those who offered explanation of their views, there seemed to be a feeling that the eldership would be downgraded if a different term were used. Although it was quite common in the Church of Scotland until the early 19th century for elders to be admitted through the taking of an oath at a Kirk Session meeting, the Panel recognises the importance of elders being appointed in the context of a congregational act of worship; but we doubt whether ordination is the most appropriate term. It is applied almost universally throughout the world church to the initiation of ministers with laying on of hands. It is confusing when the same term used for ministers' initiation by Presbytery is applied to a different rite, carried out in a different way, by a different agent, appointing office-bearers to a local congregation. Although the elders' ordination in current practice is not repeated if they move, it carries no entitlement to office unless they are re-invited to serve. In an age of increasing mobility, when many parishes experience a rapid turnover of population, the custom of bestowing non-transferable ordination must result in a large but unregistered corps of ordained personnel who are not doing the job for which they were ordained. This is a situation the Reformed Church has always been at pains to avoid in relation to the ordained ministry. Where the population is static, lifelong office gives the impression - uncongenial to contemporary thought—of a perpetual élite. It is the Panel's view that for the concept of the eldership which we have outlined some other term, such as commissioning, might be more relevant and helpful than ordination. This would avoid the contradiction of appointing people for life to do a job for a fixed period.

The Kirk Session is an admirable model for the corporate leadership that has been central to the Panel's thinking throughout this Report. One negative value of this is that elders can safeguard congregations from the foibles and idiosyncrasies of transient ministers. Much more positive is the benefit of having policy and planning formulated by a group who represent the congregation and who are identified with it and know its membership. Most congregations in our towns have Sessions bigger than the whole Church was at Pentecost. In the power of the Spirit they are potentially an explosive force for good. With the knowledge that elders acquire through their pastoral care; with their shared experience of living on the frontier between the Church and the rest of society (a frontier all too unfamiliar to many ministers); with the benefit of diverse backgrounds, occupations, temperaments, Sessions have tremendous opportunities to recognise and foster the gifts of their congregations' whole membership.

The Panel's suggestions for change have inevitably been directed to those aspects of the eldership which appear to us either negative or institutionalised. They are not made in any spirit of disillusionment. We believe firmly that the eldership is one of the Reformed Kirk's distinctive strengths—which is why it matters so much to revitalise it. From a complex and confusing heritage the Panel seeks to offer a pattern for the future which combines the best of our diverse traditions. We hope it is a pattern which loosens the rigidity at present surrounding the eldership, which liberates more members' gifts for service in the Church's courts, and which allows more members of the body of Christ the opportunity of guiding the Church's affairs for a while rather than requiring the same few to do it for life.

# Leaflets from the Stewartry

## *Colin R Williamson*

*There follows the text of a series of leaflets prepared for use in the charge of the Stewartry of Strathearn. Some of it is specific to those congregations but much will be of use to the whole Church of Scotland. The A4 tri-fold leaflets were printed in colour with a consistent design and appropriate clipart illustrations.*

### A. HOLY BAPTISM

This leaflet is designed to explain something of the Church's belief about baptism and also to tell you how baptism is administered in our churches.

### What is Baptism?

Baptism is the doorway by which we enter into membership of the Church. It is a personal sign and seal to the baptized of God's love and it binds the baptized into life-giving relationship with our Saviour, Jesus Christ. The phrase 'grafted into Christ' is used in the service and we think of a young fruit tree stem grafted into root-stock from which it will take its life and grow.

### Why did the Church devise baptism as the way of entering its fellowship?

It didn't. It was Jesus who commanded his Church to make disciples and to baptize. Jesus himself was baptized and took his stand with us. He lived the perfect life which God expects from us. He gave his life on the cross to bear away the penalty of our sin and failure. For us to be the children of God, Christ must be in us and we in him. This is what baptism is about.

**Adults can choose what to believe; infants cannot. Are baptism for adults and for children different?**
No. The very same thing is taking place. Remember, baptism is not a sign of what *I* have done, *my* repentance, *my* faith. It is a sign and seal of what Christ has done for me. The great events which won my salvation were done long before I could offer anything in return.

Certainly an adult comes with his/her own desire to be baptized and is able to affirm his/her faith at the time. Where someone is able to make these promises, they will be admitted to membership of the congregation at the time of their baptism.

**Is it not wrong to impose belief on a child?**
If the person being baptized is an infant, nothing is being *imposed* upon him/her. Remember, the baptism would not be taking place if the parents or guardians did not believe the Christian Faith to be true and something of the greatest value which they wished their child to share.

Natural birth gives an identity to the child. He is the child of his parents whether he wants it so or not - he has no choice in the matter. He does have every choice in how he will respond to that given fact. He can disown his family and cut them out of his life completely, or he can grow to a mature relationship with them where his own personality is shared freely and lovingly.

So it is with those baptized as infants. The reality is that God loves this child and all that our Saviour achieved was done for him/her. We believe this and so we wish the sign and seal be given to him/her - a birth into the fellowship of the Church. But we also know that God does not coerce belief. Love cannot be commanded. The reality of belonging is there but the baptized person is just as free to disown his spiritual identity as he is to grow to mature loving response. God's promises never rob us of our freedom.

## What is required before baptism may be offered? (The adult)
In the case of an adult what is required is a commitment to Jesus Christ as Lord and Saviour and a desire for admission to membership of the Christian Church. Normally the candidate will have attended a course of instruction in the Christian Faith. Such courses are organised regularly by the Earn Valley group of churches. At the same time, the Kirk Session must agree that the candidate should be added to the roll of the congregation after baptism.

Whilst we may experience several points in life when we renew our Christian commitment, God's commitment to us does not need any such expression of renewal. Baptism, in other words, cannot and need not be repeated. A public profession of faith may be celebrated more than once but no-one who has been baptized, say as an infant, can purport to receive baptism a second time.

## What is required before baptism may be offered? (The infant)
By the law of the Church of Scotland at least one of the parents, or other family member (with parental consent) must be baptized and either a member of the congregation or intending to become so. It makes no sense to present a child for baptism where there is no commitment to the Faith and to the Church on the part of parents. If what is signified in the sacrament has little value for his/her parents the baptized person will soon notice and act accordingly!

Baptism should take place in the parish or community church where the baptized child is to grow up. The local Christian community have a vital part to play. If, for some particular reason, a child is presented for baptism at one of the Stewartry churches but lives elsewhere and the parents are not members of the congregation the minister will issue a form for completion by the parish or other local church at the place of residence. This will certify that the local church is aware of the arrangement and is in agreement with it.

The promise by parents to bring the child up in the worship and teaching of the Church is not a condition of the baptism; it is a consequence of it. It is the responsibility of the family to see that the child attends Sunday worship and Sunday School. The best way, the only true and honest way, to do this is to be there with the child.

**What happens at the service?**
Holy baptism is a sacrament. That is to say, it is one of the very special actions which Jesus commanded the Church to fulfil and in which he would be known to be present amongst his people. A sacrament follows the preaching of the Word and forms the climax to which the whole service has been heading.

The family will take their normal places in church at the beginning of the service. In most cases of infant baptism mother and baby are present from the beginning but if baby is clearly unhappy they may leave at any point to wait in the vestry, hall or session house until recalled by an elder at the appropriate point. After the offering, the minister will welcome the family at the front of the church where seats are provided near the font.

**The service for an infant**
There is a statement about the Church's belief regarding baptism, followed by the first question to parents.

> In presenting your child for baptism, desiring that he/ she may be grafted into Christ as a member of his body the Church, do you receive the teaching of the Christian faith which we confess in the Apostle's Creed?
> Answer - **I do**

The Creed is then said by the congregation. This is followed by a prayer for the Holy Spirit to bless the sacrament. There are then words addressed to the child. Then, the father holding him/her, the child is baptized into the name of the Father and of the Son and of the Holy Spirit. There follows a blessing upon the child and a declaration that he/she is received into membership of the Church. The parents are then reminded of their responsibilities and are asked:

> Do you promise, depending on the grace of God, to teach your child the truths and duties of the Christian faith; and by prayer and example to bring him/her up in the life and worship of the Church?
>
> Answer - **I do**

The congregation then promise to play their part in the nurture of the child. The service concludes with a prayer for God's grace to help us all live up to the promises we have taken.

## The service for an adult

This follows the same pattern as that for a child with the obvious difference that the adult candidate speaks for himself/herself. The question before baptism is:

> In seeking baptism, do you reject sin and confess your need of God's forgiving grace; and believing the Christian faith, do you pledge yourself to glorify God and to love your neighbour?
>
> Answer- **I do**

Following baptism the questions prescribed by the Church of Scotland for Public Profession of Faith will be asked:

> Believing in one God, Father, Son and Holy Spirit, and confessing Jesus Christ as your Saviour and Lord, do you promise to join regularly with your fellow Christians in worship of the Lord's Day?
>
> Do you promise to be faithful in reading the Bible and in prayer?

> Do you promise to give a fitting proportion of your time, talents, and money for the Church's work in the world?
>
> Do you promise, depending on the grace of God, to profess publicly your loyalty to Jesus Christ, to serve him in your daily work, and to walk in his ways all the days of your life?

The members of the Kirk Session will come forward to give a handshake by way of personal greeting.

## With infant baptism, what about Godparents?

Godparents have not been given as formal a role in the Church of Scotland as they have in some other traditions and there is no reference to them in the service. Remember that baptism in our Church is celebrated as a sacrament by the whole congregation who are asked to welcome and nurture the baptized and in that sense every member is a 'godparent'. If there are friends who are Christians and are willing and able to support and encourage the child then their special involvement is welcome. They may wish to stand with the parents at the font.

Normally the mother will carry the baby until the point of the baptism when she will pass him/her to the father. The child remains in the father's arms for baptism.

## Proof of baptism

Every baptized person, adult or infant, is issued with a Certificate of Baptism. This is an agreed ecumenical certificate accepted by all the major Christian denominations. If requested, the baptized person's birth certificate can be endorsed on the reverse side. (Proof of baptism may be asked for in certain circumstances e.g. when marrying a Roman Catholic or when applying to live and work in some Arab countries).

The occasion may arise when a person does not think that they may have been baptized as an infant, and having come to a living faith in adulthood, they wish now to be baptized into membership of the Church. Every effort should be made to establish whether or not they were baptized as an infant. If the matter remains uncertain, it is possible to administer 'Conditional Baptism' ('If you have not already been baptized I baptize you ...').

## B. CHILDREN AND THE CHURCH
This leaflet sets out the place of children in the life of our congregation.

There has been a gradual change in attitude to children within the Church of Scotland in recent decades. This has largely been the result of renewed interest in the theology of Baptism as well as changes in the culture of Scotland generally.

Until the 1950s, children were not in short supply in the Sunday Schools and organisations of the Church. There was an expected progression from the 'Beginners Department' through Bible Class and Youth Fellowship to Communicant's Class and 'Joining the Church'. Children had their place and that was in Sunday School. They were spoken of as the 'Church of Tomorrow' and they could generally be left to the Sunday School to incubate. Their only experience of worship was the first hymn, the opening prayers, and the strange device known as the 'Children's Address' which was really there for the over 60s. The 'Children's Address' was an interruption in the flow of worship and rarely did much for children, since its moralising was above their heads and its tone was often so patronising as to be insulting.

Today we are no longer assured of a constant flow of replacement children. Those who do join us are likely to have at least one committed Christian parent - in other words, they come belonging to a family. Already these children face challenge to their faith since it is very likely that their peers will scoff at their Church and Sunday School belonging. They are, after all, a minority in the Scotland of the 21st century.

What can we give them? We can offer a radically different attitude to them from that which the Church showed to children 20, 30, 40 years ago. In the first place we have a much more mature understanding of Baptism. In line with the other major Christian traditions we have recognised once more that by the Grace of God, Baptism into Jesus Christ, whatever one's age, brings the individual into membership of the Church, the Body of Christ. Profession of Faith in mature years is a celebration of that belonging - it is not a 'joining'. Once we recognise that the baptized child is gathered into Christ we see that he or she is not a potential member but a little brother or sister, fully part of the family of Faith.

What does this mean in practical terms? In the human family, young members have special needs in terms of physical, mental and spiritual nurture. They have responsibilities laid upon them in terms of the basic rules of the home and they have their part to play in its good running. By the same token, even the very youngest child is due not only care, but respect. 'To be seen and not heard' ignores the fact that the child too has a contribution to make and a view to be heard.

On Sunday morning, when the congregation gathers for worship, there are important matters to consider.

1  Children have a right to be present with us. Sunday worship cannot exclude any member of the Christian family.

2  In line with Church of Scotland policy, no baptized person will be excluded from the Lord's Table, and children are welcome to take communion when they come with their parents.

3 Does our worship need to develop so that it is more inclusive? We must not have 'kiddies' bits, far less a 'dumbing down' of the service. This doesn't work for children; it is tedious for adults and, one suspects, is an unworthy offering towards God. But when children are regularly present, for instance for the prayers of intercession, language should take account of that presence. Might children not have a role to play verbally (with prayers from time to time), or in action (helping with the offerings, with a candle, bringing in the Bible, hymn books etc.)?

4 Babies and toddlers should always be welcome. The natural place for them to be is with their mothers and we will be delighted to see baptismal vows honoured and glad that a child's earliest memories are of Church as a natural and welcoming place to belong. Babies and toddlers will make some noise and we will be happy that mothers are free to move out of the service to the crèche area if the child has clearly crossed the decibel threshold, and free to come back in if he or she has calmed down. Parents will judge when noise is clearly preventing worshippers concentrating on the service but they should always he assured that their presence with their child is appreciated by the rest of the congregation.

Children's ministry in the Stewartry is centred at Dunning and Forteviot but in all our churches we will respect our children and show interest in them. In a culture where Faith and Family are under attack we are fortunate to have little brothers and sisters like these.

---

'Let the little children come to me; do not stop them; for it is to such as these that the kingdom of God belongs. Truly I tell you, whoever does not receive the kingdom of God as a little child will never enter it.' And he took them up in his arms, laid his hands on them, and blessed them. *St Mark 10:14-15*

---

The promise of the congregation in the baptismal service:

Do you renew your commitment, with God's help, to live before all God's children in a kindly and Christian way, and to share with them the knowledge and love of Christ?
**We do. We will nurture one another in faith, uphold one another in prayer, encourage one another in service.**

Heavenly Father and giver of all grace, we ask your blessing on those who in baptism have received the seal of the new covenant and been made heirs of your heavenly kingdom; that through the prayers, the teaching and the example of those who love and care for them, they may grow up in the faith of Christ crucified and in the fellowship of his Church, to serve you faithfully all the days of their life; through Jesus Christ our Lord.

---

## *The Children's Charter* (United Reformed Church)

1. Children are equal partners with adults in the life of the Church.
2. The full diet of Christian worship is for children as well as adults.
3. Learning is for the whole Church, adults and children.
4. Fellowship is for all, each belonging meaningfully to the rest.
5. Service is for children to give, as well as adults
6. The call to evangelism comes to all God's people, of whatever age.
7. The Holy Spirit speaks powerfully through children as well as adults.
8. The discovery and development of gifts in children and adults is a key function of the Church.
9. As a Church community we must learn to do only those things in separate age groups which we cannot in all conscience do together.
10. The concept of the 'Priesthood of all Believers' includes children.

## C. MAKING YOUR PROFESSION OF FAITH

We are delighted that you have decided to make profession of your Christian Faith. This leaflet explains the setting for this and sets out the questions which are used during the service.

Profession of Faith is a celebration of your belonging within the Church of Jesus Christ. In past times it was often called 'joining the Church' but that was a misleading phrase. As a baptized person you are not a stranger coming in from outside. You are already a member by the grace of God because Jesus has done for you all that is necessary to be a child of God. What you are doing now is saying 'Yes!' to it all. A son or daughter does not join the family at their coming of age party - they celebrate their belonging and as mature people set their own seal on what has been given to them through the years. They assume equal responsibility with the other members of the family.

Before making profession of your Christian faith it is likely that you will have been part of an enquirer's group or 'Communicants' Class'. The purpose of the group will have been to concentrate the mind, to give time to looking at some aspects of the Faith. As you can appreciate the surface has only been scratched but it may be that a door has been opened just a little for you to explore the vast world of Christian belief, spirituality and worship, Church history etc. The minister will be only too happy to point you in the direction of further study. In no sense is Profession of Faith a statement that 'I now know it all'. The Faith is a mystery of God's love which we can never box up and at its heart is a relationship not a set of theories. In that sense, Profession of Faith involves trust - a willingness to say, 'There's a lot I don't understand but somehow I believe I hear the Lord's voice calling me and as a free mature person I am willing to trust him. I will take my stand as a Christian. I believe he decided for me long ago; now I decided for him'.

What part does the Church play in all this? The Christian Faith is a faith held in common by a community - it is not a lonely journey but one undertaken by pilgrims together. So it is important that your Profession is not something done in a corner but is to be celebrated by the family of believers. They will pledge their support for you as companions of the way and, in turn, they will be greatly encouraged by the stand you are taking with them.

In practical terms, for the Church of Scotland Profession of Faith means that you become a member of a congregation. As we have said, you already belong to the Church by baptism but Profession of Faith results in your name being added to the congregational roll - the list of local disciples upon whom the Church relies if the Gospel is to be proclaimed and lived out in a parish.

For us here, the Church of Scotland congregation is The Stewartry of Strathearn. As a member you will probably join in the life and worship of one of our area churches particularly; but do remember that there are four churches within our group and you are equally welcome at any centre.

Profession of Faith will normally take place at the Eucharist (Holy Communion). This is because it is at the Sacrament that we are most aware of what our Lord has done for us and offered to God on our behalf: so our own offering of faith finds its proper route to God through the great offering of Jesus.

After the Word part of the service (the Bible readings and the sermon) and just before the Communion we present our own offerings - money offerings, bread and wine and any other offerings we want to present to God. This may include a special dedication of a gift or the offering of service by youth workers etc. It is at this point that you offer your profession. The minister will invite you to come to the front of the church. He will introduce this part of the service and will then ask the questions appointed by the Church. Please remember that these questions are not a test ('Say 'Yes' to these and we might let you in!') or in any way intended to be a burden - quite the opposite, they are designed as a means whereby you can make your profession. Each person will respond 'I do' in turn. After the questions there is a short prayer and a blessing given to each person. As a token of welcome to membership of the congregation, the minister will then invite the elders present to come forward and shake your hand. After this you will return to your seats and the service proceeds.

---

Do you believe in one God, Father, Son and Holy Spirit; and do you confess Jesus Christ as your Saviour and Lord?

Do you promise to join regularly with your fellow Christians in worship on the Lord's Day?

Do you promise to be faithful in reading the Bible and in prayer?

Do you promise to give a fitting proportion of your time, talents and money for the Church's work in the world?

Do you promise, depending on the grace of God, to profess publicly your loyalty to Jesus Christ, to serve him in your daily work and to walk in his ways all the days of your life?

## D. HOLY COMMUNION – EUCHARIST

Holy Communion, the Lord's Supper, the Mass, the Breaking of Bread - by whatever name Christians know it - this is the central act of worship of the Christian Church. The name common to all traditions is *Eucharist* from the Greek for 'thanksgiving'.

The Church carried over from the worship of the Jewish synagogue the reading of Scripture, the singing of Psalms and the offering of prayers. But the new element in worship, indeed the only instruction which Jesus gave his people about worship was to 'do this in remembrance of me'.

We can imagine the first Christians gathering in someone's house on Sunday (not yet a holiday), possibly after the day's work, and sharing a meal. During the meal the leader would take bread and break it, take the cup and bless it and distribute to the gathering. Until the Lord's coming again Christians will do this in great cathedral, in tiny chapel, in the home of the sick, at conference or on battlefield. And in doing this they will be most truly and clearly the Church, the body of Christ.

### What is happening in Eucharist?
When the bread and wine are set apart with thanksgiving to God and prayer for the Holy Spirit to bless and use them, the risen Lord Jesus Christ is really present to his people. '*Re*-membrance' here is more than looking back - it is making present now all that our Saviour is, his life, death and resurrection, his ascension and his coming again at the end time - all this is present to us at Eucharist. In the Sacrament God places into our empty hands the perfect life of Jesus with all his merits. At last we have a worthy offering to hold up before our Father God. So we are strengthened and equipped for our life of discipleship.

## What does the word Communion mean?
First and foremost communion means being at one with the Lord Jesus Christ and through him with God.

In the sacrament we are at one with all our fellow Christians. That is why Christians should be reconciled with one another before coming to table (St Matthew 5:24). The style and language of worship around the world may be very varied but in the Eucharist we are one in Christ.

In the Eucharist we have communion also with the saints of God from earliest time and with those who are still to be born who will belong with us in the Lord.

## Who is entitled to participate?
Normally Holy Communion is for the baptized. In the Church of Scotland we invite members baptized in infancy to make profession of their faith in adulthood but they are in no way barred from participating in the Eucharist before making that profession.

There may also be times when it is appropriate for those who are not yet baptized to come to Communion. An early Scottish reformer said that the Communion is a 'converting ordinance'. But encountering the Grace of God in the sacrament would naturally call for a response of faith to follow.

## In what sense are the bread and wine the body and blood of Christ?
Unlike some other traditions the Reformed Churches do not teach that the bread and wine (the 'elements') are literally changed into the body and blood of Christ. But we do believe they are more than empty symbols. The Lord is true to his promises by the power of the Holy Spirit. In the whole action of taking, blessing, and sharing, the

risen Christ is present to us in a wonderful mystery of grace where earth meets heaven.

## If Eucharist is so important, why is it so seldom celebrated in the Church of Scotland?

The reformers, including Calvin and Knox, wished the Lord's Supper to be celebrated every Lord's Day but were hampered by the superstitious reluctance of people in the 16th century Catholic Church to communicate often. The best they could achieve was monthly celebration. In Scotland, Knox had the added problem of scarcity of reformed ministers to preside. Infrequency of celebration for these reasons came to be accepted. In more recent times some congregations of the Church of Scotland have moved to monthly celebration. The over-solemn, wordy communion services of past years have generally been replaced by newer orders which have more of a spirit of celebration and it hoped that the reformers' dream (and Jesus' instruction!) will gain favour. It is the Kirk Session of each congregation which sets the times for Holy Communion.

## Can I participate in the sacrament in any tradition of the Church?

It is by the Lord's invitation that we come to the Table. He is the host, not the Church. You will find a welcome to Communion in all the Churches of the Reformation including, nowadays, the Anglican Churches. The Orthodox Churches and the Roman Catholic Church do not extend this invitation. It is the view of the Roman Catholic Church that Eucharist is a sign of unity and cannot be shared until that unity is achieved. We may feel it best simply to accept that this Church has barred us even if the Lord himself has invited us!

## How do we take part in the Church of Scotland service?

**We come!** We make it our priority to worship our Lord in the fellowship of the congregation.

**We prepare.** However we do it, we come ready to recognise the presence of Jesus in the service, listening for his word, open to a sense of his nearness.

**We take part in the service.** Holy Communion uses prayers, creeds and texts which go back to earliest Christian practice. We say or sing them.

**We share bread and wine**. Once, in the history of our Scottish Church, we would have taken our seats at a long table. Unfortunately that practice was lost and usually we remain in our pews, served by the elders. In some churches bread is passed from which each person breaks a portion. In others the bread is in small individual pieces. Three of the Stewartry churches use individual glasses for the wine. At Aberdalgie the common cup is still in use.

Some folk may have a problem with the bread (an allergy for example), others with the wine (as in the case of an alcoholic). You can make your communion 'in one kind' by taking only bread or only wine if this is necessary.

---

Holy Communion - 'The medicine of Immortality'

*St Irenaeus, 2nd century Bishop of Lyons*

God has more room in your soul, through your receiving of the Sacrament, than he could otherwise have by your hearing of the Word only. Thus the Sacrament is very necessary, if only for the reason that we get Christ better, and get a firmer grasp of him by the Sacrament, than we could have before.

*1589 sermon by Robert Bruce,*
*minister of the High Kirk of Edinburgh.*

**Prayers before Communion**
Lord Jesus, you have invited me to meet you in the sacrament because you love me. Here you will entrust yourself to me, all you have done for me, all you will do for me. It is not my worthiness that is celebrated here but yours, not my faithfulness to God but yours. Forgive my failure and my sin. Let me relax, body, mind and spirit in your company; and when I rise from table send me out in your strength to the life you wish me to live.

In this communion I rejoice in my belonging in the company of the saints. Lord God, bless my sisters and bothers who share this sacrament in this congregation and around the world. May your Church be one that the world may see and believe. With those I have wronged I seek reconciliation. Those who have offended me I forgive.

## E. INTERCESSIONS IN THE SUNDAY SERVICE
In the course of a service of public worship a number of types of prayer are offered. There are prayers of confession, seeking God's forgiveness. There may be collects, short formal prayers which often reflect the theme of the day. There will be thanksgiving prayers. Most prayers are led by the minister but there is another type of prayer which is very properly voiced from the congregation.

Intercessions express the hopes and concerns of a Christian community. They are true 'liturgy' (the Greek is literally 'the work of the people'). Here we express our loves, our fears, our solidarity when we hold up the world in prayer to our Father in heaven. We pray for Christ's Church; we pray for our nation and our communities; we pray for people, situations and issues where God's help or direction is needed.

We do this because our Lord told us to and because the Apostle Paul told us to. We do it because we believe that in the mystery of our relationship with God prayer makes a difference. We do it because while we are together as a congregation we are already beginning our work of discipleship together before we disperse.

It really does not make a lot of sense for the ministers always to be the ones to lead intercessions. Different eyes look upon the world in different ways. People's circumstances and experiences vary greatly. What a wealth or interest and concern is represented by a congregation; in terms of intercessions the minister is only one person, and we should not be limited by his/her experience, knowledge or style of speech.

We hope that gradually intercessions may be given back to the people. To begin with, we plan that from time to time members who have offered to lead these prayers will do so in one of the Stewartry churches.

## Practical Questions
*Would I have to write my own prayers?*
This is probably the best thing although it is perfectly acceptable to use a book as a guide.

*What help may I expect in preparing my prayers?*
The ministers will be available to help or consult. They will not expect to vet or approve prayers but will give advice as requested.

*What style should I use?*
There are some standard forms of intercessory prayer and it would be best if you stick to one of these. Examples are given later in this leaflet.

*Are there some things which should always be prayed for?*
It is normal always to offer prayer for the Church (worldwide and/or local) and for the nation, the Queen and our government (It is important for the National Church to hold up its rulers in prayer to God and

Saint Paul instructs the Church to do this). Prayers of intercession in our service normally conclude with a 'Thanksgiving for the Faithful Departed'. This is an important prayer not least because it assures the congregation week by week that loved ones who have died are held in the love of God.

*Do I come out to the front to lead the intercessions?*
No. The congregation will be aware from the service sheet that the prayers will come from the congregation on that Sunday. You will have a hand held radio mike and will simply speak in your normal voice from your pew. You will have clear written cue from the minister as to when to begin.

*How often will I be asked to lead intercessions?*
Only certain members will feel that leading prayers is a ministry for them but it defeats the purpose if a few folk are over used. We shall prepare a calendar (similar to the Scripture Readers' rota). This will give very good notice. It may be that intercessions are led by a member only in one of the four churches every few weeks in the early stages. You will not necessarily be in the church in which you normally worship. For this purpose you belong to the worship team of the Stewartry.

Let us remember always that prayer for the world and for the coming of God's Kingdom is the work of our Risen Saviour. It is his constant prayer which matters. The Holy Spirit will catch up our lisping prayer so that it becomes an *Amen* to his great prayer for us.

## Styles of Intercession
There are basically two styles:
1) Prayer (addressed directly to God)
2) Bidding (addressed to the congregation) often followed by silence and sometimes by a short prayer addressed to God

The following are examples.

1) God of love and power, we pray for your Church in this parish and throughout the world, that through the courage and faith of your people your word may be preached and lived.

   We pray for the Queen and those in authority that in the fulfilling of their duties they may be guided by your Spirit and upheld by your grace.

   We pray for our community, our country and the nations of the world that following the ways of truth and justice they may be free from bitterness and strife and by the power of your love live in peace.

   We pray for all who are in trouble, that those who are sick may be cared for, those who are lonely sustained, those who are oppressed strengthened, those who mourn comforted and that those who are close to death may know their risen Lord.

   We give thanks for those who have died in the Faith, especially those known to us, who have entered into the joy and peace of your nearer presence. Grant that we may follow their example and come to share with them the glory of everlasting life, through Jesus Christ our Lord.

2) In peace let us pray to the Lord;
   for the Church of Jesus Christ in all the world; for this parish and its worshipping communities; for our ministers and elders and all who belong with us;

   *silence*

   Lord God. grant that we, and all who confess your name may be united in your truth, live together in love, and reveal your glory in the world.

for the nations of the world; for Elizabeth our Queen; for all in authority; for the communities in which we live and work;

*silence*

Righteous God, guide the people of this land and of all the nations in the ways of justice and of peace, that we may honour one another and serve the common good.

for those in any trouble this day; the sick, the poor, the oppressed;

*silence*

Merciful God. save and comfort all who suffer, that they may hold to you through good and ill, and trust in your unfailing love.

Let us give thanks for the saints who have lived and died in the Faith

*silence*

God of our fathers, we rejoice in the faithful witness of your people in every age and pray that we may share with them the joys of your eternal kingdom.

Accept these our prayers for the sake of your Son our Saviour Jesus Christ.

(Example 2 has both bidding and direct prayer. Biddings alone might be used with silences with a prayer at the end commending our prayers to God.)

## F. ANOINTING OF THE SICK

The peace of the Lord be with you.

We have come together in the name of the Lord Jesus Christ who restored the sick to health and who suffered and gave his life for us. He is present with us as we recall the words of the Apostle James,

'Is there anyone sick among you? Let him call for the elders of the Church and let them pray over him and anoint him in the name of the Lord. This prayer made in faith will save the sick man. The Lord will restore his health and if he has committed any sins they will be forgiven'.

We now entrust N... to the grace and power of Jesus that the Lord may ease his/her suffering and grant him/her health and salvation.

Let us seek God's forgiveness:

**I confess to Almighty God that I have sinned through my own fault in my thoughts and in my words, in what I have done and in what I have failed to do. May Almighty God have mercy upon me and bring me to everlasting life.**

God gave his only Son that whoever believes in him should not perish but have everlasting life. Receive the forgiveness of God and the power of the Holy Spirit to live for him.

### St Mark 4:35-50

With the coming of evening that same day Jesus said to them, 'Let us cross over to the other side'. And leaving the crowd behind they took him just as he was in the boat; and there were other boats with them. Then it began to blow a gale and the waves were breaking into the boat so that it was almost swamped. But he was in the stern, his head on the cushion, asleep. They woke him and said to him, 'Master do you not care? We are going down!' And he woke and rebuked the wind and said to the sea, 'Quiet now! Be calm!' And the wind dropped and all was calm again. Then he said to them, 'Why are you so frightened? How is it that you have no faith?' They were filled with awe and said to one another, 'Who can this be? Even the wind and the sea obey him.'

Lord God, loving Father, you bring healing to the sick through your Son Jesus Christ. Hear us as we pray to you in faith and send your Holy Spirit upon this oil, your own gift. May your blessing come upon all anointed with this oil that they may be freed from pain and illness and made well again in body, mind and spirit.

+ In the name of the Father and of the Son and of the Holy Spirit +
*(Anoint head and hands)*

Through this holy anointing may the Lord in his love and mercy help you with the grace of the Holy Spirit. May he pour his strength into your weakness and bless you with the peace of his presence.

**The Lord's Prayer**

The Lord bless you and guard you
The Lord make his face shine upon you and be gracious to you;
The Lord look kindly upon you and give you peace.

The blessing of God Almighty
The Father, the Son and the Holy Spirit
Be upon you and remain with you today and for ever.

## Commendation for the Dying

Good Shepherd, you gave your life for the sheep; we commit into your merciful hands the spirit of this your servant. Let not the shedding of your own blood be in vain for him. Wash away the stains of his past sins; let your love be with him even now; and when he passes through the valley of the shadow of death, receive him into the arms of your mercy.

Blessed Jesus, whose soul was exceedingly sorrowful even unto death, comfort the soul of your servant in this hour of his greatest need.

## The Blessing

God the Father, who has created you, bless you.
God the Son, who has redeemed you, bless you.
God the Holy Spirit who has poured out his grace upon you, bless you.
The Holy Trinity be now and evermore your defence, assist you in this your last trial, and bring you into the way of everlasting life.

O God the Father of Heaven;
**Have mercy on the soul of your servant**
O God the Son, Redeemer of the world;
**Have mercy on the soul of your servant**
O God the Holy Spirit, the Comforter;
**Have mercy on the soul of your servant.**
O holy, blessed and glorious Trinity, one God;
**Have mercy on *his* soul.**

Be merciful; blot out all *his* iniquities, O Lord.
Be merciful; defend and deliver *his* soul, O Lord.

From all dark and disbelieving thoughts; from all snares and temptations of the devil; from all distrust of your infinite love and mercy;
**Defend and deliver *his* soul, O Lord.**

From all agony and distress of mind or body; from all clinging to this vain world; from all excessive fears of dying;
**Defend and deliver *his* soul, O Lord.**

By the infinite merits of your sacred Passion; by the pangs of your crucifixion; by your unknown weight of agony; by your giving up your spirit into your Father's hands;
**Defend and deliver *his* soul, O Lord**

By the burial of your sacred body in the tomb; by the passing of your blessed spirit into the abode of the dead; and by your preaching to the spirits in prison;
**Defend and deliver *his* soul, O Lord.**

By your glorious resurrection on the third day; by the rolling away of the stone from the grave; by your victory over death; by your leading captivity captive;
**Defend and deliver *his* soul, O Lord.**

By your glorious ascension to the right hand of God; by your blessing of the apostles; by the promise of your perpetual presence;
**Defend and deliver *his* soul, O Lord.**

By your sending the Holy Spirit; by your all-prevailing intercession; by your preparing the heavenly mansions for your redeemed; by your coming to receive them to yourself;
**Defend and deliver *his* soul, O Lord.**

Son of God, hear us.
Lamb of God, you take away the sin of the world;
**Grant *him* your peace**

Lamb of God, you take away the sin of the world;
**Have mercy on *him*.**

---

**The Lord's Prayer**

**Psalm 23 (read responsively)**